D1563817

Eye of the Century

DATE DUE			

FILM

JOHN BE

EYE OF THE CENTURY

FILM, EXPERIENCE, MODERNITY

FRANCESCO CASETTI

TRANSLATED BY ERIN LARKIN WITH JENNIFER PRANOLO

COLUMBIA UNIVERSITY PRESS · NEW YORK

COLUMBIA UNIVERSITY PRESS
Publishers Since 1893
New York   Chichester, West Sussex

Library of Congress Cataloging-in-Publication Data

Casetti, Francesco.
    [Occhio del Novecento. English]
    Eye of the century : film, experience, modernity / Francesco Casetti ;
translated by Erin Larkin with Jennifer Pranolo.
        p. cm. — (Film and culture)
    Includes bibliographical references and index.
    ISBN 978-0-231-13994-6 (cloth : alk. paper) — ISBN 978-0-231-13995-3 (pbk. : alk. paper) —
ISBN 978-0-231-51149-0 (ebook)
        1. Motion pictures—History.   2. Motion pictures—Social aspects.   I. Title.

PN1993.5.A1C37413   2008
791.4309—DC22

                                                                2007053009

Printed in the United States of America

c 10 9 8 7 6 5 4 3 2 1
p 10 9 8 7 6 5 4 3 2 1

References to Internet Web sites (URLs) were accurate at the time of writing.
Neither the author nor Columbia University Press is responsible for URLs that
may have expired or changed since the manuscript was prepared.

BOOK + JACKET DESIGNED BY THE *STATE OF EMOTION*

CONTENTS

ACKNOWLEDGMENTS

IN THE MANY YEARS I have been working on this book (and it is up to the reader to decide if they have been well spent or not), I have incurred many intellectual debts, which are impossible to relate in detail here. I will limit myself to remembering those who, through conference invitations and collections, allowed me to progress in my research: Giuliana Bruno, Paolo Bertetto, David Bordwell, Domenec Font, Elio Franzini, Miriam Hansen, Leonardo Quaresima, David Rodowick, Ayako Saito, Tom Gunning, Steve Ungar, Federica Villa, and Giulia Carluccio.

Among the friends and colleagues who read portions of the manuscript, I want thank for their precious advice Gianni Canova, Ruggero Eugeni, Maria Grazia Fanchi, Anne Kern, Pietro Montani, Peppino Ortoleva, Guglielmo Pescatore, Francesco Pitassio, Antonio Somaini, Pierre Sorlin, Massimo Locatelli, and Giacomo Manzoli. Luca Mazzei and Silvio Alovisio were extraordinarily helpful in locating materials. A special thanks goes to Francesca Piredda and Deborah Toschi for their revision of footnotes. For the realization of the English edition, I'm deeply indebted to Erin Larkin, for her patience in translating my Italian, and to Jennifer Pranolo, for her merciless scrutiny in revising the manuscript. Jeffries "Toby" Levers was generous in his stylistic suggestions for the final English version. Also, my copyeditor Roy Thomas at Columbia University Press did wonderful work on the manuscript. My editors, Elisabetta Sgarbi at Bompiani and Juree Sondker at Columbia University Press, deserve a special mention for their positive attitude.

This book has a special tie to Yale University. I finished the book during my residency there as a visiting professor in 2005; the English version was improved with further references (and in some points rewritten for the sake of clarity) during the spring semester of 2007, when I again taught at Yale. I'm deeply indebted to Dudley Andrew, Giuseppe Mazzotta, and Penny Marcus for making possible my teaching and research experience at Yale. Discussions with David Quint, Christopher Wood, and Brigitte Peuker were incomparably productive. A special thanks to Charlie Musser for his "Wednesday night dinners," so rich in intellectual and personal exchange.

This book was written at a time in which recognition for my teachers is becoming ever more acute, and my need to repay what I gained from them ever stronger. Thus I dedicate this work to those from whom I have learned the most: Christian Metz, Lino Micciché, Gianfranco Bettetini, and Giovanni Cesareo; and to my students, past and future, with the hope of having taught them, too.

Eye of the Century

A Hundred Years, A Century

In an article appearing in the Torinese newspaper *La Stampa* in 1908, art critic Enrico Thovez linked a recent invention with the new century. This invention—the cinema—would become the unmistakable emblem of its time. Thovez writes:

> If, in order to give the name to a period of time, we call upon the individual or idea that had the greatest influence on its minds, that most profoundly dominated human existence, we can anticipate the answer: the current century . . . will simply be the age of film. For no work of art, scientific invention, economic trend, enterprise, thinking or form of fashion can compete in terms of breadth of achievement, depth of diffusion or universality of consensus with this humble wooden box, its handle turned by some poor wretch perched in the shadows, as the interminable strip of celluloid, sown with its microscopic images, unwinds with a gentle humming sound.[1]

The millennium came to a close as film celebrated its one hundredth anniversary. The two destinies Thovez invokes—that of film and that of the twentieth century—have perhaps run their course. With the advent of the digital age, for example, cinema no longer depends on the photographic image, and earlier technological, social, or political advances have been surpassed or repudiated as well. The bold prescience of this long forgotten essayist is, however, striking. The twentieth century *was* the age of film—or, at any rate, it was largely perceived as such. Film's "microscopic images" mirrored the trajectory of this century, recording events as they took place, asserting themselves as a widespread presence, and becoming constant points of reference. Thus, it is worthwhile to inquire what cinema gave to and took from its age, in an exchange based on open and reciprocal complicities. The project of this book will be to trace how cinema—through a series of negotiations—molded modern cultural and intellectual history. Indeed film was not only the perfect translator of the last century but also an active agent determining how its turbulent decades would unfold.

Much has been written in recent years on the close relationship between film and twentieth-century modernity. Such studies have examined, for example, ways in which film has constructed new forms of subjectivity, redefined space and time, expressed social, racial, and gender identities, as well as contributed to the mass industrialization of culture.[2] While I will be navigating some of these studies, I want to consider, first and foremost, the import behind Thovez's prophecy. I will be addressing one key point: how is it possible to define the gaze that film claimed for the twentieth century? Is it true that film, in dialogue with its time, experimented more than any other art with new forms of vision that have become a common language? And what forms of vision did it inaugurate? How did film introduce these visions into the everyday? The following pages will focus on the idea that film was the "eye of the twentieth century." Not only did it record a large number of its events, but—by recording them—it has also been able to structure a reflexive spectatorial experience in which to receive them.[3]

I understand that this metaphor of the eye presents some risks. It is no longer "fashionable" to speak of the gaze: many prefer to thematize vision within a wider framework of perceptual, affective, cognitive, and social processes.[4] As the trend of these critiques demonstrates, the eye itself is often no longer considered a sensory organ, but is instead inserted within a larger matrix of analytic intelligibility. Yet we must not forget that film, from its inception, was first and foremost identified and publicized as a marvelously unprecedented *optical* device. As Eugenio Giovannetti, an Italian film critic, wrote at the moment of the rise of sound film: "At the cinema, all eyes—even the near and farsighted—see clearly, deliciously clearly; herein lies the originality of the cinematographic performance, which we have all but forgotten."[5] At the cinema we experience an almost inescapable sharpening of our visual capacity, whatever biological flaws might naturally hinder it.

Second, it is perhaps no longer even "fashionable" to speak of film in and of itself. Most recent scholarship tends, in fact, to place cinema within a cultural studies context of public entertainment, urban life, the spread of mass communication, production, distribution, and consumption.[6] Early studies emphasized film's mimicry of theater, painting, literature, etc. Some scholars advanced more surprising connections: in the aforementioned article, for example, Thovez inserted film among the "surrogates" which typify modern times. As the trinket-like celluloid imitations substitute real ivory, real tortoiseshell, real amber, so the celluloid filmstrip gives "a cheap substitute for the hard-won constructions of genius."[7] Yet even in the most charged of these scholarly treatments, film is recognized as a peculiarly singular phenomenon. Film requires specialized attention in and of itself. It has its own identity.

What kind of gaze, then, did twentieth-century cinema construct? Chapter 1 will examine the reasons for the particular synchrony between film and its time, and will attempt to gesture toward its relevance with respect to contemporary culture. Three characteristics seem to stand out. The first is film's nature as a medium—not just an art—in an age that prizes the communicative dimension as a guarantee of immediacy, nearness, and accessibility. The second characteristic concerns the rites and myths that film created on screen and in the theaters, in a century that had a special need for original images and imaginative behaviors to reflect the issues of emerging social orders. The third is the compromise that film succeeded in achieving amid the different demands of modernity. It united conflicting stimuli in an age torn by strife and dilemma, offering them up in their mundane, yet at times touching and magical, everydayness. The ability to communicate, the power to shape or define, the drive to negotiate: these are the three central characteristics of film's "gaze."

The last characteristic—this aspect of negotiation—is the most decisive for understanding film's "gaze" as I will define it. At stake, in fact, is a gaze that functions as an *oxymoron*: that is, it is capable of operating on opposing fronts, and at times collapsing them. Chapters 2 through 6 will explore this oxymoronic quality of the "gaze." Within its negotiation of twentieth-century modernity, film arbitrated at least five conflicts among opposing stances. It cultivated a partial gaze, tied to the singleness of each take and its point of view, yet at the same time ready to grasp the totality of the world through movement and editing. Film developed a composite gaze, in which reality and fantasy merge, but in which the two planes are often carefully distinguished in order to avoid any confusion between them. In the same way, film promoted a penetrating gaze that utilizes the enhanced prosthetic vision of the camera, but which is also deeply anthropomorphic. Film fostered an excited gaze, rich in perceptive stimuli, but also attentive to maintain spectator orientation. Finally, film elaborated an immersive gaze that gives the impression of being inside the seen world, but which at the same time maintains the sense of distance. Each of these gazes combines two different qualities, balancing them. The threats inherent to one characteristic (the limited seeing tied to a point of view; the mechanical vision linked to a prosthetic camera; the overwhelming sensation due to excitation; etc.) are compensated by means of the other characteristic (the multiplication of the shots; the humanlike behavior of the camera; an implied observer who "masters" the depicted events; etc.). The result was an ever inventive synthesis of gazes that strived to bring about true compromises without ever sacrificing the complexity of contradiction. We thus have a vision that, in making opposites permeable, modeled itself on an oxymoronic principle.

In its search for compromises, film did not conceal tensions, but tried to obtain an advantage from them. In constructing its gaze, the stances of the epoch were combined at the price of slight displacements and condensations. Merged with the sense of totality, a fragment was no more a "single" piece, but a temporarily detached portion of a vaster reality. The need to maintain a reference to the human transformed the mechanical into a familiar presence. Connected with a sense of orientation, excitation became a simple "cadence" in the narration. Framed by the eye of the cinema, the forces and counterforces of modernity changed their orientation and their inflection. Film "rewrote" its epoch in order to answer the question of its time.

This "rewriting" was in accordance with the basic proprieties of the cinema. Each filmic image is a partial record contained within the frame, "capturing" new sides of reality through the mobility of the camera. The cut from one shot to another gives each image the quality of a shock; editing can control its emotional power. Closeness and distance with the depicted world are defined by the apparatus. Basic proprieties were important in defining the possibilities of cinema. Yet the compromises that film defined were attempts to answer the needs of its time. Cinema was a medium subordinated to the social. As Balázs suggests, "technical development depends on social causes, and inventions take place when it is time for them to come."[8]

The formulas in which these various compromises were realized varied through time. Mainstream cinema of the thirties to the fifties did not respond in the same way as auteur cinema of the sixties and the seventies. The former carefully searched for "balanced" solutions; the latter was open to more dynamic and precarious answers. But if is true that the "classical" cinema systematically looked for compromises, it is also true that it displayed different strategies: one only needs to compare narratives based on a strong convergence of values around the hero's vision with stories based on "dual focus" narratives, in which we have the co-existence of two perspectives.[9] Hollywood's modes of representation are characterized by a very articulated history.[10] At the same time, the post-classical cinema (as well as the pre-classical and the anti-classical one) brought a more conflicted dimension to light—even though such conflicts hardly ever seemed irremediable. The fact remains that film developed its gaze by intercepting the impulses of twentieth-century modernity. It guided them in a particular direction, regulating their intensity, combining them, tying them to certain patterns or exigencies, finally giving them a model against which the spectator could compare him or herself. Film gave form to the modes of vision of its time, negotiating ongoing cultural processes, but ultimately it was the century's most astute director. Film's gaze was revealing. By fine-tuning a means of observation, film helped us to see better, and to see into the spirit of this particular time. Not surprisingly, we are dealing here with a disciplinary gaze as well: in opening our eyes, film told us what to look at and how. In this sense, film gave us a script for reading the modern experience: it not only proposed a reading of that experience, but at times imposed a pattern for its expression and communication.

This reflexivity of film's function, which I will discuss further in chapter 7, explains how cinema was simultaneously a form of thought, on the one hand, and a discipline, on the other. By negotiating the questions of its time, cinema influenced the articulation of the mental categories used to face reality. And by giving the audience some ready-made formulae, it guided our eyes. Nevertheless, these formulae were always imposed through entertainment and play. If cinema ended up functioning as a "discipline," it was a "discipline" which sought to embody the presence of a desire and the idea of freedom. Let us call it an *unimposed discipline*. This paradox confirms the oxymoronic nature of its action in an age that embraced the paradox as one of its most essential traits.[11]

A quick remark about my methodology may be helpful. The analysis will be guided by both theoretical texts and films, which I will read sometimes in a "heterodox" way. There will be a large variety of references: I will turn to both well-known film scholarship as well as less known contributions, masterpieces as well as B-movies, film as well as philosophical and literary essays. This assemblage of divergent documents and the logic with which I pull them together will not obey philological criteria. Rather, the goal is to collect a network of discourses that can function as a "gloss" for the cinematic phenomenon and give it meaning on a collective stage. Therefore, we will put into play the way in which cinema presented itself to the eyes of society, and how it rendered itself a conceivable experience.

Such attention to the intersections between gaze, discourse, and experience will ground this study. The purpose is to illustrate how this circuit of discourses gave meaning to film within twentieth-century modernity, and—in a magnificent form of specularity—it is film that bestows meaning on the modern experience. Through the elaboration of its gazes, the cinema furnishes the bordering frame within which the age makes itself knowable—and bearable—to its subjects and spectators.

The Gaze of Its Age

SEEING

Stupor, appreciation, expectation. Since its invention, film has provoked debate about its significance and much speculation about what it might contribute to the new century. The conviction soon emerged that film could make us look at the world anew. It taught us not only to take a second look at the world, but to look in a different way. Film set our sense of vision free, restoring it to us with an invigorating potential.

This idea became a leitmotif of film criticism in the 1920s. Bela Balázs summed it up in a formulation that would become popular:

> From the invention of printing, the word became the principal channel of communication between men . . . in the culture of words, the spirit—once so conspicuous—became almost invisible. . . . Now film is impressing on culture a change as radical as that of the invention of the press. Millions of people each night experience with their own eyes, sitting before the screen, the destinies of men, their personalities and feelings, states of mind of every sort, without needing words. . . . *Man will go back to being visible.*[1]

Balázs said it clearly: film restores human visibility, and gives reality back to the gaze. Some of his contemporaries expressed it similarly. For example, Sebastiano A. Luciani:

> The art of film has rendered us sensitive to the dynamic beauty of the face, in the same manner in which the theater made us sensitive to the voice. Where we once saw—in art and in life—only partially expressive masks, today we can say that we see faces.[2]

Or Jean Epstein:

> The lens of the camera is an eye without prejudice, without morals, un-
> touched by any influence; it sees in the face and in gesture features that we,
> consumed with our likes and dislikes, habits and thoughts, are no longer able
> to see.[3]

And for Abel Gance, this notion assumed a jubilant tone:

> The cinema will endow man with a new sense. He will see through his eyes.
> He will be sensitive to brilliant versification as he has been to prosody. He will
> see the birds and the wind come to rest. A ray will shine down. A street will
> seem as beautiful as a Greek temple.[4]

Film taught us to look at the world as we had never been able to before.
This idea recurs in many contemporary works.[5] It is supported by another belief that in some ways clarifies and radicalizes it: if film reconquered
and recast our manner of seeing, it was not only because it embodied the
gaze of the human eye, but because it embodied the gaze of the twentieth
century. The camera captured what lay before it in forms that revealed
the attitudes and orientations with which people were compelled to look
at the world around them. On the screen, more than a reality objectively
recorded, we saw reality in the spirit of the time.[6]

Frequently, the same scholars who emphasized the renewal of vision
with film became its chief interpreters as well. Luciani, for example, goes
on to comment:

> The telephone, automobile, airplane and radio have so altered the limits of
> time and space within which civilizations have developed, that today man
> has ended up acquiring not so much a quickness of understanding unknown
> to the ancients, as a kind of ubiquity. Film seems the artistic reflection of this
> new condition of life, both material and spiritual.[7]

Scholars from related fields also seized onto film's power to reclaim the
visual dimension and thus to interpret its time. Only a few years later,
Erwin Panofsky stressed the way in which the figurative and plastic arts
"start with an idea to be projected into shapeless matter, and not with
the objects that constitute the physical world." This journey from the abstract to the concrete allows them to transmit an "idealistic conception"
that is no longer in line with their times. With bodies and things at its

point of departure, "it is the movies, and only the movies, that do justice to that materialistic interpretation of the universe which, whether we like it or not, pervades contemporary civilization."[8] Film's tendency to lay bare the spirit of its age did not, however, necessarily require that it function merely as a mirror. Siegfried Kracauer, who gave careful attention to the typical themes running through early cinema, pointed out that even the most fantastic of these "reveal how society wants to see itself."[9] The pervasive thought is that film, in its complexity, is a sign of its time. Léon Moussinac observed in 1925: "Within the great modern upheaval, an art is born, develops, discovers its laws one by one, moves slowly toward its perfection, an art that will be the very expression—bold, powerful original—of the ideal of the new age."[10]

Keeping all of this in mind, let us move ahead to the German cultural theorist and critic Walter Benjamin and his canonical essay, "The Work of Art in the Age of Mechanical Reproduction."[11]

SYNCHRONIES

According to Benjamin, every phase of the history of man grasps reality in its own way: "Just as the entire mode of existence of human collectives changes over long historical periods, so too does their mode of perception."[12] The kind of gaze that a historical period adopts manifests the concerns and interests of that period, and refers back in turn to the underlying social processes that feed these concerns. Benjamin suggests that twentieth-century modernity is dominated by two tendencies, "both linked to the increasing significance of the masses in contemporary life."[13] The two tendencies are "the desire of the present-day masses to 'get closer' to things spatially and humanly, and their equally passionate concern for overcoming each thing's uniqueness."[14] We see here on the one hand an attempt to overcome distance, a need for nearness; on the other, a sense of universal sameness. With their emphasis on proximity and equality, these two tendencies legitimate a novel stance: what surrounds us must be captured in a plain and direct manner, without hindrance or restraint—even if, by necessity, through mechanical reproduction.

Film is an exemplary tool for attaining this end. Its gaze breaks down conventional barriers between ourselves and reality:

Our bars and city streets, our offices and furnished rooms, our railroad sta-
tions and our factories seemed to close relentlessly around us. Then came
film and exploded this prison-world with the dynamite of the split second, so
that now we can set off calmly on journeys of adventure among its far-flung
debris.[15]

Its gaze is able to draw us into the very fabric of things:

Just as enlargement not merely clarifies what we see indistinctly "in any
case," but brings to light entirely new structures of matter, slow motion not
only reveals familiar aspects of movements, but discloses quite unknown aspects within them.[16]

This is a gaze that can astonish us with the rapidity of its insight. While
the traditional arts stimulated contemplation, floods of filmic images
provoke continuous shock.[17] The filmic gaze is a leveling gaze that can
reframe everything and everyone within a principle of equality. Benjamin
writes: "the newsreel offers everyone the chance to rise from passer-by to
movie extra."[18] Finally, it is a gaze that can dispense with the uniqueness
that characterizes the traditional work of art, since it can be replicated
on every film print and during every projection. Speaking about actors,
Benjamin notices: "now the mirror image has become detachable from
the person mirrored and is transportable."[19] Of course, there are contrary
impulses as well. Cinematic technology operates as a filter; habit leads
to inattention; the "optical unconscious," giving the spectator the knowledge of things that could never be seen previously,[20] complicates the
relationship between observer and what is observed. Nevertheless it is
true that film celebrates and manifests the nearness and the sameness of
things. It does so in conjunction with an age that privileges these values
by stripping any "aura" from the work of art, which is transformed from
an object of veneration to a mere object of display.[21]

Here it becomes important to define more precisely film and its relation to the century it represents. If these two spheres really do converge,
at what points do they meet? And how does this convergence mutually condition each? What kind of film and what kind of modernity does
this convergence produce? In short, what made film an interlocutor for
modernity?

I will try to answer these questions by following three parallel paths.
To begin with, it is film's power as a medium that played a decisive role

in creating the convergences we have identified. It acted primarily as a means of communication—even more than as a means of expression. And it did this in an age which saw the media, rather than the traditional arts, as the preferred instrument for exploring and unifying experience. Film was the medium of choice in a profoundly "mediated" era. It was significant too that film not only highlighted the questions of its time, but recast them, making them its own, and at the same time giving them an iconic value in the eyes of all. It did this in a period when cultural institutions charged with elaborating social values and concerns were in deep crisis. Cinema redefined the conceptual field at a time when this function was partly unfilled. Yet film would not have been so successful as a medium if it had not been able to resolve contradictory impulses and *negotiate* compromises between them. Let us remember that this was an age that had numerous and distressing conflicts in need of mediation. Film is a space of reconciliation: it forces us into contact with reality, but is simultaneously grounded in distraction. It offers fantastical images and ideas but reincorporates them in plausible scenarios. It provokes and stimulates, but also organizes and disciplines.

First, film is a medium for the exhibition and exchange of proposals; second, it is a sphere in which the impulses of its time can be reworked and made iconic; and third, it is a space in which these contradictory impulses can come to the negotiating table. In the remainder of this chapter I will elaborate on these three theses with the help of three essays by Louis Delluc as well as other theoretical texts from the 1920s. I have privileged the 1920s here because the debate of this decade is highly interesting. It occurred after two decades of examining film as a surprising modern experience, and it came before the "standardization" of film's linguistic and expressive devices in the 1930s. The 1920s constitute an essential hinge between moments of utopian euphoria and subsequent systematization. What unfolds in this decade is the attempt to gradually transform a novelty into an *institution*.[22] We have various positions scattered over various geographical poles (Paris, Berlin, Moscow, Rome, America), but also a largely common concern. In this framework, Delluc's relevance lies in his basic attitude: suspended between the defense of traditional values and attention to the clashes within them, he is more subtly contradictory than most early critics, and shows the complicated way in which awareness of cultural change often develops.

"DE L'ART ET DU TRAFFIC"

It quickly became clear that film was, more than anything else, an instrument of communication in the broad sense of the term. Undeniably, film also claimed for itself a place in the field of aesthetics: the terms "fifth art," "eighth art," and even "seventh art" prove this (the last, coined by Ricciotto Canudo, having come into everyday use).[23] But however much its expressive possibilities were extolled, its masterpieces enumerated, or its influence on other arts recognized, the aspects of film that stood out most prominently were its popular appeal, the universality of its language, and the industrial quality of its production. Critics sometimes seemed uncomfortable acknowledging these latter characteristics of film as an object of mass consumption. Rather than recognize them, they recycled old categories from the field of art history such as authorship. Yet even those who most wished to incorporate film into the aesthetic traditions of the past (beginning with Canudo himself)[24] had to realize it was a new form of experience that demanded new critical canons.

Louis Delluc's short essay, "The Fifth Art" ("Le cinquième art," 1919),[25] seems exemplary of this critical dilemma. Delluc begins the piece with his usual mélange of aesthetic dissatisfaction with the cinema and hope for what it could be: "An art, of course it will be an art." He goes on, however, to list a series of characteristics that point to a different line of criticism. First he points out film's spatial diffusion: "Film goes everywhere. Theater halls are built by the thousands in every country, films have been shot all over the world." Next, he acknowledges its extraordinary power of persuasion: "The screen . . . has more impact on the international masses than a political speech." He notes as well the instant stardom that film offers its actors: "A year—even six months—is sufficient for a name, a grimace, a smile to compel recognition from the world." And similarly, the attention it stirs in the public: "It is a powerful means to get the people to speak." Finally, he stresses the importance of not only the commercial but also the technical dimension of cinema. American supremacy in the field, he argues, is linked to the "technical improvement of the image, lighting, sets, and scripts, which gives a harmonious nature to their science." In the conclusion of the piece Delluc revises his opening thoughts: "We are witnessing the birth of an extraordinary art: perhaps the only modern art that already has a place apart and one day will have astonishing glory; for it—and it alone, I tell you—is son of the mechanical and the human ideal." Delluc echoes here, in more positive terms, the withering definition of cinema that he provided some lines earlier: "This expressive industry is heading toward the simultaneous perfection of art and traffic."

Art and traffic. In this biting characterization, Delluc not only expresses the need to draw attention to a dimension other than—though linked to—the artistic; he also offers a powerful image of what makes a medium. What, in fact, do we normally mean by this term? A medium is, above all, a means of transmitting sensations, thoughts, words, sounds, and images. Its main objective is the spreading of information and, in the case of mass media, the widest spreading of information that technology will allow ("film goes everywhere"). The pursuit of this objective gives rise to three closely interrelated features which define all media. In order to spread information, a medium must also be able to gather, readapt, and conserve it: a medium works on content in order to render it consumable (the happy fate of "a name, a grimace, a smile"). By spreading information, a medium grants its audience the opportunity to enter into contact with the information being offered, the source or agent offering that information, and finally its other audiences; it works to produce a system of relationships that is as interactive as possible. Finally, a medium cannot distribute information without the appropriate technical apparatus: it depends on a host of reproductive technologies, from which it seeks the greatest possible efficiency (the role played in an "expressive industry," by "the improvement of image, lighting, sets," etc.). A medium, then, is a conjunction of content, interaction, and technology that is locally optimal for information transfer. From this we can deduce that a medium is always and necessarily representative, relational, and technological.[26] The ground for these subsequent determinations is, in every case, communicability.

Delluc, perhaps unintentionally, paints just such a picture. In fact the faces of the medium (implicating representation, relationship, and technology), together with its primary vocation (communicability), have a strategic value in any society. In one way, they allow three branches of activity to be interconnected: the construction of images of real or possible worlds, the definition of interpersonal and group relationships, and the fine-tuning of a device may all join together in a single communicative gesture. In another respect, they permit the medium to enter into the nerve center of a society. The action of a medium overtly influences the sphere of symbolic, social, and technological procedures, and thus touches the most delicate nodes of a human community. It is in this connection that Marshall McLuhan would speak, years later, of the means of communication as the "nervous system" of a society: they elaborate information, share it, and channel it into technological equipment, just as nerve endings and synapses expand and distribute impulses in the human body. In both cases, the organism becomes dependent on its communicative network.

Returning to Delluc, it is clear that we search his criticism in vain for a full treatment of what constitutes a medium. It is interesting, however, that in trying to define film, he juxtaposes the word "art" with terms like "expressive industry," "efficiency," "conversation," "mechanical" and above all, "traffic." Film can be many things, but it is what it is because it marries the ability to fine-tune content, the capacity to kindle relationships, and the capability to set a machine in motion. It does so by virtue of its vocation as a means of transport and exchange—the very site of "traffic." Herein lies film's distinctiveness, as well as its modernity.

If Delluc was not fully conscious of the nature of the medium, Benjamin certainly was. The term *medium* in fact recurs in Benjamin's work, though he intends it in a sense slightly different from the one elaborated here.[27] In his pages, the medium's central feature—its commitment to constructing consumable representations, interactive relations, and efficient technologies—is paired with a historical period that revolutionizes at a stroke social relationships, systems of production, and indeed man's very way of seeing the world, under the triple sign of immediacy, equality, and industrial organization. Mass media can contain the conflicted dimensions of the modern age, while traditional forms of art find themselves unable to confront these dimensions. The inevitable conclusion is that in an age that Benjamin identifies with mechanical reproduction, what is exemplary are visual media, since they seek increasingly to share their content, broaden their reception, and accelerate the development of their technological base. Conversely, traditional art is held at a distance, and worshipped without any true reason.[28] It is much better to recognize that traditional art set itself off from the contemporary scene,[29] and to ask it to abandon its "aura" and to become a communicative medium itself.[30]

Benjamin wrote extensively about this transformation of art into something that fits the term *medium*. I will not summarize all of his argument here. Yet is it evident that in modernity—an age of desacralization—the communicative substitutes for the aesthetic. The aesthetic, if it is to survive, seeks refuge elsewhere—for example, in the experimental fields where meaning is formed before it becomes "common sense."[31] It may also fold itself, with the artist's apparent reluctance, into the communicative realm of commodified media. Within this frame film's role becomes clear. No longer simply art—or not sufficiently art—it is exposed as a medium, and as a medium it displays the best of itself. Film offers its content in the broadest and most practical form possible; at the same time, it creates collective cultural ties of enormous strength and employs a technology of previously unimagined probative power. Film embodies the modern age precisely because it comprehends the dimensions and exigencies of that age to the fullest extent possible.

IF ORESTES BECOMES RIO JIM

Though film's manner of recording the world evinces a strong synchronicity with its time, this should not be understood as a passive absorption of signs. Neither what we see on screen, nor the affect that it inspires in us, is a simple imitation of what lies before the camera. On the contrary, the depictions of the world in a film are often quite idiosyncratic. Films are therefore active contributors to the world they represent.

We can explore this mutual transference by returning for a moment to the 1920s debate regarding the widespread popularity of the cinema. In particular, the lecture Louis Delluc gave at the Colisée cinema in January 1921, entitled "Cinema, the popular art" ("Le cinéma, art populaire"),[32] is instructive. The talk began with the legendary phrase, "Ladies and gentlemen, the cinema does not exist"—a further expression of Delluc's constant concern for what he thought of as the unrealized artistic potential of the medium. As usual, however, his attention also pointed elsewhere: specifically, to the universal audience which film had won. The reasons for this rampant enthusiasm were threefold. Above all, film, as already mentioned, speaks a "universal language" and thus speaks to all. Next, film cultivates a "universal taste," based on the affirmation of ostensibly universal values, such as love, duty, and revenge. Finally, film promotes what we might call a "universal synchrony" through the collective and simultaneous viewing of the same spectacle by thousands. Delluc posed: "Film spectators gather in the amphitheater of the whole world. The most diverse and extreme beings witness the same film at the same time the

world over. Isn't this magnificent?" These elements of film as a phenomenon allowed Delluc to make a connection that is only initially surprising. Film recapitulates the defining characteristics of Greek tragedy on a
global scale. It has the same popular character: it promotes broad access,
a common idiom, and collective participation. Moreover, it exhibits the
images and deeds an entire people regard as their own—the myths and
rites of an entire community. In this sense, there is a continuity between
the new theaters and the ancient amphitheaters. Rio Jim, the protagonist
of a western played by William Hart, is a direct descendent of Orestes,
just as Louise Glaum and Bessie Love are, respectively, those of Clytemnestra and Electra.[33]

Delluc's curious intuition further illuminates—through reference to
film's ability to resuscitate myths and rituals—a film's fundamental characteristic as a mode of communication. We are confronted with a source
of images and socially relevant behaviors that function as "models." Now
let us take a closer look at its underlying processes.

Every medium assumes control over what it transmits, even if only
through its transmission. Whenever it receives external stimuli—pieces
of reality, social discourse, fragments of latent drives—a medium always
"adapts" them to fit its own demands. In making them its own, it selects
and reorders them, often paraphrasing or even blending them with one
another. These elements combine to form a new shape. A medium never
simply transmits preexisting contents without in some way reforming
them. The same holds for the social relationships that it engenders. Here
as well, despite the best efforts of a medium to replicate existing relations in an adequate way (as the telephone replicates the mode of face-
to-face communication), it inevitably privileges one sensory channel over
another (the aural over the visual), or alters the spatiotemporal circumstances of the act (by the sacrifice of real presence), or alters the intent of
its actors. We are not dealing with a copy here, but with a reformulation.

This "rewriting" has a strong interpretive value, and in this sense it
constitutes a true redefinition of the reality to which the medium refers.
But this "rewriting" goes so far as to define reality. By establishing this
reality for a series of recipients, it also fixes the traits with which it will
be interpreted. From this point of view, the "filtering" action that a medium carries out is an action that "guides" perception and behavior: when
a medium speaks to me or causes me to act, it suggests what I must

(and must not) take into consideration, and how I must (must not) do so (this reality or action instead of that one; this feature or mode instead of another). Thus, on the one hand it gives me a key to reading existence, while on the other it binds me to a certain line of conduct. In establishing a reality or behavior, a medium offers a "formula" for understanding or interpreting the world, and at the same time a "standard" to which my interpretation must conform. Herein lies the medium's power of definition. This power is directly proportional to both its capacity for producing adequate images of things and to the breadth of currency that these images enjoy in my cultural context.

This is, in broad outline, the process by which the medium gives a *form* to its context.[34] Let us now return to Delluc. His essay on the new medium captures not only film's power to engender interest and participation in its fantasies but also its ability to construct imaginary symbols and behavioral patterns in which a society is able to see itself. Delluc brought to the fore film's nascent capacity for just this sort of "putting into form." It is in this aspect of filmic communication that Delluc finds parallels with Greek tragedy. Rio Jim—and his embodiment of the mythological cowboy figure—epitomizes the sentiments, desires, and values by which contemporary society wished to live. In the same way, the dilemmas that pervaded ancient Athenian society were condensed and revealed for the benefit of all. In the modern age film is the most appropriate medium for a reproposal of myths and rituals, a set of symbols and deeds that trace and condition collective experience. Film is a machine that exposes what stirs beneath social surfaces. But it is also party to the process: through its suggestions, it advances new models of understanding and behavior (that is, new categories of mind and action). It is at once a witness and a fully active protagonist.

Film's ability to find new forms in the spirit of its time began to constitute a fundamental principle of the medium in the 1910s and 1920s. Film's most essential moments were those in which it retranscribed the real, offering a new image of it, which became ours as well. A striking American article by Rollin Summers, which appeared ten years before Delluc's, sets the parameters of the issue:

> Every art has its peculiar advantages and disadvantages growing out of the particular medium in which it expresses itself. It is the limitations and the

advantages of its particular means of expression that give rise to its particular technique. An observation of the limitations and advantages of motion photography will suggest the particular technical laws of the moving picture play.[35]

Summers points out that every medium is characterized by a set of possibilities and limitations. The more a medium works on these possibilities and limitations, the better it obeys its internal "laws." What follows is an immediate approval for all of those moments in which film gives form to the real, using the processes that conform to its "laws." A film gives the best of itself when it widens the radius of its visual exploration, puts rapid scene exchange into play, and drives actors to naturalistic acting. Conversely, it shows its worst when—imitating the theater—it aims to express thoughts, uses fixed scenes, and accepts contrived acting. This evaluation formula, which David Bordwell[36] rightly posits as the basis for the traditional theoretical canon, had many followers. We find it again in the work of scholars such as Eugenio Giovannetti, who underscored the "predilections of film,"[37] or Erwin Panofsky, who demanded that cinematographic style respond "to the specific conditions of the medium."[38] It found its clearest formulation in Rudolf Arnheim, particularly in his 1932 *Film (Film als Kunst)*: "In order that the film artist may create a work of art it is important that he consciously stress the peculiarities of his medium. This, however, should be done in such a manner that the character of the objects represented should not thereby be destroyed but rather strengthened, concentrated, and interpreted."[39] The cinema must follow its own inclinations: only this allows it to speak clearly.

I have had good reasons for beginning this discussion with Delluc. His work is devoted to both filmic representation and forms of reception. In this light, Delluc's examination of myths and rites is interesting. But this work of "giving form" is not limited to the medium's technological dimension. Technology must also measure itself against social and symbolic needs that are often overdetermined. It is indicative that Delluc called these key elements of society *rites* and *myths*. This work of "giving form" does not merely have an aesthetic value: on the contrary, it extends into "everyday" production and fruition. Film is a medium that operates precisely in the everyday. It is a "laboratory" of new symbols and practices; indeed, it is an open laboratory—an unending process—and a common laboratory, belonging to all. In this sense, the reference to Delluc's myths and rites acquires additional weight.

"*LAIDEUR ET BEAUTÉ*"

We have already seen how film is able to gather the signs of its age, reorganize them according to its own principles, and make them worthy of this new form as recognizable and recognized models. Film cannot be considered, though, a simple mirror of its time. In shaping the themes and behaviors that pervade social space, it became also a source for new ideas. As a medium, it carried out this action in everyday reality, competing with other communicative channels: from newspapers to light fiction, from popular music, illustrations, and theater to etiquette guides (in addition, naturally, to the traditional arts, scientific research, and behavioral guidelines proposed by large institutions, etc.). In other words, film elaborated mental models and behavioral canons in a larger network of social discourses.[40] In this network, film occupied a role of utmost importance for its ability to set out and circulate its own ideas, for the perceptiveness with which it operates, and finally for a third characteristic that I will now address.

We should return to a piece by Delluc, "The Photo-plastique in Film" ("La photoplastique au cinema," 1918).[41] I return to Delluc—the ambiguity of his position notwithstanding, suspended as it was between a nostalgia for high expression and the understanding of the radical change in progress—for it is precisely this ambiguity that is fruitful. Not surprisingly, its opening is striking: "Nudity in film will one day assert and establish itself. Nothing is more photogenic. Haven't you noticed how it is already used? Film heroines spend all their time in evening gowns." Film is an exhibition space for bodies, so much so that to satisfy this need, films require that their characters wear clothes that are not always appropriate to the narrative situation. This passion for the unclothed body can be malicious as well: the reference is to Max Sennett, whose films seem deliberately set at a pool's edge, on the beach, or in a ballroom; they are "all fantasy, filled with an almost cubist brusqueness that conjures away the knowing debauchery." And yet film seems to redeem such a display of nudity. "This penchant for the skin's effect . . . never offers anything ugly." Film avoids vulgarity, even when it seems to threaten the screen, for at least two reasons. First, it transforms the bodies it (even shamelessly) displays. Nudity is photogenic: and the photogeneity redeems and exalts. Next, because film tolerates neither the immediate nor the excessive: it has internal measure. In this regard, it is interesting to note how actors learn from watching their own images on the screen: "The first films in which women, such as Francesca Bertini, showed their arms and breasts were awful films. Nevertheless, the physical beauty of the performer appeared as genuine—at least—as it does now. The years have taught it to measure its grace." The conclusion is unavoidable: "Film notices, conserves, advises. Having for once been delivered from ugliness (or else all the ugliness of which it is capable), it often creates an intelligent and new beauty."

Delluc again offers a useful starting point to widen our frame. In the game that he describes, we see how film is situated before two possibilities: it can pursue libertinism (perhaps seasoned with an "almost cubist brusqueness" that gives the body further plastic starkness), or it can bring the representation of nudity back to more classical standards (thanks to the filmic image's power to transform what it captures). The two paths subtly conflict: one can lead to pornography, the other risks becoming abstraction. Film however pursues both: it accepts one as a necessary attraction, and gives a strong pedagogical importance to the other. What is realized is then a more "inclusive" rewriting: the screen glows with the display of skin, but will avoid ugliness, in favor of a bright and gratuitous beauty.

Film often carries out this job of assessment and rewriting. Or, to put it better, it *negotiates* between its various permeating impulses. It does this not only between ugliness and beauty but also with many other opposites it inevitably encounters, whether they be aesthetic or moral choices, courses of action or basic values, personal opinions or collective attitudes. Film measures itself against a large spectrum of alternatives, alternatives that it, in turn, moves to measure against each other. The age it faces is, moreover, marked by a great variety of currents. Let us take, for example, the phenomena and subsequent changes in the years of its birth and development: the scientific discoveries and their application to industry, the broadening of the market and necessity for new products, the demographic upheaval and the explosion on the scene of new ranks and social classes, the construction of networks of transport and communication, the intensification of movement and contact, etc. An entire frame of life changed, and with it, the traditional frames of reference.[42] It is precisely here that the Benjaminian need for availability, nearness, and efficiency emerged. Also pushing to the foreground was an appreciation for novelty, activeness, speed, repetition, individualism, etc. Perhaps as a reaction, or a sense of nostalgia, there was also the need for withdrawal, placing distance, naturalness, stability, and slowness. Meanwhile, despite the increasing closeness of the world, a subtle sense of the loss of reality asserted itself in the background; it was accompanied by a sense that the self was somehow lost, even as all individuals seemed propelled toward the center of history.

Film calls this variety of references to account; it summons them to its table, and puts them side by side; it readapts them, if necessary, searching for a form that might make them appear compatible. The cinema shapes the stances that it encounters, and in doing that it *negotiates*. In the essay that spurred this discussion, Benjamin offers some fine examples of this complexity—a complexity that remains to be clarified. After noticing that films "jolt the viewer" with "an alluring visual composition or an enchanting fabric of sound,"[43] he also remarks that they produce a "distracted perception," one in which shock effects are transformed into habit: "Reception in distraction—the sort of reception which is increasingly noticeable in all areas of art and is a symptom of profound changes in apperception—finds in film its true training ground."[44] Even as he points out film's ability to exalt the powers of sight, he notes how the camera introduces a new kind of gaze: at the moment in which the world is filmed, "a space informed by human consciousness gives way to a space informed by the unconscious."[45] Finally (and in some ways the weightiest detail) though he emphasizes film's tendency to put us in contact with things, Benjamin concludes that its apparatus unavoidably veils the direct gaze of the world: "The vision of immediate reality [has become] the Blue Flower in the land of technology"[46]

Film is thus able to work with seemingly opposite impulses: it seizes them, draws them together, and reassembles them. It succeeds in holding together excitement and habit, consciousness and unconsciousness, immediacy and mediation. What is more: it is even able to negotiate between the aesthetic and the communicative. For if it is true that the age demands that the communicative enforce its own principles, it is also true that it cannot—or will not—completely give up the aesthetic, with its traditional values. Here we have the significance of Delluc: his battle for art is indeed a step backward with respect to Benjamin's considerations on the age of mechanical reproduction (but also to Kracauer who, in an extraordinary essay on Berlin's cinemas, condemns the increasing desire to return film to the dignity of the traditional masterpieces, instead of allowing them to express the superficiality, breakdown, and fragmentation consonant with mass society).[47] This battle of his, however, indicates the necessity of continuing to bring to account certain traditional categories; if for no other reason, it is through them that the new medium can appear a socially positive, socially legitimated phenomenon. Film plays along: it is a medium, but one able to cloak itself in art (perhaps the promise of art, or of a popular art). In this way, it puts forth the new, while equally demonstrating its power to call the old into account, to salvage some of its worth, to graft itself onto tradition, to carry on its inheritance. Raymond Spottiswoode, seventeen years later, would determine the point of compromise: "communication is an indispensable objective of works of art"; moreover, "the spectator will . . . establish perfect contact with the artist if he is aware of each detail in theme and technique which the artist made a vehicle of communication."[48] The best comes from the marriage of these two fronts.

So film *negotiates*, and it negotiates its own basic limits as well. This effort of rewriting is often related to the search for *compromise*. Often, in fact, the convergence in film has the effect of rendering "innocuous" solutions that might otherwise seem too unilateral or dogmatic. In these cases, choices contemplated within social space (such as, to use Delluc's words, the "rough" representations of cubism, but also the tensions of a crowd that seem to smooth themselves out in the cinema) are recovered and softened, weakened even: the cinematographic medium can, in this way, become more easily and more abundantly their bearer. Yet, though film aims at compromise, it is equally able to practice radicalism: perhaps not in mainstream production, distinguished by a broad acceptance of ideas, but at least in circles where it promotes experimentation, authorship, and the pursuit of expressivity. Even in these cases, however, we are confronted with an exercise of negotiation: a careful consideration of the different forces that hold claim to film rightly results in exasperation. At the same time, even the simplest choices can reveal an element of radicalism: created from compromise, they seem completely innocuous, yet seethe with the passions from which they are born. It is not by chance then that the most advanced cinema (as, moreover, often happens in the avant-garde) makes choices that, though seemingly "scandalous," soon reveal themselves to be perfectly practical. In the same way, it is not by chance that a closer look at classical Hollywood (which best represents mainstream production) reveals a cinema that is much less classical and much more risqué than most reconstructions would have us believe.[49]

I would add that film carries out this work of negotiation both in the broad space of culture, as well as in the more specific space of its own reception. I mean that comparison and rewriting concern both the dynamics that are at the very foundation of the construction of a filmic text (and that lead precisely to one solution or another, chosen from various possibilities), and the dynamics of consumption (in which the reciprocal comparison lies between the filmic text, with its points of view, and the spectator, with his/her expectations, abilities, knowledge, etc.). The cinema "regulates itself," both in the circuit of social discourse and within its own vision. In this "auto-regulation," film finds a point of equilibrium, claims it, and puts it into view. There it is ready, as such, to turn its own proposal into the next element at stake, which must be balanced against the situation created as soon as it is put into public circulation.[50]

Thus, a negotiation takes place during a filmic text's preparation and consumption, sometimes in the name of compromise, sometimes under the weight of exasperation. This negotiation accompanies a rewriting of the drives that run through the social space maintained by the film, demanding that—in accompanying this work—they nourish and feed on it, too. There is, in fact, a total complicity between film's attempt to "give form" to what it encounters, and its ability to "negotiate" among the different forces and counterforces enveloping it. In short, film "gives form" to its own time, and in doing so—indeed, in order to do so—it negotiates; it negotiates in light of this "giving of form" and uses its own form for further negotiation. Its third advantage (being, additionally, a means of communication and a medium capable of articulating persuasion) is precisely its capacity for dialogue; and this at a time more tumultuous than ever, in an age that discovers a renewed need for mediation, since its traditional means—entrusted to institutions and processes rendered obsolete—are clearly inadequate.

FILM, TWENTIETH CENTURY

We can therefore return to the problem posed earlier. If film embodies the gaze of the twentieth century, what guarantees this convergence?

What nourishes their coming together? And what effects does this have on the participants?

Film comes to this meeting with three features. It is a medium, in an age that looks to the media rather than art. It is a medium that "gives form" to the ideas that circulate in the social space, in an age searching for new forms of representation and relation—new myths and rituals. And it is a medium that negotiates between often contradictory demands, in an age when the conflict between differing values is open and often dramatic—an age when traditional clearinghouses seem to fail. These three characteristics directly influence the type of gaze that film adopts. At stake is a gaze with the power to give evidence and circulate what it fixes in its lens: film, as medium, displays and shares its proposals. Once again, it is a gaze able to clarify and guide: film—as a device that "gives form"—offers models of interpretation and behavior. These models become, in turn, canonical, despite a certain levity granted by the quotidian nature of its actions. Finally, we are dealing with a syncretic gaze, which measures itself against various positions and, at the same time, seeks to individuate feasible resolutions. Film, as a device of negotiation, seeks to rewrite what it encounters. Vividness, exemplarity, practicability, syncretism: these are, after all, the dimensions in which film works to "tune in" to its times. Many of the recent definitions that have tried to focalize the role and action of film within the frame of modernity (as, for example, the idea that it acts as a "public sphere," or the idea that it supplies a "vernacular" language) could find more precise answers by looking to these features.[51]

It remains to be said that we are obviously not talking about "all" cinema, but a "certain" cinema. In particular, we are talking about a cinema that looked to and could assume the form of a real *social institution*: that is, a system both recognized and recognizable, given recurrent features, and well ensconced in its own context. Moreover, it is precisely the cinema that criticism—represented here by Delluc—attempted to "institutionalize," beginning with the early postwar years. It was a cinema that would see its greatest moment in mainstream production and the so-called classical age; but it was also a cinema that knew, both within and beyond this production, how to articulate its ideals, making them assume shapes that, with time, would best respond to the needs of society. No institution is static: even cinema—even this cinema—must know how to modify its art for communicability and its points of negotiation.

Accordingly, it has been a certain cinema—certainly not cinema "in itself"—that has embodied the gaze of modernity; similarly, it has been a certain modernity that has found in film its embodiment. This meeting has relegated other possible trajectories and realities to the background: "other" cinemas—perhaps only imagined, only potential—and "another" twentieth-century modernity—perhaps only hinted at, or rendered invisible. Every convergence is also the story of omissions and rejections. To follow the ties between film and its time, it is therefore necessary to work at two levels, both onstage and off. In the previous pages, we brought to light the cinema that characterized the stage. We will go on, aware that even the backstage has its importance. But it is on the stage itself—if only by convention—that the main performance takes place.

Framing the World

MORE, LESS

Since its invention, film has distinguished itself in its unprecedented visual capabilities. Yet its particular "gaze" has presented many ambiguities. A parallel reading of two books by Bela Balázs—*The Visible Man* (*Der Sichtbare Mensch*, 1924) and *The Spirit of Film* (*Der Geist des Films*, 1930)—gives us precious proof of this fact.[1] In *The Visible Man*, the idea emerges of a device that leads us to regain our sense of sight. Balázs writes:

> The lens of the cinema reveals to you the single cells of the vital tissue, it makes you feel the material and substance of the concrete life anew. It shows you what your hand—that you neither observe nor notice at all—does while it caresses or hits something. You live through it without seeing it. It reveals to you the intimate face of all of your vital gestures through which your soul appears and you are not conscious of it. The lens of the cinematographic apparatus will project on the wall the shadow with which you live, without seeing it, and it will recount the adventure and destiny of the cigar in your oblivious hand, and the secret life—the unnoticed life—of all the things that accompany you throughout your existence.[2]

Film offers to the gaze what we would otherwise let slip away. It opens (or reopens) our eyes and allows us to seize the reality in which we are immersed. This is true above all for the human face. Framing it, film restores to us its entire range of features, laying bare "type and personality, hereditary and acquired elements, one's fortune and will."[3] As a result, film ends up giving back to us the polyphony of sentiments occurring on the face. The face "becomes the everything in which the drama is contained," particularly with the close-up.[4] Indeed, every shot brings us straight to the heart of things. It returns the substance of what has been captured; it makes us experience the breathing of the entire world. Balázs illustrates this effect, for example, when he describes the portrayal of the crowd: "With a series of close-ups, of medium close-ups and detailed shots, it shows us the single grains of sand that make up the desert, so that even in the presence of the total picture the buzzing life of atoms lingers. In such close-ups, we feel the living spiritual material of which the masses are part."[5]

Six years later, in *The Spirit of Film*, the need for the camera to masterfully command the sense of sight persists, but the glances it casts on the world reveal a more subtle quality. A face on screen not only incarnates the elusive spirit of its subject but also revives the experience of being seen by someone, in a certain way, from a certain perspective. "A *physiognomy* in and of itself does not exist. There are only those we see," Balázs explains, "and they change, according to the point *from which* we see them. The physiognomy depends on the point of view; that is, the shot. The physiognomy is not only an objective fact but also our relationship with this fact. A synthesis."[6] Thus, film redeems the human gaze, at the same time anchoring it in a perceptive act. A seeing subject, a seen object, and a mode of framing this relationship all come into play in the cinematic gaze.

The consequences of this relationship are crucial. The gaze loses its immediacy: in seeing reality on the screen, we inevitably bring ourselves out in the open. "In the image, we see our position at the same time, or our relationship to the object,"[7] Balázs observes. Moreover, the gaze loses its neutrality: in seeing reality on the screen, and in seeing it from a certain perspective, we adopt a certain attitude and orientation. "Every visual angle on the world implicates a vision of the world,"[8] Balázs continues. Finally, the gaze loses its fullness: seeing reality on the screen, we see only what the adopted perspective allows us to grasp. The world, then, becomes like a kaleidoscope. As Balázs glosses it: "In fact, we do not see one image of certain things, but a hundred different images, according to the different views through which we look at them."[9] The real is no longer before our eyes, ready to reveal itself. We see that it is we who are seeing, seeing in a certain optic and partial way. In this sense, the argument of *The Spirit of Film* alters the logic of vision. And yet the desire of a productive and generative gaze lingers on. Anticipating the advent of color film, Balázs foresees that "it will be able, in close-ups, to reproduce even the most subtle nuances; it will reveal a new world of which we know nothing, although, in reality, we see it every day."[10]

It is useful to note that in the interim between the two works by Balázs, Erwin Panofsky published his celebrated essay "Perspective as Symbolic Form."[11] In that essay, attention returns to one of the key moments in art history: the perspectival representation emerging out of the Renaissance. The Renaissance conceives pictorial representation as the level intersection of a "visual pyramid." The ideal observer raises his eye to the pyramid's apex, and the entire field of vision is constituted by the lines that irradiate from this same eye. This means that the space that spreads out on the surface of a painting is presented not as reality in and of itself, but as something *seen*: what supports this perspective is the gaze that contemplates (and controls) the world. Panofsky rightly notes that the *perspectiva artificialis* appeals to a mathematical base that flattens and normalizes representation. Yet the presence of an observer in his or her singularity is never completely canceled. "Perspective subjects the artistic phenomenon to stable and even mathematically exact rules," Panofsky writes, "but on the other hand, makes that phenomenon contingent upon human beings, indeed upon the individual: for these rules refer to the psychological and physical conditions of the visual impression, and the way they take effect is determined by the freely chosen position of a subjective *point of view*."[12] It follows that the *act* of seeing continues to constitute an essential reference. However abstract the constructed gaze that organizes, the painting is always a unique "view."

The most advanced modernity, as Panofsky reminds us,[13] will be suspicious of mathematical reference and ready to emphasize perspective as "view." It might be opportune at this point to make another reference, which moves from the field of painting to that of literature, from the Renaissance to the years that saw the cinema's birth and development. I cite the ample series of prefaces and essays that Henry James wrote from the decades spanning the end of the nineteenth and beginning of the twentieth centuries.[14] Many scholars have pointed out the correlation between these writings and the birth of the cinema.[15] James recommends narrating an event as if it were passing before the eyes (or the consciousness) of a character. There are various motivations that prompt such a choice. There is the pull of finding a center to the narration that can give the story coherency and intelligibility, but also the need to intensify the tale, tying it directly to the perceptions and sensations of those acting within its diegetic world.[16] Whatever the reasons might be, to narrate means to offer an "ocular witness" of an event. James defines this "ocular witness" in various ways, all of which are significant: the *perceiver*, to underline the function of the observer within the field itself; the *reflector*, to show the capacity to shed light on events with a well-positioned ray of sunshine; and the *block*, to highlight the function of registering the consequences of the facts in one's own eyes and consciousness. The presence of the "ocular witness" is decisive. Indeed, it becomes the narrative's focal point, the true essence of the story. But its presence is decisive in another way as well: guided by it, the narration inevitably adapts a "limited perspective." What comes into view is only what he or she sees from his or her point of observation.

Let us linger for a moment on the idea of "limited perspective," illustrated by James's now-famous image: the narration as a building with infinite windows.

> The house of fiction has in short not one window, but a million. . . . At each of them stands a figure with a pair of eyes, or at least with a field-glass, which forms, again and again, for observation, a unique instrument, insuring to the person making use of it an impression distinct from every other. He and his neighbors are watching the same show, but one seeing more where the other sees less, one seeing black where the other sees white, one seeing big where the other sees small, one seeing coarse where the other sees fine. And so on, and so on . . . "[17]

The result is an undeniably personal vision:[18] perception of the world belongs to the individual—it is not a divine, omniscient gaze. This vision is thus also inevitably contingent: perception depends on the "window" through which we look, or rather, the window where we happen to be in the course of our own existence. Finally, and above all, this is an inevitably partial vision: the observer is able to gather only a small slice of the "human drama," especially if he or she stands before a simple sliver or "crack" of vision opening onto to the world. Perception of the total picture is forever barred. This is what we can call the crux of the Jamesian lesson. Every story implicates a gaze and this gaze is tied to a point of view. The point of view coincides with the presence of an observer who, at the same time, depends upon specific conditions for observation. This point of view is the "locus" in which the gaze is incarnated in a scopic subject, and is situated in a particular circumstance. The "locus" assigns the gaze the "*ego-hic-nunc*" that makes it "worldly" at last.

If the modern gaze has a typical characteristic, it is precisely that of being a "worldly" gaze, inescapably embodied and positioned. With his valuable analysis founded in a study of nineteenth-century physiology, Jonathan Crary drew attention to the rise of the new paradigm: early physiologists stressed how seeing relies on physical and mental processes that hinge upon both the body of the observer and the situation in which he or she exists. Through this new theory, the Cartesian model—according to which the eye constitutes a simple point of passage that puts reality and its mental image in direct contact—was questioned and then eradicated. To see is to transform data, to reelaborate and reconstruct it.[19] In this context, the gaze suddenly discovers its own limits. It responds to a subject, rather than to the reality. It operates on partial elements, rather than a total appreciation. It acts in the moment, rather than outside of time. The absoluteness of the gaze seems to disappear: what emerges instead is the field of tensions in which it is rooted. This is a realm in which the task of comparing the part and whole, subjectivity and objectivity, contingency and necessity, plays an essential role.

It would be fruitful perhaps to comment further on the consequences of this new idea of vision, as others have done,[20] but let us return to Balázs and film. Our slight detour into the work of Panofsky and especially of James allows us to understand the urgency at the heart of *The Spirit of Film*—even if the Hungarian author had no direct contact with the Jamesian debate. His inspirations were, if anything, Eisenstein's films, with their idea that every representation of the world is necessarily "oriented." Moreover, Balázs worked on a theory of filmic representation that was independent of the notion of an "ocular witness" within a story. Yet there is something that ties his position to the Jamesian problem: against the backdrop of the pressures of modernity, both writers seize on the exigency of a point of view, and with it, put an end to the idea of an all-embracing gaze that is abstract and absolute. The standards for measuring vision are inverted: limitation, subjectivity, and contingency become primary. Seeing becomes a riskier endeavor.

Let us look more closely at one of these three elements: the limitation of the visual field. Each glimpse can only catch fragments of the world, and the world becomes a whole of fragments. The theory is widely circulated. We encounter it in James, with his metaphor of the house with many windows. We recognize it, as well, in Benjamin: in analyzing the features of the modern experience, he brings to light primarily its loss of coherence and unity.[21] In film, the limitations of the cinematic gaze also spring from a technical aspect. What the film is able to show is more narrow than our natural field of vision. Enrico Toddi, in an irresistibly ironic 1918 article, lamented this reduction of the visual field due to the size of the frame, and dreams of a film in which the form and range of the screen image can expand itself: "Though the camera imitates as perfectly as possible the human eye, a heterogeneous element is suddenly introduced: the molded rectangle of the frame: 25 by 19 mm."[22] Eisenstein returned to this issue in the early 1930s, questioning whether the filmic image is confined to an invariable shape, or whether it might rebel against this fate.[23] The discovery that the cinema has its own point of view would allow us to confront this problem in all of its complexity.[24]

In *The Spirit of Film*, however, Balázs does not merely discover the existence of a point of view that limits our field of observation—he continues to dream of a gaze able to seize the world in its breadth and significance, as he had in *The Visible Man*. Under the pressure of modernity, the goal of a full vision collapses. Within the scope of modernity, however, this fullness still has a chance. The value of Balázs' insights consists in having systematically inscribed in his own reflections the contrast between the overdetermination of modern vision and the absolute perfection to which it still aspires. He keeps these two poles alive, without forcing only one to emerge. From here comes the question that film poses to the twentieth-century gaze. Should it move in the sphere of partiality, subjectivity, and contingency? Or should it aspire to completeness, objectivity, and necessity? Should it accept limits or try to surpass them?

Film effectively seized this emergent duality of modern vision, assuring a dialogue between the two. With the shot, film puts a limited perimeter of vision on screen; but every film-take seeks to restore a striking, "epiphanic" vision of the world. Through editing, each shot proposes one and one vision only, but the sequencing of shots permits multiple—even ubiquitous—perspectives.

Some years before Balázs, Jean Epstein concluded his essay "The meaning 1bis" ("Le sens 1bis," 1921) with the phrase "I watch" ("Je regarde").[25] This treasonous phrase openly rewrites the Cartesian principle of "cogito," and establishes an indissoluble tie between vision, its subject, and the concrete act of seeing. Seeing—at the cinema, as well as in "real life"—is always an individual, idiosyncratic act in any given situation. It is a seeing from a point of view and therefore inevitably partial, contingent, and subjective. Yet film discloses an extraordinary capacity in vision: at the movies, we get the heart and the soul of the world. Epstein writes: "There is a pregnant air of expectation. Life sources gush from corners we believed to be sterile and explored. The skin gives off a luminous soft-ness. The cadence of the crowd scenes is a song. Look. . . . Film sees on a large scale."[26]

How, then, to penetrate this question of the unique and universal, the part and the whole, the limited point of view and that which is beyond? If it is true that the power of film lies in tackling these polarities, keeping the extremes alive, and seeking to negotiate itself among them, then it is a question of identifying a series of instances in which film performs these operations and of attempting to understand their internal logic. In confronting this challenge, I will pursue a slightly unpredictable path. I will begin with three very different films and try, with some provocation, to uncover the ties that make this path crucial.

THE EAGLE, THE FLY, AND THE EMPEROR

If I had to sum up the basic problem at the heart of Abel Gance's *Napoléon* (1927), I would say that it recounts a destiny that emerges from single ep-isodes drawn out of one life. The story begins at Brienne, Napoléan's mili-tary college. It continues at the Club des Cordeliers, where Josephine first appears. Then it moves on to Corsica, the siege of Toulon, the Terror, Ven-demiare, the Reaction: though these are only steps, they are nonetheless fulfilling a luminous path. The moral: we can only illustrate mere frag-ments of existence, but in each fragment pulses the sense of the whole.

Naturally, this question of a tension between the part and the whole is not isolated to the narrative plane. Gance's initial project envisioned the reconstruction of Napoléon's biography in six films. The film he fi-nally made was only the first installment. His ambition, then, was not just to detail the relevant episodes of Bonaparte's life but to offer its full scope.[27] The treatment of single episodes, together with the immensity of the complete picture, are proof of this desire to permeate the part with the whole. Each shot contains but a slice of reality, like each biographical episode: it is a question of restoring its limits, capturing reality within a

global vision. Gance's manipulation of certain defining cinematic techniques in Napoléon—the split screen, superimposition, rapid montage,
swish pans—seem the perfect illustration of this tension and, at the same
time, an attempt to resolve it.

Let us consider the split screen. We find a striking example in the initial episode, set at Brienne college. During the pillow fight, the screen is
divided at first into four boxes, then six, then nine, in order to depict the
many phases of a fight in progress.[28] What does this segmented composition suggest? Each portion of the screen gives us only one fragment
of the event: each is seen from a specific perspective and in a specific
instant, and therefore taken from a single point of view. Yet the entire
screen incorporates side by side the various portions of the event, combining perspectives and moments, and therefore generating a point of
view born from the sum of those preceding it. The effect is that of offering a composite whole in which the meaning of each part survives, but
in which the sense of the whole comes forward as well. The filmic image
is a true mosaic in which one can see individual tesserae, but in which
there is also a design that both incorporates and exceeds them. The act of
filmmaking thus signifies working with fragments, and above all knowing how to transcend them. At the cinema, to see means to break through
the limits to which we are anchored by everyday vision.

Superimposition obeys the same principle, thanks to the multiplication of levels of the image, and Napoléon makes frequent use of this
technique. In addition to creating metaphors, the use of superimposition
aims to combine various elements that are not easily separable. This is
again the case with the snowball fight at Brienne college. After the in-
tertitle "He gave orders in the midst of the confusion," we see repeated
superimpositions of Napoléon in close-up and the fight as it happens, in
order to underline the intimate harmony of the leader with the events
he commands. This is similarly the case at the Convention, in which we
find a quadruple superimposition—the Assembly, a stormy sea, Napoléon
among the waves, and an eagle—to mark the entire picture of all elements at play, both present and future. In this sense, superimposition offers a "comprehensive" image that gathers, unites, and fuses. We see a
single point of view, but we also see it as the product of an intersection of
several points of view. Naturally, there is the risk that individual elements
become no longer recognizable, as Gance shares: "I found some negatives
from Napoléon where there are sixteen images, one on top of the other. I

knew that it was impossible to see anything after the fifth image, but they were there, and from the moment that they were there, their potential was there as well."[29] Some intelligibility may be lost, but what persists is a feeling of density and concentration.

The same accumulative logic lies behind the use of rapid montage, which joins brief clips. *Napoléon* makes frequent use of this technique, beginning with that same snowball fight at Brienne. The tight close-up of the young Bonaparte (compressed into only a few frames) is alternated with close-ups and details of the ongoing fight, again represented through very brief fragments. In the ultra-rapid montage, the different shots are not truly present in the same image as they are in the split screen or the superimposition. Here, the different points of view follow in succession, but quickly enough as to give the impression of blending one into the next. Integration is obtained through the course of the film, rather than in the space of a single filmic image. But this is an integration in every sense: we see the close-up of Bonaparte, but we have no way of lingering upon it, and thus we end up taking it in "together" with the other fragments making up the battle scene. In short, we are dealing with a filmic gaze that frees us from the limits of a single glance. I would add that this principle emerges again—though purged of its radicality and brought to a sort of objectivity—in the shot/reverse-shot, the principle technique of the classical cinema. Here as well, we find an integration of partial elements into a comprehensive vision.

Finally, we have brusque camera movements—mainly swish pans, dollies, and fast tracks—that are often carried out by hand. These are techniques that recur almost obsessively in the film. In addition to their virtuosity, they give us the idea of an entirely unstable frame that desperately seeks to move beyond its limitations and capture new parts of reality. The lens moves without settling on anything, as if it wanted to follow the multiplicity of the world.

It is not difficult to recognize in these techniques the logic of cubist or futurist synthesis. Through them, we are similarly dealing with a mode of grasping the world simultaneously from many sides or in many moments, knowing well that the eye by itself only glimpses it from one side or in only one moment at a time. In other words, the futurist or the cubist painter knows that vision depends on a "here" and a "now," but he tries to enact a gaze that is able to penetrate them with a complex appreciation, without giving up those "heres" and "nows," and thus without being

forced into abstraction. At the cinema, this game seems almost sponta-
neous, above all when one moves from the "avant-garde" techniques like
those discussed here to more standardized techniques. I mentioned the
shot/reverse-shot as a normalization of rapid montage, but I could equally have brought up the distribution of the filmic image on different planes
of depth as a companion to the split screen or the superimposition. Beyond these possible parallels, the fact remains that film is an intrinsically
futurist and cubist art, and one in which the cubist and futurist gazes are
made seemingly "natural."

Gance's stylistic choices also recall a larger set of literary techniques
of his time. I am thinking of Blaise Cendrars, one of Gance's collabora-
tors. Describing the film experience, he writes: "Beneath the heads of the
spectators, the cone of light flickers like a dolphin. The characters, the
individuals, and the things—the subjects and the objects—spread out on
the screen. They are immersed, they turn around, they pursue each other,
they meet, with an enormous, fatal precision." We are not dealing with an
"abstract symbolism, obscure and complex, but a part of a living organism that we catch, drive out, defeat and that has never been seen. Barbar-
ian evidence." The result is that the fragments of reality come together in
a whole, like the letters of the alphabet in a new language: "Captured life.
Life of depth. Alphabet. Letter. A B C."[30]

Cendrars evokes Gance not only conceptually but also through his
writing style, replete with sliding meanings and word aggregation. But let
us return to *Napoléon*. Its final great "triptychs" represent the culmination
of a search to construct a gaze able to go beyond its own limits, to seize
the whole of a phenomenon. As is well known, *Napoléon* ends with a long
section dedicated to the Italian Campaign, in which the central screen is
flanked by two other screens. The image is tripled in width. This enlargement is twofold. In some cases, we have a vision that is wider in scope:
the two lateral screens offer some images that fit with the central one,
which produces a panoramic gaze. In some other cases, we have a composite vision: the two lateral images are like the wings of the central one,
and the result is a figurative structure similar to an altarpiece. Hence,
the landscape and the polytych: on the one hand, it is a question of seizing the entire width of the horizon, and saturating the visual space; on
the other, it is a question of gathering the whole of phenomena, resulting in a phantasmagoria. Even if these two types of "triptych" differ, the
impulse behind them is the same. In both cases, there is an attempt to

"embrace" the real, to keep it together, beyond the partiality inherent in every point of view. It does so by literally "breaking through" the screen and thus destroying the most obvious limits of the filmic vision. Simply put, in one case this action refers to the eagle—a majestic bird surveying the world from above—that often appears in the film as the young Bonaparte's companion, foreshadowing the destiny of the future emperor. Walter Benjamin could have made reference to an eagle when—discussing masses and film—he writes: "A bird's-eye view best captures assemblies of hundreds of thousands."[31] In the other case, the reference is to the fly—an insect with a kaleidoscopic gaze—that is often evoked by theorists of the age, who saw its faceted eye as analogous to that of the cinema. Cendrars for instance points out: "The cinema has given man an eye more marvelous than the multifaceted eye of the fly. One hundred worlds, a thousand movements, a million dramas occur simultaneously within the field of this eye."[32] The landscape and the polytych: a wider vision and a composite one. The eagle and the fly: *Napoléon* aspires to see on a grandiose scale.

The gaze that Gance imposes on his film—a gaze that goes beyond the limits of the scene to grasp the whole of reality in one single embrace—takes up, after all, the very attitude of the protagonist. It breaks barriers, not stopping at the here and now, but conquering the world. Gance is like Bonaparte: he seeks to construct an empire, a visual empire. The director's speech to his troupe on the first day of filming confirms it:

> To collaborators of all kinds, to all in leading and secondary roles, operators, painters, electricians, stagehands . . . to all, but particularly to you, the extras; you will have the weighty load of finding the spirit of your forbearers; you will present, with your good-spirited unity, the awesome face of France from 1792 to 1815. I demand more: the need for the total oblivion of small personal considerations and an absolute dedication.[33]

Filming is like going into battle, and thus demands the same kind of attitude. Conversely, if Gance was inspired by Bonaparte, Bonaparte behaves like Napoléon. His gaze throughout the film is directly modeled after the operating film reel. His vision is characterized by speed, by ubiquity, by synthesis, which are characteristics typical not only of this film but also of the cinema in general, and characteristics typical of modernity.[34] This identification reaches its culmination in the dialogue between the future emperor and the late great fathers of the Revolution: the vision of the film and the vision of the protagonist line up perfectly.[35] But precisely when we are ready for the apotheosis—and in the screen explosion, we have confirmation that the Hero, in making History, is also capable of seeing its realization to the end—it is here that two other scopic subjects—the eagle and fly—insinuate themselves. The construction of a visual empire must draw upon other kingdoms, such as the animal one. Who is, ultimately, *watching* in the film? Who is the owner of the gaze: who is really able to pass from a narrow vision to an all-embracing one? And what kind of whole is in our gaze?

In one way, the multiplicity of scopic models that has emerged doubtlessly carries a limited sovereignty. *Napoléon* embodies Bonaparte's gaze, but his gaze is not exclusive. Moreover, he also proves to be a subject incapable of seeing, as the extraordinary sequence at Josephine's house demonstrates. Napoléon is blindfolded to play blindman's bluff,[36] and so robbed of his eyesight (he himself comments, "In love, one mustn't see more than this"). This blindness echoes the holes in vision such as those that Gance himself reveals with regard to superimpositions. The same holes can be perceived in a montage in which it is too rapid to see things distinctly, and in a split screen that is too complicated to be entirely understood. However full, every vision is inevitably imperfect. Yet the multiplication of scopic models offers us a confirmation that film is capable of "embracing" the world. It is able to hold all the spheres of nature in its hands—the human, the animal, the mineral, the vegetable. In taking possession of these realms, it is also able to adopt their various points of view.

Blaise Cendrars's *The End of the World Shot by the Angel N.-D. (La fin du monde filmée par l'ange N.-D.)* provides an excellent example of the same move.[37] This unrealized film project tells a mad story of God as producer and proprietor—having nothing better to do than film the history of the universe to its end, and then rewinding the film to its beginning. In this script, God's vision becomes a string of single shots, taken by the cameraman Angel Notre-Dame, each describing a single moment of the history of the universe. And, at the same time, God's film involves the entire History of the universe, from Genesis to the Apocalypse and back. So, *The End of the World* can be read as cinema's most radical dream of appropriating reality through a gaze that adapts itself to all situations in order to grasp their entirety. Both in Cendrars's script and in Gance's film, this gaze must be, however, a *plural gaze*. That is to say, a gaze that recalls many sources, many moods, many points of view, and weaves them together without ever being able to prevail over them completely. Corresponding to this gaze is an idea of the whole as a *partitive unity*; its various elements converge, making their presence known in a play of superimpositions and fusions that is never restrictive.

Richard Abel emphasizes the nature of the "deliberately plural discourse" in *Napoléon*, analyzing with great acumen its implications at thematic, stylistic and syntactic levels.[38] He takes into account the film's slightly disordered gigantism, its frequent changes in rhythm, the introduction of digressions and narrative deviations, the uncertainty in the structure of the enterprise itself. What interests me, however, are the implications of this plural gaze. Caught between singularities that carry with them inevitable limitations and a whole that in itself risks never being realized, film seeks a mediation. It finds this in a gaze that weaves scopic subjects and combines and superimposes points of view in an image that grows ever wider than a single frame. Certainly, the result has a decentered and dispersive quality that renders the total creation unstable and in some way elusive. It is, furthermore, the conquest of a visual empire that opens itself to its deconstruction. Nonetheless, this plural gaze seems a necessary response to the tension between the parts and the whole: aimed at the latter, it keeps contact with the former. It is here, then, that the three emblems I have used—the eagle, the fly, and the emperor—become, in their bizarre differences and practical incommensurability, not a common denominator, but the paradoxical triumvirate that sustains a film based on aggregation. The eagle, the fly, and the emperor: it is through their eyes that the visual realm of *Napoléon* is formed; it is through their eyes that the World and its History are refracted.

WHAT EVER HAPPENED TO THE BLACK MAN?

Robert is sought by the police; he is accused of murdering the actress for whom he worked as dramatist. He is on the run in search of evidence that will exonerate him. Erica, the chief inspector's daughter, and Old Will, a vagrant who has seen the true culprit's face, help him. The two are in the hotel hall where the murderer (recognizable by an eye tic) is likely hiding. The camera, beginning with a high full-shot of the hall, suddenly drops down, points toward a jazz orchestra, and then goes forward, before pausing in a close-up of a drummer in blackface. He has a tic. He, in turn, notices the man and woman: the camera advances, this time toward them, before resting in a medium close-up on the couple. The musician recognizes Old Will as the vagrant he had met before. He is disconcerted by his presence, as he is agitated by the appearance of the police, who are really there in search of Robert. He begins to play off tempo; at last, people begin to notice. At this moment he collapses to the ground, unconscious. Erica, stopped by the police along with Robert, dashes toward him to help. She wipes his face, and discovers the tic. The murderer is caught.

The finale of *Young and Innocent* (Alfred Hitchcock, 1937) is interesting in many ways. Let us consider the camera movements described above: first, the crane shot that, gliding in a fascinating and unyielding manner, moves from the high full-shot of the hall to a close-up on the murderer. The shot is the result of great technical skill, which Hitchcock himself recalled in his interview with Truffaut.[39] Yet it proves exemplary for the kind of gaze that it embodies and for the manner in which such a gaze treats narrative events. This crane shot, more than seeking to grasp the whole of the situation, chooses to concentrate itself on only one part of the scene. As such, this part emerges from the rest. A lone individual is singled out from the crowd in the hall, and he thus acquires a particular importance. He is the murderer who has been sought at length, and whose presence is now revealed. The vision is subject to restriction, but it acquires an extraordinary significance in exchange—it gathers only a portion of the world, but what it gathers is truly valuable. In other words, there is the choice of a detail, together with an emphasis of its importance. If we are content with a fragment, it is because it is at the heart of the action. This logic is contrary to that presented by the preceding film. In *Young and Innocent*, the gaze works on concentration instead of enlargement; on the limits of the visible space instead of what breaks through it; on the salient element, instead of the total design; on quality instead of quantity. The choice of the one makes up for the loss of the other. On the other hand, once the principle element has been identified, it makes us reconsider the whole.

It is not difficult to recognize in this dynamic the imitation of the process of *attention*. Hugo Münsterberg was one of the first to define a true psychology of the cinema. Indeed, he dedicated an entire chapter of his 1916 book *The Photoplay* to attention. "Of all internal functions that create the meaning of the world around us, the most central is the attention," Münsterberg writes. "The chaos of the surrounding impressions is organized into a real cosmos of experience by our selection of that which is significant and of consequence."[40] The process follows four stages. In the accumulation of stimuli offered by the external world, there is something that strikes us, and that in this way becomes more vivid, more clear: it stands out in the center of our own consciousness. This impression acquires importance, while all the others lose clarity, until they finally fade away: attention is always accompanied to some degree by an oversight of the rest. It is here, then, that our body reaches out toward the emphasized object: our senses sharpen, in order that the most precise impression possible is formed. Finally, "our ideas and feelings and impulses group themselves around the attended object":[41] the latter is able to order our perception of the whole, placing itself at the center of a total organization of the world. These are the four steps of the process of attention, steps that we carry out both voluntarily (when we scan the reality before us, moved by interest or curiosity) and involuntarily (when it is reality itself that attracts us and shows us what is important and what is not). One of the fundamental elements of art consists in controlling this process, in a way that the audience follows the path traced by the work. Film excels in this action, having several expressive means that it employs to elicit and orient attention. Among them are captions (which indicate where our attention should be with words), actors' movements (which always catch our eye and hold its attention), and the layout of action along the depth of field (which magnifies the foreground while shading the background). Above all, there is the close-up: through it, as Münsterberg notices, "any subtle detail, any significant gesture which heightens the meaning of the action may enter into the center of our consciousness by monopolizing the stage for a few seconds."[42] In parallel, "the detail which is being watched has suddenly become the whole content of the performance, and everything which our mind wants to disregard has been suddenly banished from our sight and has disappeared."[43] Through the close-up, a film concentrates on what matters, even if it is only a detail. By virtue of its relevance, such a detail redefines and recalls the surrounding whole. In this way, the observed world acquires a new face. It is outlined according to our mental processes. As Münsterberg writes: "It is as if that outer world were woven into our mind and were shaped not through its own laws but by the acts of our attention."[44]

Let us return to *Young and Innocent*. The camera movement discussed above—followed by another crane shot, which concludes with a medium-close shot of Erica and Old Will—seem literally to mime the movement of our attention. The eye reaches out to the detail, which breaks away from the rest and finally becomes the center of the action. Yet there is an essential difference between the two camera movements. While the first presents an "objective" vision, which implicates the simple identification of the murderer, the second offers a "subjective" vision (we see Erica and Willie from the murderer's point of view) and the sketch of an interpretation (the murderer connects the elegant man before him with the vagrant he had met previously, and concludes that he has been discovered). Thus, we pass from the objective to the subjective, and from identification to interpretation. Attention implies both dimensions: if it gives importance to a portion of the world, it also compels the body and the senses to reach out toward the object. And if it isolates a detail, it also demands the reconstruction of the entire situation around it. In this way, *Young and Innocent* seems to want to saturate the entire process of attention. In fact, a detective film could not function in any other way. It is a genre in which the protagonist seeks to recover clues from the world at large, and, with the clues as starting points, it tries to reconstruct the crime. It is a genre that focuses on the objective identification of telling signs, but also on the subjective interpretation of the facts as they have taken place.

Hitchcock is most certainly playing with this objective-subjective dialectic. More specifically, he is suspicious of interpretation. It is not by chance that the film is full of misunderstandings that stem from the incorrect reading of details. Think of the two women on the beach where the body of the actress resurfaces. They see Robert leave. Is he looking for help or is he fleeing? But let us also recall Erica's aunt as well. During her little party, she realizes that Robert and her niece are embarrassed. Do they have something to hide, or are they simply in love? To identify something or somebody implies interpreting as well, but the interpretation is not always certain and, above all, it is not always good. Hitchcock's ironic play goes even further. During the beach sequence at the beginning of the film, he gives a close-up of a flying seagull and its strident cry. Its presence, though strongly featured, does not have a precise function or significance. The bird just reminds us that identifying something or somebody implies interpreting as well, but our attention is not always led in one particular direction, and sometimes it is openly fruitless (unless, through some mad game of philology, one can link the seagull in *Young and Innocent* to the birds of the eponymous film, or through Norman Bates's work of taxidermy in Hitchcock's *Psycho*). In short, the steps to interpretation are many, and they are filled with obstacles and traps. The fact remains, however, that *Young and Innocent* seems to want to remind us, with irony and reserve, that attention and interpretation are connected, and that fixing the eye on a detail always implies arriving at an understanding. In this light, attention leads to the construction of a new form of the whole. It is not based on a gaze that seeks to conquer the entire world by enlarging it, but on one that fixes on a simple portion of reality and finds in it the keystone to the entire situation. Thus, a whole is not the sum of the parts; if anything, it is an investment in only one part, in the conviction that it will open up to the whole. What counts is the significance of the detail, its strength. That means that we have an *intensive whole* (to paraphrase Pudovkin),[45] in contrast to the *partitive unity* put forward by *Napoléon*. And we are dealing with a *penetrative gaze*, as much as the former was a *plural gaze*.

In *Suspension of Perception: Attention, Spectacle, and Modern Culture*, Jonathan Crary explores the development of the strong interest in attention that occurred between the nineteenth and twentieth centuries.[46] It emerged against the backdrop of a profound transformation of the idea of perception itself: the world no longer seemed comprehensible "in terms of immediacy, presence, punctuality."[47] On the contrary, it seemed to escape a subject who is ever more convinced that his or her "perceptual and sensory experience depends less on the nature of external stimulus than on the composition and functioning of our sensory apparatus,"[48] and who liberates "the perceptual experience from a necessary relation to an exterior world."[49] Seeing (though seeing is not exclusively at stake) is thus articulated through subjectivity, contingency, and limitation. Attention is the answer to this problem, as it restores a structure and functionality to perceptual processes. In subdividing the world into centers of interest, it disciplines the subject's body and eyes. In bringing portions of the world into close-up, it offers the subject the idea (or the illusion?) that its relationship with reality is still efficient and fruitful. Making the whole turn around the fragment, it offers the path to an otherwise impracticable synthesis. Attention can then appear to be "an imprecise way of designating the relative capacity of the subject to selectively isolate certain contents of a sensory field at the expense of others in the interests of maintaining an orderly and productive world."[50]

Film's role becomes apparent within this framework. It is a medium that privileges exercises of attention, in order to secure a cognitive control over reality. The close-up is an exemplary field for such exercises. Epstein depicts it in his essay "Magnification" ("Grossissement," 1921) as a perfect synthesis that unites concentration, interpretation, and mastery of the object. Epstein writes: "The close-up limits and directs attention. I have neither the right nor the means to be distracted. Present imperative of the verb 'comprehend.'"[51] But film's control over reality is also exercised through more complex techniques.[52] I am thinking in particular of the analytic editing—*découpage*—in which the passage from one shot to another follows the movement of one ideal observer's attention within the story: we are able to investigate the represented space, at the same time finding ourselves always at the right time and place. As a result, we can say that we have the world depicted on screen "in our hands." Pudovkin explained it perfectly in his *Film Technique*, a book that was to be influential both in Europe and America. What he calls constructive editing "[builds] the scene from separate pieces, each of which concentrates the attention of the spectator on only that element important to the action. The sequence of these pieces must not be uncontrolled, but must correspond to the natural transference of attention of an imaginary observer (who, in the end, is represented by the spectator)." Moreover, "This guidance of the spectator's attention to different elements of the developing action is, in general, characteristic of film. It is its basic method."[53]

About fifteen years after Pudovkin, André Bazin returned to découpage in terms that were not dissimilar.[54] Bazin recognized that the technique had been exhausted, substituted by the long-take and by depth of field, which seem to leave the observer in control of his or her eyes, without waiting for the director to impose a particular vision. Yet these two new techniques do not imply a radical reversal of the game: the ball simply passes to the spectator instead of the film, and the weight of voluntary attention supersedes that of the involuntary. Spectators in the theater can thus regain the role they risked losing—a loss that could potentially have led to distraction.[55] Thus, we are not spared visual stimulation, fixation on a detail, and its emergence from the whole. It is simply that *we* perform this on the film instead of the film performing it for us. We need a center of attention around which a situation is made to move. This center of attention is of course fragile and temporary. Hitchcock's lesson is still relevant here. The so-called "modern cinema" will insist on this fragility, rendering any presumed crucial point banal or even ridiculous.[56] But it is also a center of attention able to capture our gaze and reflect it all around. A fragment, precisely. Nothing more than a fragment, but one around which the whole is redistributed.

WITH CLOSED EYES

There is, however, one more path by which film seeks to offer a total vision, despite the inevitable partiality of the gaze. It is no longer a question of adding fragment to fragment, in order to construct a whole as the sum of its parts—nor is it a question of making the fragment grow, to grasp in it all that keeps the whole together. Instead, we are dealing with the recognition of what is missing from the fragment, and placing the true core of the action there. In short, this third path avoids the "logic of the emphasis," which leads either to widening the gaze onto other portions of the real (to have more information available), or limiting the gaze to only one detail (in order to properly accentuate it). On the contrary, it obeys the "logic of litotes": if the image is limited, we can benefit from its limits.

Fritz Lang's M (1931) can help us to introduce this topic.[57] I am thinking especially of the first sequence, opening with a fade-in. A group of children are singing a nursery rhyme, "Schwarz Mann." A woman interrupts them, ordering them to stop singing the lugubrious song. The woman chats with Elsie's mother, who is waiting for her daughter to return from school. The cuckoo clock strikes noon. The schoolchildren leave, and Elsie is among them. A friendly policeman helps her across the street. Elsie's mother sets the table. Elsie skips down the street, playing with her ball. She bounces it off the poster promising a reward for the capture of a serial killer—the shadow of a man falls on the poster. The mother is in the kitchen, and the clock strikes twenty after noon. There are steps on the stairs, but they belong to two other schoolchildren. Next to Elsie, a man with his back turned buys a ball from a blind man. Someone rings the doorbell, but it is the mailman bringing a dime novel. The mother calls for her daughter in vain; the clock strikes one o' clock. The stairs are deserted. The attic is empty. There is an empty plate on the table. In the park, Elsie's ball rolls in the field. The ball purchased earlier gets stuck in some electrical wires. A gust of wind blows it away. Fade out.

M opens with this sequence, which is dominated not only by a crime but also by the fact that the crime is removed from view. The film gives us this information without showing it to us, almost obeying the women who told the children to be quiet and stop singing "Schwarz Mann". An obscene act, the crime is kept off the scene. The result makes evident the partiality of the cinematographic gaze. In showing one thing, it can and perhaps must leave something else out, even though what escapes us is sometimes at the heart of the story. Everything visible is accompanied by the invisible, and the invisible may constitute the essential.

In the film's opening, the invisibility concerns an event that we do not see, since it takes place in a space beyond the limits of the frame—off-screen. We must remember that Lang often uses offscreen space. He does so in this same film, which also offers us many examples of a minute exploration of setting. For example, let us recall the scene in which beggars search the house where the murderer has hidden. The struggle between one of them and a guard is discernable, though not shown. Lang does this in other films as well: we have only to remember the beginning of *The Big Heat* (1953). We observe a hand taking a gun from a desktop, then we hear a shot, and finally we see a head collapsing onto a desk. Once again, there is a crime—this time self-inflicted—that our gaze is denied. Besides these examples from Lang's work, the use of offscreen space is a technique that brings us to film's basic foundation. It stresses how the filmic image is bordered: a rectangle (or squarish)—that is, a space limited by four sides. The borders serve to circumscribe the world on the screen and, at the same time, to differentiate it from the real world of the spectator. In this way, the rectangle's sides are like the frame of a picture or photograph, which both identifies an image and separates it from its surrounding environment. These borders also serve to define the portion of space caught by the camera, contrasting it with other ones that could have similarly been shot, like window jams that cut one glimpse of landscape and not another.[58] The edges shut in, but they also separate. Particularly in the second case, such borders separate a space that is well in view from one that seems reachable by the camera (were it to extend the shot and reposition itself, as it is able to do). In short, edges of the screen separate an "in" space from an "off" space that is potentially within reach. This almost but not-quite-accessible view makes what is excluded from the screen all the more clear.[59] Consequently, there is always something in a film that we do not see that exists alongside what we do see. There is always something that we do not see *precisely because* we are seeing something. The offscreen space thus reminds us of a basic truth: at the cinema, exhibition always implies concealment.

But there is also a second invisibility in M's opening sequence. We see the serial killer buy the ball for Elsie, but we cannot make out his face. Here, what is beyond our gaze is not an event confined outside the borders of the image (in the "off" space), but a hidden detail within the image (in the "in" space). The image hides something within its own folds. Thus, it is a question of an invisibility that penetrates the visible, more than circumscribing it. The scene is well within view, though it nevertheless is seen as a shadowy area.

It is once more appropriate to recall that Lang often resorts to this second order of visibility in representing the "invisible." In M, the killer's face is hidden for most of the film, and when it is at last revealed, it appears deformed by the grimaces he makes in the mirror. The opening sequence of *The Big Heat* proceeds to the widow of the man who has committed suicide. She finds the letter on the desk, opens it, reads it, and runs to make a telephone call. The spectator is not shown the pressing contents of the message. Something is under our eyes, but we cannot grasp it. This "shadowy area" takes us back to film's basic mechanism as well. In a film, what falls under our eyes really hides a significant part of itself, on at least two levels. In one respect, the filmic image possesses such complexity that it is nearly impossible to completely decipher. It "unfurls" without allowing all its contents to come into focus. It is also for this reason that classical film composition created zones that were endowed with an immediate significance, such as the image's center. Such zones helped us not to get lost in the potential convolutions of the image.[60] In another respect, the filmic image is formed by running the film in the projector. Through projection, however, both the single frame and the black leader between one frame and the next are made imperceptible (that is, we cannot see the two elements that constitute the actual material form of the image). This means that we see something on the screen, but we do not see the foundation of what we are seeing: the filmic image can "unfurl" because its constituent parts "withdraw."[61] Again, at the cinema, exhibition always implies concealment.

Thus, the visible and the invisible are inextricably interconnected. In this context, the whole at which the gaze is directed changes. It appears as a *dislocated whole*: present, perhaps, but not before our eyes. Enclosed by four borders, often not entirely discernable,[62] the filmic image will always be a fragment, a glimpse of the world that gathers only "heres" and "nows." Yet it is precisely "beyond" what the image shows us—if not "beyond" the filmic image in itself—that we find the key to *everything*. "Beyond" what the image shows us, it is often hiding the root of what we see. In Lang's film, it is the evil that inhabits the earth; elsewhere, it is desire, utopia, the divine design, the unexpressed, etc. More generally, in the off-screen or a fold within the scene, we may find what constitutes the source of the events—what represents the potentiality that finds in the image a single realization, a proof. It sets itself as the all-encompassing realm to which every aspect of film refers. But there is also a "beyond" the image itself. Outside the four edges that designate the rectangle of the screen, there is a theater of spectators. Before the scene portrayed there was the camera in action. And, hidden in what we see, there is the black interval between one frame and the next. These radical "offscreens," which the image can never depict, refer us to the image's origin and destination, and recall its conditions of existence. They, too, constitute a horizon, not of the filmed, but of the filming. These various "offscreens" are what render possible the single result taking shape before our eyes.

Thus, "beyond" the image, "beyond" what it portrays, in this space of the potentially represented and filmed (the representable and the filmable), is that in which we can find the whole that is denied to the screen. This is a whole that is *dislocated*, as it is not directly before our eyes. But it is also *whole* in every sense: an infinite horizon to which the image and its depiction are inclined, placing themselves, in their temporariness and incompleteness, as its concrete expression.[63]

Victor Freeburg dedicated an entire chapter of his *The Art of Photoplay Making* (1918) to this space "beyond" the image.[64] He focuses first on that portion of film which is "off stage," subtracted from our vision, outside the edges of the picture. Then he offers examples of images that hide something within themselves, either because they keep the filmed object at a distance (and thus make its borders more vague), or because they transform the actors into simple silhouettes (and thus obscure the details of their bodies), or because they present shadows instead of objects. Freeburg praises the use of these techniques: "Let [the screenwriter] rather suggest part of his picture by leaving it outside the frame. Or let the scenario writer utilize the vague and subtle effect of distance."[65] He does so essentially because, in this way, film restores to the spectator his or her power of imagination, which would otherwise be taken by a meticulous and exhaustive reproduction of reality. Undoubtedly, "the motion picture has the amazing power of capturing physically and projecting onto the screen a vast number of things which in stage play had to be left entirely to imagination,"[66] as Freeburg notices. Yet no film truly succeeds in making us see everything; we continue to exercise "the mind's eye as well as the body's eye." For Freeburg, this use of imagination—stimulated by the absence of something on the screen—often borders on *fancy*. But it is also fundamentally the *suggestion* of what is not there, an evocation so strong that the absence becomes in some way a presence. Consequently, Freeburg can talk about his experience as spectator, emphasizing his ability to see and feel even what the film does not offer. For example, he relishes his capacity to infer actions omitted from the film as seemingly uninteresting (either parallel to the story being told, or coming before or after it.) But he also enjoys the capability of hearing sounds in a silent sequence. Through these mental exercises, it becomes clear that the filmic image has its limits, despite its extraordinary power: but it also becomes clear that precisely, owing to these limitations, we search, and find—in our imagination—the whole.

Freeburg's considerations can be tied to contributions by early twentieth-century psychologists who analyzed film from a perceptual and cognitive point of view. For example, a 1911 study by Mario Ponzo pointed out that sensorial associations triggered at the cinema allow us to see and hear what is not there.[67] But I will jump ahead now and complete this discussion with a later text: *Notes on Cinematography* (*Notes sur le cinématographe*) by Robert Bresson. This text spans the beginning of the 1950s to the mid-1970s and is worth reading even without familiarity with Bresson's films. From Bresson's aphorisms in this work emerges the idea that the more film accepts the limitedness of the screen, the greater the extent to which the sensory horizon can be stretched. "One creates not through adding, but taking away,"[68] Bresson intones. Therefore, "Do not show all the sides of things. A margin of the indefinite."[69] Working with actors also reflects this principle: "Model. Withdrawn into itself. Of the little that is let to escape, take only what suits you."[70] All of this is not, however, for the sake of minimalism. It has to do with capturing the essential, as these messages illustrate: "Drain the pond to get the fish"[71] and "Model, its pure essence."[72] Bresson strives to achieve that breadth of vision that is possible only by closing one's eyes: "Your film must look like what you see when you close your eyes."[73] What is therefore opened through the invisible is the presence of a potentiality, of a stimulation of imagination. The screen, seemingly empty, can thus contain the whole.

I will not go beyond this bit of wordplay. Some terms, like "imagination," require deeper analysis.[74] Simply put, the idea that the image is always inadequate is as prominent in filmic practice as it is in the theorization of film (and we may wonder, in fact, why movies did not develop into an art of the invisible rather than the visible).[75] This deficiency is not, however, a disadvantage: through it, the breadth of horizons irretrievably lost by the single image can be recuperated. Only as a part can the image aspire to recover the whole.

NOSTALGIA FOR SOMETHING

Let us try to bring together some of the threads of this exploration. Film seems suspended between two great poles. On the one hand, its gaze has proven limited, tied as it is to a point of view (that of the camera and its operator). The world is always captured on the screen from a certain perspective, which inevitably emphasizes one piece and not another, one feature and not another, one phase and not another, etc. On the other hand, film's gaze possesses a particular force: reality appears on the screen in all of its richness and density, liberated from the habit and indifference that has obscured our normal view. But herein lies a basic problem: how to maintain this force, while simultaneously managing its limitations? How to restore the sense of the whole of things, despite the inevitable partiality of the pieces? How to develop the potential of the gaze, making up for what it loses?

Nineteenth-century modernity had already encountered a similar tension. There we find a progressive and powerful extension of the dimension of sight. We have only to think of the growing diffusion of images in books, newspapers, city walls, the presence of performances and optical devices such as the panorama, diorama, phenakistoscope, praxinoscope;[76] the rapid success of the photograph, in both everyday and institutional practices (with its ever more widespread use for medical and police purposes). In parallel, we have only to think of the two factors that allow the eye to conquer new segments of the world. The first is the progressive development of artificial light, with the gas lamp, then the arclight, and finally the incandescent electric light. The second is the availability of new methods of rapid transport, such as trains, that come into common use by the century's fourth decade. They allow vision to pass over the horizon, and thus to widen the range of its perception.

Yet this broadening of vision[77] has its inverse. As the world seemed to become wholly visible—either directly or through images—shadowy zones and blind spots emerged. The experience of the train ride is exemplary in this regard. As the train advances, new and different horizons come into view. Though the landscape seen from the window moves too quickly, it seems screened-in by passing poles, vanishing when the tracks climb the viaducts, disappearing suddenly as the train passes through tunnels.[78] This "loss of landscape" is a widespread given: it goes back, for example, to Monet's series of paintings of the Rouen cathedral, to his desire to grasp the world in its single moments, capturing all its variations, resulting in a quasi-unintelligible painting.[79]

The gaze thus widens, and at the same time encounters black holes. Film in some way absorbs this situation, and bears witness to it. On the one hand, it exalts its own visual capacity and, on the other, it denounces its limits, attributing them a point of view. Beyond bringing this dialectic to light, film also works to intervene in it, to make the two poles converge. Each frame gives us back only a fragment of the world: it is enough, however, to condense into one image many gazes, to select the significant details, to go beyond the edges of the picture, and this partiality will be corrected. The sense of the whole can then be restored, though *a posteriori* and imperfectly. It is sometimes a question of a *partitive whole*, in which the fragments make themselves known as such and nevertheless they add to each other. At other times, we have an *intensive whole*, in which the fragment is loaded with references and becomes the center around which the entire action develops. Finally, there is a *dislocated whole*, in which a return to the beyond takes place. These wholes keep open the interplay between the two opposing exigencies—the pleasure of the larger vision and that of the detail—without necessarily ending the game.

The negotiation between these two measures has had different moments of equilibrium throughout the course of film history. One moment is the typical preoccupation of classical cinema with visibly recuperating what would ordinarily escape the gaze (the shot/reverse-shot technique serves this end); another is "modern" cinema's preoccupation with marking the fact that a certain incompleteness persists and cannot but persist (it is one of the effects of de-framing).[80] In this light, after World War II, "modern" film is permeated by a sort of painful awareness tied to the idea of the "impossible whole." The French critic Serge Daney made reference to this, speaking of films in which "the sphere of the visible ceased to be available in its entirety: there are now absences and holes, necessary voids and full abundances, images forever absent and gazes always failing."[81] The eye no longer seems to have a "hold" over reality, and makes room for a nostalgia for that which is eclipsed.

In this vein, I would like to conclude with a film that introduces the modern cinema, though it also represents the culmination of the classical. I am referring to Orson Welles's *Citizen Kane* (1941), an extraordinary reflection on visibility in the world, and in particular on the strength and limitation of the gaze.

Let us think about the narrative structure of the film, which is based on a series of flashbacks, plus newsreels, framed by a prologue and an epilogue.[82] This structure tells us that every story is inevitably a biased account, with a narrator and point of view. The newsreel obeys this principle as well, and thus does not put into play facts, but rather a certain way of referencing or not referencing them; it is, in truth, the omission of a detail (what does Kane's last cryptic word—"Rosebud"—mean? What is not said and not seen in the reportage?) that redirects the investigation. The various versions that Thompson the journalist gathers shed light on different dimensions of the story because they are based on different points of view; each reveals one thing, while hiding others. The most resounding example is Susan Alexander's operatic debut: it is recounted from two opposite perspectives that collect the facts as seen both from backstage and from the audience. It is the same episode, yet it seems another. Nonetheless, the inevitable partiality of each account can be redeemed in at least two ways. In the first place, each witness's account, once narrated to the journalist, becomes public. In this way, each loses its status as an individual vision and becomes a vision shared by the collective. Subjectivity becomes intersubjectivity, and partiality, once shared, acquires fullness and weight. This always happens at the cinema. If it is true, as Balázs maintains, that every frame reflects a point of view, then this point of view—made of a million spectators—becomes a collective gaze. Consequently, what appears on the screen is a part of the world that everyone sees. In the second place, the accounts of each witness intersect, completing each other reciprocally. What one does not see the other sees, and vice versa. This is the principle of the shot/reverse-shot: the alternation of shots allows the combination of both views of the scene. The joining of flashbacks in Citizen Kane forms an immense Shot/Reverse-shot on the life of a man: like a puzzle, the pieces complete each other, little by little. And yet two half-truths do not make the whole truth. Details can be added to details, but what truly matters can always slip away. In fact, it is not by chance that none of the witnesses can tell us what "Rosebud" is. No account contains the key to the mystery. The puzzles that help Susan Alexander pass the time at Xanadu remain incomplete.

One could protest that we do finally see the sled stamped with its name in the epilogue.[83] "Rosebud" appears at the end: the invisible offers itself up to be seen. In retrospect, the final sequence, more than resolving the enigma, shows us the density of its mystery. The clarity with which the object sought in vain is placed in sight—an obvious, excessive clarity—serves only to elicit our suspicions. On the one hand, we can and perhaps must ask ourselves if this sequence does not also have a view of its own or if, moreover, it cannot but have one. It thus becomes legitimate to read this as an act of omission. It effectively leaves something out of the scene; Kane himself is by then irretrievably removed from the gaze. On the other hand, it is precisely its audacity that makes us understand that we have already seen what it is showing us, without seeing it. The sled was already present in the key scene of Kane's farewell to his childhood home, without us realizing it. Similarly, Kane's comfort object, the snow-globe that he holds in his last moments of life, was already present in the scene of his encounter with Susan Alexander. There is always something that is taken away—offscreen, among the folds of the image.

Thus, the sled sequence shows us how vision is directed at the whole and, at the same time, can never be complete. In this picture, "Rosebud" becomes the name of all that is not perceptible to the eyes, of what escapes, what is lost. It is not a coincidence that Citizen Kane is punctuated by a string of losses that recall each other in turn, which demand impossible ransoms. Let us remember, for example, that the protagonist meets Susan Alexander the evening in which he goes in search of furniture from his old family home. Later, he will force his new wife to become a singer in order to realize her own mother's unfulfilled dream. In other words, if "Rosebud" brings us to the sled, the sled brings us to Kane's childhood, which leads us to his mother, who brings us to other dreams that lead to another possible life. Bernstein, when questioned by Thompson as to "Rosebud"'s significance, gives the only right response: "Maybe that was something he lost. Mr. Kane was a man that lost almost everything he had." To see is to lose. It is a place of conquest, but also of tragic loss. It is filling one's eyes with an image of the world, but also letting this image be transformed into a falling tear.

"Cinema . . . appeases a certain sense of nostalgia that lies dormant in our hearts, nostalgia for countries never seen that will perhaps never be seen, but where it seems that we have already lived in a preceding life,"[84] remarked the Italian journalist Fausto M. Martini in 1912. That is cinema: nostalgia for something.

Double Vision

In realizing a single point of view on the world, the shot not only bears a limited gaze rather than an all-encompassing one but also a subjective gaze instead of an objective one. Béla Balázs developed this theme in *The Spirit of Film* (*Der Geist des Films*), particularly in the chapter "The Shot."[1] He analyzed both the subjectivity of the camera ("the camera shot corresponds to an inner shot"), and that of a character who offers onscreen his or her vision of things (in this way eliciting an "identification" on the part of the spectator, who is able to feel "the sense of space and position of the protagonists" like "no other art can give us").[2] This subjective dimension of the filmic image is such that Balázs asks, "Is objectivity no longer possible in the cinematographic image? It certainly is. It is, however, nothing but the impression of objectivity . . . that is possible to achieve. And the objectivity expressed by the film shot is naturally a subjective arrangement of the observer."[3] Thus, everything is subjective at the cinema. Balázs is aware that this subjectivity is a risk: filmic images could be reduced to abstract impressions (as in "absolute film") or simple representations of the psychic process in itself (as in "surrealist film"). So, precisely at the moment in which Balázs emphasizes the subjectivity of the shot,[4] he also recognizes the presence of an objectivity. The filmed event "occurs in a determined space and time. This sense of the determination of time and space gives the things represented a reality that goes beyond the image. They still seem facts, to which the images are simple reports."[5] In other words, things have an existence that goes beyond the cinema. What appears on the screen is also reality in and of itself.

Subjectivity and objectivity operate side by side. Balázs wrote at a moment in which film was institutionalized as a story of images and sounds.

He was thinking of film as a form of "literary" expression, in which an "author" lays out his or her "self."[6] Yet the problem that he raised directly implicates the properties of the filmic gaze as such (property in its double meaning: what kind of gaze, and whose gaze?). To better understand the ways in which subjectivity and objectivity advance their own "causes," as well as influence each other, let us look at two articles: though different in tone and method, they both reveal a line of thought that has existed since the advent of film. The first was inspired by psychoanalysis. Entitled "The Psychological Value of the Image" ("La valeur psychologique de l'image"), it was signed by Dr. René Allendy and appeared in the prestigious series *Cinematographic Art* (*L'art cinématographique*), which was published between 1926 and 1928.[7] "There is a principal difference between the two orders of reality: the image can simply be a sensorial fact of vision—the direct perception of the exterior world in its clearest characteristics—but it can also be understood as the subjective representation that we make of the outward world, beyond visual data. In this way, we in fact possess the ability to create images: the imagination."[8] If the image "comes from the vision that perceives it," it appears objective. If it "comes from the imagination that creates it,"[9] the image appears subjective. The film that

> is not an image of the first degree, but is instead one that transforms the screen into an image of an image, represents both elements: real pictures of the objective world as the gaze perceives them, and unreal creations of our imagination. These are the two paths by which film can move us. It can take one or the other, or it can mix them, as it mixes immediate reality with a hint of memory and the product of dream in each of our consciences.[10]

Film gives space to the subjective and the objective; primarily, though, it superimposes them. In this way, it mimics our own psychic process, in which we superimpose immediate data and our own mental elaboration, even when we deal with a witnessed fact.

The second contribution, from noted philosopher Georg Lukács, was written thirteen years earlier and published in the *Frankfurter Allgemeine Zeitung*.[11] Lukács noted that reality is not physically present onscreen (as opposed to the theatrical stage), yet it takes on such empirical weight that what we see automatically seems possible.

> "Everything is possible": this is film's *Weltanschauung*. In every single moment, the cinematographic technique expresses absolute reality—even if

in a merely empirical way—of the moment itself. "Possibility" is no longer a category in opposition to "reality." Possibility and reality are placed on an interchangeable plane. "Everything is true and real, everything is equally true and real": this is what film sequences teach us.[12]

Film, in offering things up with such extreme precision, gives its images a strong "life truth" (which is, adds Lukács, often disquieting). This "life truth" makes even what is not real seem real. As a result, the cinema elides "strictly natural reality and extreme fantasy." Filmic images offer what exists *de facto* and what is only imagined, and with the same concreteness. It is no wonder then, that "in a drunkard's room, the furniture moves by itself, his bed flies with him beyond the city."[13] On the screen, the set has the same value as a real experience. Under the gentle nudge of the "evidence" it provides, what is real and what is virtual can go hand in hand.

These articles by Allendy and Lukács, though quite different, help clarify the dialectic between objective and subjective vision introduced with Balázs. First, they confirm how film is able to offer both immediate data (or "reports") and a mental reworking of them (or "inner shots"). On the screen, we have both "visions" and "things." Second, the subjective dimension pervades a range of phenomena, going from the moment in which, observing the world, we make it our own, to the moment in which, through our imagination, we give life to an imaginary world. There is continuity between the interpretation of the real and the construction of a fantastic reality: the action of a subject is vital to both. Third, there is also a continuity between immediate data and a mental elaboration or reworking of that data. On the screen, reality is always an observed reality, and observation (like the imagination) is based on concrete objects and situations. When everything appears perfectly subjective in a film, it is because the inevitable choices of the camera are emphasized (in other words, the presence of a gaze). When everything appears perfectly objective, what is foregrounded is the feeling that film offers things up—that is, the capacity of the object to assert itself onto its own observation. The subjective and the objective dimensions are strictly interdependent: the problem lies in the placement of emphasis.

Let us go over this slippery terrain with the help of a most diverse set of examples. We will examine how film sought to make these two dimensions emerge: how it characterized and contrasted them, but also how it put them together. Using their uncertain borders as starting point, we will pass to the ways in which they distinguish themselves. We will examine their reflections on the reality depicted onscreen—suspended as it is between the return of what is real and the invention of what is possible—and we will conclude with the investigation of how film as witness leads to an equilibrium between the two forces.

AND WHAT DO YOU KNOW ABOUT HIM?

The first film that we will examine, Jean Epstein's *The Three-Sided Mirror* (*La glace à trois faces*, France, 1927) dates from the same period as the Allendy article. My analysis here will focus on the film's narrative structure, rather than its figurative elements and audacious syntax.

The film presents a series of stories that refer to each other, beginning with a prologue, which poses an opening riddle that refers to the identity of the protagonist. Four episodes follow, the first three of which (entitled "1," "2," and "3," respectively) are dedicated to three women: Pearl, Athalia, and Lucie. The fourth and final episode, entitled "He," is devoted to the male hero. In the three episodes dedicated to the women, they relate their relationship to the man, each giving a different picture of him. In the man's episode, we realize that he does not seem to correspond to any of the three accounts offered. The film ends with a highly symbolic image: a three-paneled mirror in which the man's face is reflected into three figures.

Clearly, this narrative structure contains a topos that will recur in numerous variations, not the least of which is *Citizen Kane* (Welles, USA, 1941) or *Rashomon* (Kurosawa, Japan, 1950). *The Three-Sided Mirror* presents itself not as a story of facts in the strict sense: the narrated events mix with the way they are experienced by their protagonists. We are not told (or, rather, not shown) who "He" is, but instead who "He" is in the minds of people he has met. In this sense, the film fosters a gaze that takes into account both events and experiences. Things are what they are, but they are also what they end up being in the eyes (and minds) of those who live them. This is a gaze in which perception and interpretation, reality and possibility, readily blend.

Let's examine this scenario more closely. Here, the gaze is born from the presence of an observer, before even that of an observed object. What is seen depends on who does the seeing: on his or her position, on the way in which he or she looks at things, on the interests that emerge, and so on. In each part of *The Three-Sided Mirror*, there is a different gaze— each attributed to a different observer—and thus, sustained by a different point of view. What Pearl sees is neither what Athalia nor what Lucie see. On the other hand, it could not be any other way. Even the camera gaze follows the same rule: in the section entitled "He," the film seems to give us a more direct version of the facts, one that is no longer tied to the impressions of the three women. Yet this same section—coupled with the others—shows us that even here there is an observer, a point of view. This time, it belongs to a machine, and even the camera has its own positions, its own interests. When we the spectators—after having seen the protagonist through the eyes of Pearl, Athalia, and Lucie—are placed before a "he" devoid of their filter, we continue to see him filtered through an eye, a new eye of glass. Reality in its immediacy is irretrievably lost to us.

Some crucial passages of "Meaning 1[bis]" ("Le Sens 1[bis]"), one of Epstein's most beautiful essays, come to mind.[14] In it, Epstein distances himself from the naive idea of documenting the real. Many believed that the cinema was able—even required—to help us to see nature directly. Epstein cites no one specifically, but we might recall both the appeals of a "reactionary" critic like Paul Souday—who would save the cinema only for this[15]—as well as a 1914 address by the president of the French Chamber of Deputies to professionals of the field: "There is a series of areas that belong only to you: that of your beginnings, science, the life of plants, animals and man. . . . Then nature, landscape, travels."[16] Against these hypotheses, Epstein commented with great irony, "Serious and insufficiently over-cultured gentlemen applaud the life of the ant, the metamorphosis of larvae. Exclusively. To instruct others' youth."[17] The cinema is quite a different matter. It is a new eye, but one that has a way of understanding things all of own. "This vision has a way of seeing all its own, just as the other does."[18] In particular, it gives us "only symbols of reality, constant metaphors, proportionate and suitable. And not symbols made of material—which does not exist—but of energy; something that in itself does not seem to exist, but for its effects when they touch us."[19] This means that when the cinema captures, it captures to the core, but not what we mistakenly believe things to be in and of themselves, in their literalism. It captures what it can gather through the eyes, which results in sometimes unpredictable realities. "Think about it: that eye sees waves that are imperceptible to us; onscreen love holds what no love has had until now, its own piece of ultraviolet."[20]

Love in ultraviolet is a beautiful symbol that shows how the camera does not offer us a direct reflection of things, but a personal, often deeper, restitution. It filters and interprets reality as Pearl, Athalia, or Lucie do. It is a tendentious witness, as all witnesses are. But it also carries out this work of filtering and interpreting, going where the human eye cannot, some steps higher in the spectrum of light. After all, it cannot be attributed with the same subjectivity as a human being: "The Bell-Howell is a metallized, standardized brain, produced and circulated in some thousand specimens, which transform the surrounding world into art."[21] Epstein pointed to both the camera's capacity to transform the observed object and its mechanical quality, which makes it "a subject that is object, void of conscience, that is lacking hesitation and scruples, lacking venality, satisfaction, possible errors. It is an absolutely honest artist; it is exclusively an artist, a model artist."[22] I will return to this characterization later in the book. Here, I will only say that it is equally an observer and a player in the story. We access things through its eye. This eye—gathering what others do not see—functions as an intermediary of the world. Finally, this intermediary gives a subjective tone to everything, as Balász pointed out. As a machine, however, its "subjectivity" is beyond that of a simple psychological dimension. This results in a pronounced lack of clarity with respect to what we see as spectators: an indeterminateness that *The Three-Sided Mirror* seems to thematize. We perceive a mediation. Perhaps we even enjoy this mediation. But we do not know who is responsible, to what extent, or at what cost. We see that someone is seeing: But who? And how? And what does it contain of the real, once captured by a gaze?

The Three-Sided Mirror accentuates this uncertainty by suggesting that reality—and in particular, the character "He"—does not wish to offer itself up for definitive understanding. "He" is what appears from time to time, and that's that. There is certainly an allusion to Pirandello here, which was not hidden in the film's publicity:[23] the character—indeed, more than one—is always superimposed over the person, and in the dialectic between the two, the former wins. Going one step further, we could cite Goffman and the construction of the self through its representation for the benefit of the others.[24] Conversely, we could recall the numerous social situations, tied to urban life in particular, in which appearance is a decisive factor in acquiring a sense of self.[25] We find ourselves faced with the essential questions of modernity: the emergence of an identity based not on belonging, but on a complex and reciprocal game of relations between individuals. We are not what we are by nature or by destiny, but what we are in the eyes of an other. *The Three-Sided Mirror* confirms this assumption by telling us that the real is always filtered through a gaze and, moreover, that it is nothing more than what is presented for view. This, of course, does not prevent a large part of the world from attempting to reassert itself. In this regard, the film's conclusion is symptomatic: in the protagonist's mad car race, a bird hits him in front, forcing him off the road and leading to his death. The bird—more a symbol, like Coleridge's albatross—heralds the "return of the real." Yet the conclusion of these events does not coincide with the conclusion of the film. The last image is an image within an image: a three-paneled mirror appears on the screen, and "He" is reflected in each of the panels. There is no face: there are only masks, masks to which we must refer in our search for the truth.

I would add that in this game of appearances, the cinema functions as a cause more than effect. If the face is confused with the mask, it is because we film it. In the following passage, dated 1914, an anonymous journalist who signs as "Fantasio" understood this: "The cinema is so deep-seated in our habits, our existence, that we no longer know if our pain or joys are real or simply a mise-en-scène captured by the lens. We are not convinced of their sincerity if not by taking them in some night on the cinema's luminous screen."[26] It is the cinema that forces reality to make its appearance and, in the end, establishes its own law of truth.

But let us return to *The Three-Sided Mirror*. The film seems to do away with reality: never offered in its totality, it is always subject to filters and interpretations. Reality is always a qualified appearance. The world returns because there is an eye that follows it. And if it returns, it is only in a form conceded by the eye. The presence of multiple observers, each with particular traits, results in a kaleidoscopic picture. In addition to the camera's perspective, we experience that of Pearl, Athalia, and Lucie. As a consequence, we are left with a situation involving many and coinciding components: the eye of a mechanical device that, in Epstein's words, is a subject as well as object; human eyes, tied to character's visions; and a reality that plays with its own eradication, offering us perhaps some umpredictable sides, but ones that are always filtered by something or someone. Clearly this situation is rife with ambiguity—indeed there is no possibility of a decision.[27] What do we see? And with whose gaze?

The answer is found in the narrative structure of the film, which raises a terrain on which things become more practicable. I am referring to the sectional subdivisions, each with a different title, either specifying the number of the version presented ("1," "2," and "3," which in turn reference the three women), or conversely the observed object ("He"). This is the film's ordering principle: thanks to it, we know through whose eye we are watching things as they happen, and in this way we know how to understand them. The effect is one that redistributes and reorganizes an otherwise unsolvable mix. Everything tends to blend, yet we can also make distinctions. Chaos is in some way transformed into a cosmos.

Cinema will manifest precisely this concern each time that it tries to distinguish—through a typology of gazes—the camera's vision from that of the characters, and the vision of a camera as neutral witness from that of a camera ready to openly reinterpret the world.

A FACE, THE EYES

This typology of gazes is the product of a patient and continuous work, which began early in film history and became established in mainstream production. This is not the place to reconstruct such a process, however briefly. But it is useful to look at its outcome, with the help of a film from the late 1940s, *Dark Passage* (D. Daves, USA, 1947).[28]

The first part of the film is dominated by one character's gaze. We see things from the point of view of a faceless escapee from San Quentin. In the second part of the film, we get a more direct vision: the fugitive gets plastic surgery, and we see his face. Subsequently, we no longer follow his actions from his perspective. This two-part division is actually much more subtle. In the first part, the shots from the fugitive's point of view dominate, but they are not exclusive: we see through his eyes—especially when he encounters nearby objects (when he turns on the radio, or opens the tap) or when he looks his interlocutors in the face (in particular, Irina, the woman helping him)—yet events are often presented in the manner that a neutral on-the-scene witness might see them. The first sequence is a good example. After an establishing shot of the prison, we have the image of a truck transporting trashcans. We understand that one of them is carrying the man. Only when the trashcan rolls off the truck do we see the landscape spin, as if it were seen by someone hiding inside. We follow him in a full-length shot as he climbs out of the trashcan, then we return to seeing things through his eyes as he moves forward and crouches down. His escape to San Francisco will alternate between these two types of vision: in particular, when the fugitive, Vincent, gets into Irina's car, we abandon his gaze (there is also a diegetic motivation: he is hiding under a tarp); only when they arrive at her house are we put back in his shoes, adopting his point of view. Thus, a double register: we see with the character's eye and we also see him from outside. We are far from the position taken in *Lady in the Lake* (R. Montgomery, USA, 1947), which is in some ways extreme: the entire film is shot from the point of view of the protagonist, a detective working on a clearly delicate investigation.

The second part of *Dark Passage* reestablishes a more direct vision of things. We see the protagonist's actions without passing through his eyes. I must emphasize, however, that we arrive at this point through a sequence that puts us in the fugitive's head. After he has plastic surgery, which changes his appearance and renders him unrecognizable to the police (in other words, it enables him to become Humphrey Bogart and us to finally see the actor's face), there is a long moment in which we see his dreams in an extended series of abstract and spectral images. Then, when Vincent fully enters the action, the general atmosphere becomes all the more threatening and dark. The spectator feels assaulted by the unavoidable events, exactly as the protagonist does. Thus, the reference to what Vincent Perry has seen and lived does not disappear. If anything, it contracts and expands. Here, we are brought to the searing conclusion: Vincent is in front of the ocean, in a café he told Irina about before escaping San Francisco once and for all. Their music begins, and suddenly she is in the same café. He sees her, and they begin to dance. The sequence (certainly a tribute to Bogart and Bacall) is so utterly improbable and, at the same time, so dazzling that it lies beyond any strict definition in terms of the gaze and its ownership.

This is a general outline of the scopic system in *Dark Passage*. It would be interesting to explore why late 1940s Hollywood production felt the need to experiment with a vision attributable to a central character on such a grand scale. *Dark Passage* is one example; *Lady in the Lake* is another. Still, we cannot leave out those films characterized by long oneiric sequences (*Spellbound*, A. Hitchcock, USA, 1945) and lengthy flashbacks (*Letter from an Unknown Woman*, M. Ophüls, USA, 1948; or *A Letter to Three*

Wives, J. L. Mankiewicz, USA, 1949). A widespread need for more introspec-
tive narrations emerged, tied to the success of psychoanalysis, the need
to value the individual, and also the call to explore new expressive solutions. I would like to underline yet another element. This search seems
rooted in the idea that it is possible—indeed necessary—to emphasize
what Balázs identifies as the subjective dimension of the gaze: this emphasis must also foreground a specific "agent" to whom the subjectivity can be attributed, and in this way must identify this subjectivity as a
specific form of gazing. In other words, the filmic image's subjectivity can
be emphasized, as long as it is anchored to a shot "seen by a character"
(the so-called point-of-view shot), which is quite distinct from its inverse,
the shot "seen by no one" (which we may call the "impersonal shot"). The
effects are many. The two great dimensions that were, for Balázs, natural
to film—the "inner shots" and the "reports"—are identified in two distinct
types of shots: the point-of-view shot and the impersonal shot. The former refers to the character's vision and could turn into imagination or
nightmare, the latter is a neutral and immediate insight. Translated into
a point-of-view shot or an impersonal shot, the subjectivity and objectivity that are latent in film become clearly placed in opposition. As an
effect, they are transformed from intrinsic qualities of the filmic image
(as they still were in Balázs) into simple narrative processes. We are no
longer dealing with two inherent and converging faces of a filmic image:
we are confronted with two modes of telling a story, with two "grammatical categories" that are easily distinguishable as such.

   Dark Passage is exemplary in this regard. Everything hinges on the fact
that the shots either imitate Vincent Perry's gaze or come from a neutral
observer who is outside the story. The former type of shot is certainly distinguishable from the latter. Film's subjectivity is traced back to the point
of view of a character and reduced to a problem of shots.

   Not surprisingly, this brings us back to the extensive work of the
"grammarians of the cinema" of the 1930s and 1940s. I am thinking, for
example, of Raymond Spottiswoode and his *A Grammar of the Film: An
Analysis of Film Technique*,[29] published in the mid-1930s, in part influenced
by Pudovkin and his writings and in part as a response to Rudolf Arnheim
and his *Film as Art* (both of whom had a great deal of success in the United States and Europe).[30] Spottiswoode in particular connects the dimension of subjectivity to the recognizable presence of the gaze's "source,"
as well as the use of "grammatical markers." For example, "emotional or

physical disturbances are often represented by a multiplicity of simultaneous shots. They contain movements in constant conflict with one another, while the shots themselves loom out of the distance and, before coming into focus, disappear into it again."[31] It seems a description of Vincent Perry's dream. We can say more generally that these "grammarians" describe (and with it, indeed prescribe) the great processes through which we can construct an objective or subjective gaze: the particular kind of shot, forms of punctuation, use of sound, ways of editing. In this context, objectivity and subjectivity cease to be considered intrinsic properties of the cinematographic gaze. They become the product of linguistic work, but they can no longer be considered latent properties either. Brought back to linguistic processes, they are recognizable to the spectator. I would add that the work of the "grammarians" has its roots in a reflection dating back to the 1910s and 1920s. I have Hugo Münsterberg in mind. He writes: "The screen may produce not only what we remember or imagine but what the persons in the play see in their own minds. The technique of the camera stage has successfully introduced a distinct form for this kind of picturing."[32] Jean Epstein, as well, offers interesting insights. In "Magnification" ("Grossissement"), placing himself in a dance scene, he imagines himself also able to film a "double [sequence], according to the point of view of the spectator and that of the dancer, objective and subjective."[33] Finally, let me say that each nation has had its own (often multiple) "grammarians": France, for example, had Robert Bataille and André Berthomieu,[34] while Italy had Renato May.[35] The latter was particularly exacting in his insistence that objectivity and subjectivity are what would today be called "effects of discourse." He first reminds us of a precise typology: "Shots . . . seen by those outside the situation are called 'objective' [and] shots seen as if by someone in the situation take the name 'subjective.'"[36] Then, owing to the fact that this characterization comes from a narrative mode, he empties these two terms of all intrinsic value: "one shot is, in itself, neither subjective nor objective, but assumes one characteristic or the other according to what precedes or follows it narratively."[37]

Distinguishing and marking: the cinema can allow itself all the gazes that it wants (or almost all), as long as it makes it clear to whom they belong. The game of attribution is, however, naturally quite complicated and must be kept under control. *Dark Passage* exemplifies this process. In its second part—the very moment in which a visual objectivity seems restored—the films falls, in fact, into deepest nightmare. San Francisco is no longer a transparent city: anyone could be someone else (indeed, everyone is someone else). Nor is it a sunny city: everything is cast in the literal shadow of night, or the metaphorical shadow of doubt. Visual objectivity is thus tinged with tones that are not so objective. And yet, though it is pervaded by a disquiet that later aligns with the character, we know that what we see is not filtered by his gaze. We feel with him, but we do not see with him. We inhabit his skin, but are cut off from his eyes. The finale accentuates this mixing: here, we see with eyes that seemingly belong to no one, not even the neutral observer who assures the images' objectivity. Yet nevertheless we see through the eyes of desire and imagination—Vincent's, Irina's, our own. We could succumb once more to a sense of vertigo, but the words "The End" intervene, closing the adventure and beginning a myth.

THE LAW, A RIFLE, AND MEMORY

With this brief outline, I have tried to reveal the two antithetical paths that the cinema seems to pursue. On the one hand, it deals with a subjective and an objective dimension, connecting and superposing them. On the other hand, it distinguishes the two planes through a series of markers that retrace their presence into a narrative problem. Film works with the two principal levels of the image, collapsing them; at the same time, it tries to keep them separate, transforming them into clearly identifiable categories. It is likely that cinema itself creates this short circuit. While it is true that cinematic images bear witness before even offering documentation (someone has seen and now reports), they must also blend objectivity and subjectivity; similarly, they cannot but strive to set them apart. The narrative structure reveals this foundation and, simultaneously, attempts to smooth it out (thanks to one character's presence, we may compare a "subjective" vision and an "objective" vision, differentiating between them by contrasting the point-of-view shot and the impersonal shot).

I would like to focus on this short circuit with another example that particularly illustrates the nature of cinema as witness. *The Man Who Shot Liberty Valance* (J. Ford, USA, 1962) is the story of the small village of Shinbone, which is rife with abuse and violence.[38] A young attorney, Ransom Stoddard, assisted by the rough cowboy Tom Doniphon, succeeds in

bringing law and order to the town by ridding it of the bandit Liberty Valance. The film does not present these events directly, but through a long
flashback that takes up the entire film. In it Ransom Stoddard, who has
since become an influential U.S. senator, recalls events that have taken
place long before. It is, in fact, a double flashback: within the first, there
is another, entrusted this time to Tom Doniphon. He recalls the duel in
which Liberty Valance was killed, revealing how this actually happened.
We never see what took place; rather, we see how a certain character recalls these events.

What implications does this narrative structure have? And what does
it tell us about film, and ownership of the gaze? I will forgo any specific
observations on the flashback, as I did with the point-of-view shot: they
are both subjects that have been adequately studied.[39] Similarly, I will
leave aside any consideration of the history of the western, and the evolution of Ford's poetics. In the 1960s the genre attempted to shed its skin,
and the work of the director assumed a darker tone. What interests me is
how this film, during the period of classical film's decline, faces a problem
that we have found in *The Three-Sided Mirror* and *Dark Passage*, films which
are at classical cinema's margins and center, respectively. This problem
is the need to get to the facts through mediation. All stories are subjec-
tively evoked rather than objectively presented and, correspondingly, all
actions pass through some sort of conscience.

Let us linger for a moment on this contrast between action and conscience (or, if you will, between action and reflection). In *The Man Who
Shot Liberty Valance*, the polarity is established with the central pair of heroes, Doniphon and Stoddard. The first is a man of few words and many
deeds. It is he who takes the initiative at the crucial moment and shoots
Liberty Valance, though he lets everyone believe that the young lawyer
did it. His is a language of arms. Stoddard, on the contrary, is a man of
thought. More than directly interfering with events, he wants to understand what he sees, confining himself to the position of an "observer." Yet
it is precisely through reflection that Stoddard is able to impose reason on
a world seemingly dominated by brutality and abuse. His two keystones
are the book and the assembly. The book is the collection of precedents
that the young lawyer, working as a dishwasher, reads with attention, in
search of a legal solution to resolve the conflict that plagues the growing small city of Shinbone. But the book also holds the pages with which
its inhabitants learn to read, in the school established by Stoddard. The

assembly is instead the meeting in which Shinbone elects the two representatives who will go to Capital City to decide the future of the Territory,
just as the convention in Capital City will decide the representatives to
send to Congress in Washington. The book and the assembly recall two
central elements of the Protestant community of America's Founding Fathers, drawing on the Bible and the public confrontation between group
members. Here, they become two symbols of Western civilization. Yet, all
in all, they are not enough to actualize this civilization. It takes an act—
specifically a duel. Liberty Valance must be challenged. The bandit is shot
in the back—assassinated—in order to prevent him from killing Stoddard.
As the reflection gives space to action, the act produces a violence that is
justified, though not justifiable—a violence that brings us paradoxically
back to the world that should be left behind.

Such a game of reflection, action, and violence calls to mind many
sources. Hazarding a guess, I would say that Goethe's *Faust*[40] comes to
mind. We find a hero who, rereading the Gospel of John, stakes everything on action: "The Spirit's helping me! I see now what I need /And
write assured: In the beginning was the Deed!" (vv. 1236–37). At the same
time, he wants to tie this action to knowledge. "There, to stand and look
around,/I'll build a frame from bough to bough,/My gaze revealing, under
the sun,/ A view of everything I've done,/Overseeing, as the eye falls on
it,/A masterpiece of the human spirit,/ Forging with intelligence,/ A wider
human residence" (vv. 11243–11250): a desire that brings him, as Moretti
emphasizes, to an "inertia" in some way reminiscent of the spectator.
Finally, in acting, he is mixed up in violence, justified and unjustifiable,
as in the episode of Baucis and Philemon: to proceed with what today
would be called his plans of land development, he is forced to do away
with an innocent elderly couple. Action, reflection, violence: in Faust, the
three things are deeply connected. In the most advanced modernity, they
are often tragically separated: no longer are their reciprocal justifications
found in one plan. But this Goethian analysis of *The Man Who Shot Liberty Valance* would lead us too far astray. I would instead like to offer two
points.

First, the contrast between action and reflection is something that the
cinema explores in several ways, often obsessively. I am thinking of the
actor system. There is the energetic actor, a true body in movement, like
Douglas Fairbanks; and there is the introverted actor, wrapped up in his
own thoughts, like Spencer Tracy. We may also consider the typology of

shots. We have shots useful to show bodies in action, such as the medium full shot, which goes from the face to the waist (that is, from the eyes to the pistol); and we have shots more useful for showing states of mind, such as the close-up, especially when it functions as a reaction shot. Finally, I am thinking of filmic syntax. There is an editing tied to onscreen action, in which cuts are made to the actors' movements, and there is an editing tied to the exploration of the scene, in which cuts are determined by the gaze of the spectator (or by his onscreen alter ego). Naturally, this series of contrasts does not preclude an integration of the two poles, especially in the classical cinema. The man of action withdraws into himself and his energy transforms into a nervous tic, like Humphrey Bogart. There is also an alternation of various shots, in which action and reaction are regarded equally. And there is an editing which, in the name of continuity, employs both cuts on movement and cuts on gaze. Yet the polarization continues to make itself felt, in this way giving the spectator better orientation.

Second, in *The Man Who Shot Liberty Valance*, the opposition between action and reflection helps to differentiate events from the awareness that an individual can have of them. Embodied in the two principal heroes, this contrast is projected onto the entire film, leading us to recognize two different planes: that of the world, and that of thoughts—that in which things happen, and that in which one reflects upon the action itself. In one, the history of the West is made and, in the other, the story of Liberty Valance is recounted. As a result, while the facts are entangled insofar as they are known, they are nevertheless distinguishable as such. A gesture analogous to "grammatical markers" intervenes: representation (of events) creates a space for memory (someone's memory of what happened). It is, however, important that we are able to discriminate between the two planes.

How is memory shaped in Liberty Valance? We have thus far held off on giving a response. Memory seems primarily an act of reparation—toward an old friend who has died, for example. Doniphon lies in his casket, watched over by Stoddard's wife Hallie and his elderly black servant, Pompey. Stoddard recalls for the journalists what the old cowboy represented for Shinbone's story and, in this way, returns to him the merits that his solitary existence had prevented him from receiving. Memory, then, restores a life to us. The first descriptions of the Lumiére shows focused on this idea of return: they saw in the new invention of the cinema a device able to keep our dead friends and relatives with us. As Boleslaw Matuszewski wrote: "Cinema holds thousands of images in one scene and, made up of a bright source and a white sheet, makes the dead get up and walk. This simple exposed celluloid ribbon constitutes not only a historical document, but a piece of history, the history that has not disappeared, that does not need a genius to be resuscitated."[41] Lucio D'Ambra put forward the same idea, almost to the letter, in his 1914 proposal to found a cinema archive or museum. He spoke of films as "strips of miniscule photographs that, with a jet of light projected on a white screen, re-animate what was, give life back to death, remake the past into present, and miraculously capture, allowing us to recall when we want the 'fleeting moment.'"[42] In the same year, the president of the French Chamber of Deputies, addressing the cinematographic community, reiterated that through the cinema, "we see the beings we have lost, for whom we weep, live again before our eyes." He added that if the invention had been made earlier, we would have had the opportunity to see "Bonaparte in his Italian campaign, the 'Tennis Court Oath,' Molière acting before Louis XIV, Mohammed, Caesar."[43] In 1922, Elie Faure imagined that the inhabitants of a planet two thousand light years away could have filmed Christ's death with a powerful telescope, and sent it back to us as living memory.[44] Bazin's landmark essay, "Ontology of the Photographic Image,"[45] claims that cinema is intrinsically a memory device that serves as a remedy to death. The filmic flashback highlights this ability.

Memory's reparation has a second objective as well: it heals violence. Hallie is in the other room, watching over Doniphon. Years before, she had almost married him, before the young lawyer charmed her away from the coarse cowboy. Even Stoddard has in some way mortally wounded someone, though in a symbolic way. Just as Doniphon shot Liberty Valance in the back, Stoddard took Doniphon's future from him, leaving him alone. Remembering the episode in some way rights the wrong: violence is denounced, and excuses are offered for it, though posthumously. Again, this element of memory refers back to the cinema in general. I am thinking in particular of its social use, as an instrument of celebration. The filmic image not only preserves the filmed reality from change and deterioration, but it also gives us that reality in its purity. It is the opposite of the use we explored in *The Three-Sided Mirror*. Cinema not only brings us a reality as seen by somebody, it also breaks the masks that it encounters, freeing the underlying face of reality from its constraints. "The cinema is a terrible revealer of secrets, unconscious but very cruel. Brought to the screen, the most cautious and astute man loses his mask; he is revealed for what he in fact is, just like the man are the earth, sea, and sky, all of nature, veiled and otherwise impenetrable," said Alberto Savinio in 1924.[46] This idea of a preserving and purifying memory seems the basis of a suggestion put forth in 1925 by Jacques de Baroncelli: if there is another great flood, "it will be enough for the few superstitious on an Ararat far away to have saved some rolls of film so that, after the catastrophe, not only the image of the swallowed-up civilization can be re-created, but its secrets, resources and power."[47] The cinema gives us back the world as it was before its ruin. I would add that this function of preservation is mirrored in a complementary function, that of proclamation: memory can extend to utopia. The last remarkable chapter of Vachel Lindsay's 1915 *The Art of the Moving Picture* signals this utopian power of the cinema, in its construction of a purer universe. Lindsay writes:

> Oh you who are coming tomorrow, show us every-day America as it will be when we are only halfway to the millennium yet thousands of years in the future! Tell what type of honors men will covet, what property they will be apt to steal, what murders they will commit, what the law court and the jail will be or what will be the substitutes, how the newspaper will appear, the office, the busy street . . . [48]

Furthermore, the reparation of memory reworks the truth. The long flashback reveals who actually killed Liberty Valance, and thus who liberated that part of the West from bullying and abuse. The person behind the act incorrectly attributed to Stoddard (who is rewarded with a long and illustrious political career) is actually Doniphon. The old senator's memory, offered to the journalists, reconstructs what really happened.[49] Again, there is a reference here to the cinema in general. I am thinking specifically of the debate on its use as an instrument of scientific observation. Jean Painlevé recalls in a 1931 essay how "famous researchers have discovered in animated images things that they had never perceived by their specialty, direct examination. The eye had registered them, but the effort of forced vision, the tension of concentration (either on many different points or in one place) had only an inhibitory effect."[50] In these cases, the cinema rearranges the truth of things, revealing how they are in reality. And yet, Painlevé adds, "having said this, we must not delude ourselves regarding the value of 'impartial witness'. . . . attributed to the cinema." It certainly records things in a way that is seemingly faithful, but "the terrible interpretation maintains its dominance."[51] The filmic image reflects both the world and our imagination of it, with all its distortions.

This brings us back to our film. Through his flashback, Stoddard attempts to reinstate the events that took place in Shinbone. He tries to give the dead a new life, to heal violence, to reestablish the truth. His account—a reflexive moment—rids itself of any subjectivity, in favor of objective deeds. Yet his effort is unsuccessful. He cannot be exclusively an "impartial witness"; he must account for the presence of the "terrible interpretation." Alongside his interpretation of the facts, there is a social interpretation, which has grown year after year. It is not by chance that, even though Stoddard puts things right, the journalist throws his testimony away. The legend of the West demands that the young lawyer, not the cowboy, commit this act. Between truth and legend, legend must win. For this reason, no newspaper will ever reveal what really happened.

This lays bare the ambiguity of memory. On the one hand, it offers a reparative understanding of the past. On the other, however, nothing can go against our image of the facts. A remembrance is inevitably a personal report. Moreover, offered to the listeners, a remembrance immediately becomes a story and, as such, it is destined to succumb to the great social story, which includes fantasy and dreams. It is the same for the filmic image. Even if it is presented as a direct trace of things, this image cannot be solely documentary. It provides a personal reconstruction of the events, and this is enough to distance it from simple objectivity. The image reexposes the events: it recounts. The cinema is, inevitably, a complex terrain: the subjective always lies in wait.

Told in another way, memory offers a trace of what was, yet it must also yield to the fact that every recovery is a renovation as well. It replicates the dialectic intrinsic to every work of restoration—to preserve or to reconstruct?[52] Cinema, as form of memory—memory of what passed before the camera[53]—rearticulates the same dilemma: should it preserve the traces of what is no longer or stage the past whatever the cost? *Liberty Valance* displays a desire for the first solution juxtaposed next to the inevitability of the second. By the end, the reconstruction wins over the preservation.

Stoddard's memory is not tripped up, but it does slip, and we spectators slip along with him. "Print the legend."

OBSERVING, RECONSTRUCTING, INVENTING

This long digression on memory has clarified the cinema's nature as witness. The image on the screen always gives back something that the camera has seen. As the flashback exemplifies, seeing at the cinema is always a re-viewing. It is running over with the eyes what "was." In this act of witnessing, there is always some uncertainty—something slippery, if you will. It is true that this represents a reparation (with respect to what has disappeared, the violence exercised on the past, the truth that must be reestablished). But it is also true that what is restored vacillates between different states. We can have a mere observation of what has happened, for the purpose of preserving the total objectivity of the facts (as if it were nothing more than reestablishing them). But we can also have a personal reconstruction of the events, and thus the intervention of a subjectivity acting as a filter with respect to what has happened. Finally, we can have a reconstruction that openly adds something of its own, even while giving reasons for something through the brush stroke of invention. In this case, witnessing becomes a narrative act. The confession of those present at the events becomes a story, and the recovery of those events slips into the realm of imagination. The risk remains that the latter version should triumph: indeed, "Print the legend."

It is evident that, in passing from the second to the third case (that is, from reconstruction to invention), we are faced with a different form of subjectivity. We no longer simply encounter an eye or a conscience that "filters" the objectivity of the facts, but a mind that imagines possible facts. The (subjective) interpretation of things becomes the (subjective) elaboration of a reality. Thus, Stoddard's flashback, marking for us the ambiguity of all memory restoration—suspended as it is between preservation and reconstruction—shows us also that re-creation can end up becoming a new and fresh creation. We have a story, a fictitious story, which is in essence the epic of Liberty Valance in the context of the great western sagas.

Such a dialectic runs through the very heart of the cinema. Cinema has been an excellent witness to the events of the century, but it has primarily been an outstanding narrator of fiction. Its eye has scrutinized the most intimate folds of reality, but it has also braved possible worlds, while giving all the density of the real one, to take up Lukács once again. Many have discerned an irresolvable contrast in these two abilities (critical legend would have it that Méliès betrayed Lumiére by entering the world of the imagination). In the conceptual picture that we are constructing, the two activities must be intersecting: they are both born from a "subjective" work that is, in turn, compared to and mixed with the "objectivity" of things. Briefly, to witness is to offer the story of facts as they effectively occurred. To narrate, instead, is to witness possible facts. The two gestures are in some way circular. The cinema exalts this circularity, passing from one face to another with extraordinary fluidity (which allows Godard to say that Méliès is the documentarian, while Lumière is, if anything, a narrator of fiction). It is certainly right to ask ourselves how much this circularity is excessive and how much it is instead authorized. The fact that, on the level of genre, two different categories were instituted for documentary and narrative film gives us the answer: they are two paths that often use the same methods and often obey specular forms of logic. There is, however, a series of recognizable characteristics that— analogous to the grammatical markers called to define the point-of-view shot and the impersonal shot—allow us to distinguish between different forms of discourse. In this light, observing (facts), reconstructing (a witness), and producing (a possible world) are activities that intersect more at the cinema than anywhere else. Yet it is possible to distinguish these activities, however indistinct their outline.

This game of indeterminateness and determinateness finds an interesting documentation in a curious 1917 critical text.[54] The piece, dedicated to the "cinematography of the real," defends the genre in question, though its author Giovanni Livoni denies that the cinema "portrays nature as it is." In order to have a perfect reproduction of nature, "it is necessary to photograph with special criteria, which have to have as their goal to render or represent nature as beautiful as possible: in a word, to improve upon it." Restoration of the world requires direct intervention: one cannot observe a fact without reconstructing it and, if reconstructing it, adding some bit of invention. In fact, "how many times have we seen on the screen places that we knew or that we came to know and how many times, seeing them on the white screen, did they not seem more vast and beautiful than they really are?" The cameraman, in filming those places, used all of his talents; he applied "insight, prudence, an expert eye, an innate aesthetic sense, artistic gift developed with practice." In this way, he also ended up constructing an image of things that goes beyond what exists. Only in this way could he produce a portrait that rings in some way "true." Only by forcing some elements was he able to make the "characteristics and curiosities" of what he was filming emerge. Only by becoming a bit of a storyteller was he able to be an effective witness. Livoni concludes his article with a piece of advice: "the cameraman must operate in a way that makes others believe he has shot the film in site conditions that were terribly unfavorable and dangerous. This increases his merit and thus, its value."

This text is certainly at the margins of the great theoretical debate, yet it is fairly indicative. The opportunity to distinguish between the documentary and narrative dimensions is never called in doubt. Rather, there is the awareness that they constitute two readily recognizable genres.[55] What it instead emphasized is the circularity between a subjectivity connected to an interpretation of the facts and a subjectivity that is pushed further and inserts something of itself (though its purpose is to make what is witnessed stand out better). Film's gaze is undoubtedly a slippery terrain: different forms of vision converge on it, and in doing so, they tend to overlap. But at the very moment in which we have a clear typology of the situation, the confusion fades. The filmic image represents a field of convergence for different dimensions, but it is also a place in which these qualities articulate and define one another. Thus, we can say that film inherited the capacities of both the documentary and the narrative; it put them side by side as never before, collapsing them with all the ensuing vertigo. More productively, it also reformulated their nature and identity. The cinema is precisely a site of overlapping uncertainty and elucidation.

EXERCISES IN RECOGNITION

Before concluding this analysis, I will try to further develop this idea of the ambiguity tied to cinema's nature as witness. In what way does the cinema *recognize*, or *make recognizable*, the reality to which it offers itself as witness? To what degree does it recover the existence of something already experienced and, at the same time, allow it to acquire for the conscience something unforeseen? I am taking the term *recognition* for its deeper characteristics: to recognize is to associate what is being seen to something previously encountered (the dog Argus recognizes Ulysses) and, at the same time, it means admitting the legitimacy of something that one encounters (I recognize someone's authority). It is thus an act that implies both identification and reception, *knowledge* and *acceptance*. What paths, then, does this recognition take when set in motion by a film-witness?

To start with, if it is true that the cinema presents things not as they are but as the camera sees them, it is also true that the cinema can be a site of authentic revelation. On the screen the world shows an unexpected face, which allows us to find in it what we already know, while expanding on that knowledge. Ricciotto Canudo offers a useful confirmation in his posthumous collection *The Factory of Images* (*L'usine aux images*). He writes:

> [Cinema] was born from the will, science, and art of modern men . . . , to gather, through time and space, the meaning of life, which is perpetually renewing itself. It was born to be the Total Representation of the body and soul, *a visual story made of images painted with a brush of light.*[56]

Moreover,

> [Cinema] expresses the whole of life, with the infinite range of its feelings, aspirations, defeats, and triumphs, aided by this eternal game of lights, taking in being and things only as forms of light, harmonized and orchestrated according to the inspiring idea of action. This is the secret and the glory of Visual Drama.[57]

And finally:

> Nature as character. The subconscious revealed. The immaterial . . . evoked in visible form and in movement. These are the things that no other art could touch. ∴ . . The cinema, only the cinema, can and must represent them.[58]

In these passages, Canudo is quite clear. The filmic image restores reality to us in its entire range of manifestations, including those most difficult for us to gather in our normal activity and those we are unable to gather at all. It permits a "total representation of body and soul," bringing to light the vitality of nature, the subconscious and the immaterial. This restoration of reality is not neutral: the cinema transforms what it encounters, giving it an altogether different quality. What was formerly a concrete body becomes a "form of light." Such involvement, which we can call "subjective," from the moment it makes evident the presence of action or "agency," does not imply a betrayal. If anything, as Canudo suggests, it allows an "abstraction"[59] of mere empirical data. They can be gathered beyond their mere appearance, interpreted in their essence, revealed in their plot, and put together in their most general design. In repainting the world, the "brush of light" proves perfectly able to grasp it, and thus to give it back completely. As a result, reality—in its masks and in its true face, to use our previous terms—opens up on the screen, before our eyes in all its richness. We can recognize this reality and, at the same time, connect this recognition to discovery and acceptance.

Canudo is not the only one who points out that film, as a witness, permits a recognition that leads to discovery and acceptance. The debate on animism, which swept the world when it came to the screen, illustrates this.[60] Two memorable references will suffice. Hugo von Hofmannsthal: "From the film's sparkling, the eyes gather an image of life made into 1,000 facets. This obscure and profound origin of life . . . , inaccessible to the word, can only just be realized through prayer or the stammerings of love."[61] And Antonin Artaud: "Isolating objects, film gives them a life of their own, which tends to become ever more independent and deviates from the usual meaning of such objects. [It] reveals an occult life, with which we are placed into direct contact."[62] Revelation, illumination, discovery. The terms persist, just as they recur in the reflection on the photogenic quality of being.[63]

Nevertheless, when it meets with the gaze, reality can unsettle us by unleashing trouble and unease, as well. Sometimes presented in an unexpected way, it proves almost unrecognizable. Next to the pleasure of the discovery, there is also the risk of creating true displacement, which occurs in particular when seeing oneself onscreen. Epstein returns to this moment on more than one occasion: "The uneasiness at seeing one's own cinematographic image is sudden and complete"; and again, "the initial reaction to our own filmic reproduction is a kind of horror."[64] But it is perhaps Pirandello who offers the richest description of the matter in his novel *The Notebooks of Serafino Gubbio*. Speaking of the actress Varia Nestorova, he says, "She remains speechless and almost frightened by her image on the screen—so altered and fragmented—on the screen. She sees there is someone who is herself but whom she does not know. She would like not to recognize herself in that person, but she would at least like to know her."[65] Thus, the image does not always offer us an illuminating revelation. It can also be the font of a profound unease. The cinematographic gaze often lays things too bare: "The camera lens is an eye . . . with an inhuman analytic capacity."[66] This gaze returns us to a past that has ceased to belong to us: in the filmic image, "we feel that we are fixed there in a moment of time which no longer exists in ourselves."[67] This means that a displacement intervenes when film's capacity to witness becomes too direct, too crude; paradoxically, that is, when it lacks the right measure of reinterpretation (a reinterpretation that is often an adjustment and revision). Too much objectivity is never a good thing. Neither is too much subjectivity: testimony based on an exclusively personal reconstruction makes us fall into an arbitrary story, which can be accepted only through the power of illusion. In both cases, the fact remains that there is no full and correct recognition: it is impossible either to bring an image back to one's own point of reference, or to accept this image as trustworthy. The cinema puts us in check, and we can withdraw only by ending the game.

Neither too much objectivity, nor too much subjectivity. This is film's last recommendation. After challenging the inevitable superposition of immediate data and a mental reworking of them ("reports" and "inner shots," according to Balázs), and after trying to keep the two planes separate (through grammatical and narrative markers), cinema discovers that if it wants to recognize and make recognizable the world, it must be nourished by things "as they are" and by visions "of somebody." Recognition deals with a revelation and an interpretation—it implies a world that opens itself and an eye that takes possession of this world. Thus, neither a simple subjectivity, nor a simple objectivity. But both, once again.

THE EYE AT STAKE

Let's end with a final example: a film entrusted to an exemplary "observer," which stages a game of witness and recognition, objectivity and subjectivity.

A detective, Scottie, has seen a police colleague fall to his death, and the resulting trauma causes him to suffer from vertigo. He tries to accept the situation and agrees to follow a friend's wife, Madeleine, who—convinced she is the reincarnation of an ancestor—has begun to exhibit strange behavior. Scottie falls in love with Madeleine, yet he is unable to save her when she climbs to the tower of an old church and, in an apparent fit, throws herself off. After this episode, Scottie falls into a deep depression: he no longer realizes what is happening around him, and is tormented by terrible nightmares. One day, he meets Judy, a young woman who reminds him of the dead woman. He follows her back to her hotel, and eventually forces her to dress and make herself up like his lost love. But at the moment in which Judy becomes identical to Madeleine, he realizes the trap into which he has fallen. It was actually the real wife of his friend—murdered by him—who plunged from the tower; the woman he met was her double, called to play a part so that the crime could take place without arousing suspicion. Under the guise of the fake Madeleine, he loved Judy, and now he sees her once again before his eyes. But the woman, forced by Scottie to return to the scene of the crime, climbs the tower and falls to her death . . .

I have just recounted Alfred Hitchcock's *Vertigo* (USA, 1958),[68] one of the most extraordinary meditations on vision that the cinema has ever produced, and a film that reveals all the threads we have followed here (observation, memory, reconstruction, exorcism of the dead, etc.). Let us concentrate on the process that leads Scottie to recognize Madeleine in Judy, from the moment in which he sees her for the first time, to the moment in which he is certain about what had really happened in the past. This process of recognition shows us the different sides of subjectivity and objectivity involved in the filmic gaze and, at the same time, the forms that such a gaze accordingly encounters. Scottie, recognizing Madeleine in a passerby met by chance, makes a discovery: he draws from the real what it would normally hide. And the real, for its part, opens to his gaze like an authentic revelation: the passerby is the former Madeleine. Here, the observer is like an *oracle*, facing the splendor of things and deploying a deeply personal insight. Second, Scottie gives the woman a name; he decides her identity. She says that her name is Judy, but he insists in seeing Madeleine. For Scottie, reality becomes what he decrees it to be: Judy can be Madeleine. Here, the observer's subjectivity is that of a *bureaucrat*, though an unseemly one. He is the administrative authority that defines the "who" and "what" of individuals and things. Third, in a dramatic crescendo, Scottie compels the woman he encountered to be what he has lost. He forces her to dress and make herself up as the other woman: Judy must be Madeline. The subjectivity is that of *desire*, or perhaps madness. The observer falls into a *hallucination*: the same hallucination that any film brings about when it causes us to mistake a representation for perception, according to Oudart's striking principle.[69]

Finally, Scottie wakes up from his obsession and is able to see straight once more. He sees things for what they are. But Judy and Madeline are no longer there. For this awakening to occur, the real had to withdraw; it had to die once more, as it must do under the pressure of the passing of time. The End.

This finale clarifies our entire path. Beginning with Balázs, and adding Allendy and Lukács, we demonstrated how the cinema is as radically objective as it is subjective. The camera filters and transforms, though outside a traditional psychology. On the other hand, the screen shows with the incontrovertible evidence of the real what can only be imagined. This leads to a possible uncertainty that is highlighted when the two categories overlap. One remedy is a typology of filmic gazes that attempts to distinguish, due to a series of grammatical markers, what is offered as fact and what instead appears as a mental state. In these cases, the objective and subjective dimensions of the filmic gaze are traced back to a series of essentially narrative processes, such as the point-of-view shot and the flashback, which "locate" the subjectivity in a narrative character, making it function as the alter ego of the camera or the spectator. Subjectivity and objectivity are reduced to mere effects of language. Yet the superimposition of a fact and a mental state—or better still, in the words of Balázs, of "report" and "inner shot"—continue to operate. This uncertainty is tied to the filmic gaze's nature as witness, the merging of the recording of facts and their interpretation, the repetition of what was and its reconstruction. This is true also when witness is inflected by memory, or involves a recognition. Memory, as restoration, vacillates between reparation and reconstruction. As for recognition, it needs both the revelation of the real and an interpretation by an observer. In this sense, it is decisive to understand who carries the keys to defining what appears before us, and when he/she/it does that. On this path, we may discover that film's subjectivity is connected to the presence of a mechanical device for recording the real (a subject-object), an almost official device for the handling of things (defining identity, legitimating a presence), and a social device for the preservation of memory (to make the dead live), etc. The fact remains that objectivity and subjectivity continue to overlap and, at the same time, to distinguish themselves: the cinema shapes a gaze that both joins and simultaneously divides these different levels; it unites them and separates them at the same time.

In the mid-1950s, during an extreme phase of the "ontological theories" (and in the decline of the "classical cinema"), Edgar Morin's *Cinema, or The Imaginary Man* (*Le cinéma ou l'homme imaginaire*) explored how objectivity and subjectivity indissolubly merge in the filmic experience. Onscreen, the world is presented in its immediacy, the effect of a mere recording. The spectator, however, projects him or herself onto and identifies with what is being seen, and in this way charges it with an entirely personal value. In Morin's words, image and imagination permeate each other in what can be called, under Sartre's influence, the imaginary. The penetration is total: "Cinema is exactly this symbiosis: a system that tends to integrate the spectator into the flow of the film. A system that tends to integrate the flow of the film into the psychic flow of the spectator."[70] Morin takes the process from the side of its reception: he analyzes how the camera's gaze meets that of the spectator. But his attention climbs the summit, to the camera's (or director's) encounter with the world: "Subjectivity and objectivity are not only superimposed but endlessly reborn, the one from the other, in a ceaseless round of subjectivizing objectivity and objectivizing subjectivity. The real is bathed, bordered on, crossed, swept along by the unreal. The unreal is molded, determined, rationalized, internalized by the real."[71] Moreover, these are two sides of the same coin, which in the filmic experience find their point of intersection: what comes to be seen on the screen, and how the spectator sees it; what the camera saw and what I see now.

Almost forty years before Morin, Hugo Münsterberg's *The Photoplay* shed light on film's capacity to capture the real and shape it according to our psychological processes (attention, memory, imagination).[72] We see the world in its essential state, yet we reinsert it in a mental experience. Twenty years after Morin, Christian Metz in *The Imaginary Signifier* asserts how the onscreen image inserts the action of the psychological processes (specular identification, voyeurism, fetishism) within the recording of the real.[73] In the filmic signifier there is an overlapping of extremely vivid states (all related to something that seems to be there, even if it is absent) and a desire (a desire for seeing and, more generally, perceiving).

We began with Balázs and the dialectic between "report" and "inner shot," arriving at Metz and the dialectic between recording the real and desire. It is only on this wide canvas that we can truly understand how film is able to put subjectivity and objectivity into play. It is only against this background that we can appreciate the ways in which these two essential categories take their respective shapes and mutually redefine one another. It is their inevitable meeting—together with the necessity of articulating their presence, categorizing their respective abilities, and defining their significance—that constitutes one of the richest terrains on which film is wagered. Here, it defines the modes of its own gaze. Here, the eye is at stake.

The Glass Eye

THE MECHANISM OF LIFE

"A hand that turns the handle"—so says Serafino Gubbio, operator at the Kosmograph film company and narrator of Pirandello's early twentieth-century novel *The Notebooks of Serafino Gubbio*.[1] He feels like "A hand that turns the handle": a person so connected to a machine—the camera—that he becomes a mere appendage. This machine is, in appearance, a "little device," yet its action is nonetheless devastating. It consumes and changes the shape of whatever passes before it. "The machine is made to act, to move, it swallows up our soul, devours our life. And how do you expect them to be given back to us, our life and soul, in a centuplicated and continuous output, by the machines? Let me tell you: in bits and morsels, all of one pattern, stupid and precise."[2] The "little device" separates the person being recorded from the real world, transporting him to a sort of other world. The actors, removed from direct contact with the audience, Gubbio goes on, "feel as though they were in exile. In exile, not only from the stage, but also in a sense from themselves. Because their action, the live action of their live bodies, here, on the screen of the cinematograph, no longer exists: it is their image alone, caught in a moment, in a gesture, an expression, that flickers and disappears."[3] Finally, the "little device" demands true servitude from the person controlling it, in this way confirming what seems the vocation of all mechanical devices, "these monsters, which ought to have remained instruments, and have instead become, perforce, our masters."[4] To devour, to separate, to subdue: the final effect is an emptying one. The filmed body "[is] so to speak subtracted, suppressed, deprived of [its] reality, of breath, of voice, of the sound that [it] makes in moving about, to become only a dumb image which quivers for a moment on the screen and disappears, in silence, in an instant, like an unsubstantial phantom, the play of illusion upon a dingy sheet of cloth."[5] The operator in the camera's service similarly loses all feeling. An operator must have "impassivity in face of the action that is going on in front of the camera." This impassivity makes him, in the end, like a thing ("I was a thing: why, perhaps the thing that was resting on my knees, wrapped in a black cloth"), rendering him machine-like ("I ceased to be Gubbio and became a hand").[6]

The "little device" is not unique in doing this. The world is populated with mechanical devices that subdue those they should serve, that swallow up life and reduce it to mere semblance. Pirandello offers more than one example: Zeme the astronomer's telescope ("You imagine that it is your instrument. Not a bit of it! It is your God, and you worship it!"); the monotype that substitutes for the old printing presses ("a monstrous beast which eats lead and voids books"); and, above all, the player piano "the man with the violin" must play alongside, which represents the very negation of freedom and creativity (so much so that the musician is forced—along with his instrument—to "accompany a roll of perforated paper running through the belly of this other machine!").[7] After all, the world itself has become a "clamorous and dizzy machinery . . . which from day to day seems to become more complicated and to move with greater speed." This is a machinery that offers a series of strong and overwhelming stimuli. At the very onset of the novel, the ironic description of the "mechanism" of modern life offers proof: "Today, such-and-such, this-and-that to be done hurrying to one place, watch in hand, so as to be in time at another. 'No, my dear fellow, thank you: I can't!' 'No, really lucky fellow! I must be off . . . ' At eleven, luncheon. The paper, the house, the office, school . . . "[8] Here, everyone risks becoming a "doll," moved by a "too obvious spring in its chest," whose arms can be made to open and close at will. Everyone is required to renounce his or her person, in order to become puppets called to act a part that is a pale "metaphor" of the self.[9]

The cinema, then, does not constitute an exception. In a world of machines—in a world reduced to machines—the cinema obeys a general rule. If anything, it brings this situation's paradoxes to light. In one way, in fact, it covers the deceit: thanks to photographic reproduction, it makes its representations look perfectly real. Those who work at Kosmograph can stage the most vague and improbable events, for example. The "little device" perfidiously "gives an appearance of reality to all their fictions."[10] In another way, however, the cinema renders our gaze even more acute.

In truth, it will perhaps never succeed in doing what the painter Giorgio Mirelli does in his portraits of Varia Nestorova—that is, it will never reveal the profound personality of those around us (on canvas, Varia is truly herself, while onscreen she is another person whom she neither recognizes nor knows).[11] The cinema succeeds in laying bare the subtle logic at the foundation of the "mechanism" of the modern world. It has only impassively gathered "life as it comes, without selection and without any plan." The cinema succeeds in "presenting to men the ridiculous spectacle of their heedless actions, an immediate view of their *Passions*, of their life as it is. Of this life without rest, which never comes to an end."[12] On the screen, in spite of everything, we see what we have become.

The cinema can do even more: it can, in fact, embody the logic of the "mechanism" in which we are caught up. It is enough to let the camera move as it knows how to do: here, a vision of things from a mechanism's point of view will emerge; here, new ways of looking at the world will be revealed, which we can make our own. There is a famous moment in Pirandello's novel, in which a description of a car passing a carriage is drawn by contrasting two "takes" from the two vehicles. This passage offers a splendid demonstration of how the cinema can mobilize a new kind of mechanical gaze, which may become a shared form of perception:

A slight swerve. There is a one-horse carriage in front. 'Peu, pepeeeu, peeeu.' What? The horn of the motor-car is pulling it back? Why, yes! It does really seem to be making it run backwards, with the most comic effect. The three ladies in the motor-car laugh, turn round, wave their arms in greeting with great vivacity, amid a gay, confused flutter of many-coloured veils; and the poor little carriage, hidden in an arid, sickening cloud of smoke and dust, however hard the cadaverous little horse may try to pull it along with his weary trot, continues to fall behind, far behind, with the houses, the trees, the occasional pedestrians, until it vanishes down the long straight vista of the suburban avenue. Vanishes? Not at all! The motor-car has vanished. The carriage, meanwhile, is still here, still slowly advancing, at the weary, level trot of its cadaverous horse. And the whole of the avenue seems to come forward again, slowly, with it. You have invented machines, have you? And now you enjoy these and similar sensations of stylish pace.[13]

On the screen, besides seeing how the "mechanism" of the world has reduced us to a series of images, we can see how this "mechanism" permits us—even demands us—to see.

The cinema appropriates life, transforms it, and empties it. But in the meantime, it gives rise to a gaze that is renewed in its precision. It swallows us, it sends us into exile, it renders us insensitive, yet it helps us see things in their reality and from a new perspective. In this sense, it is an ambiguous machine. Pirandello wrote *Shoot!* at a moment in which the technological explosion (less evident in Italy, though no less shocking)[14] led to questions on the nature of machines. Industrial technologies cease to be simple "tools" at the service and the direct command of man, and become "machinery," almost fully autonomous devices that force man to adapt to their functioning; and at times they even become "technical macrosystems," an integrated and autonomous apparatus in which man completely disappears.[15] They bring about a transformation of man from master to slave, as well as the transformation of the surrounding world from natural to artificial. Pirandello points out this dual destiny in his parallel descriptions of Serafino Gubbio's "little device" and the "mechanism" of life. It is at the heart of numerous critical observations of the period. I will limit myself to mentioning only two, which are different but complementary. The first, *Letters from Lake Como* by Romano Guardini, is a sorrowful reflection on the sunset of an old culture: "the human world tied to nature, the natural world filled with humanity, is waning away."[16] The second, *Technics and Civilization* by Lewis Mumford, is a broad and acclaimed history of the development leading to the culture of the machine. Mumford writes: "From the beginning, the most durable conquests of the machine lay not in the instruments themselves, which quickly became outmoded, nor in the goods produced, which quickly were consumed, but in the modes of life made possible via the machine and in the machine. The machine challenged thought and effort as no previous system of techniques had done."[17] Both authors put forth urgent concerns. Both conclude—albeit with quite divergent motivations and emphases—that one can and must reorient technological development, rewriting it into a new culture. In this way, it can be utilized to the end, without defeating man or the environment.

Let us return to the cinema. It is evident that a Pirandellian reflection on the camera leads us directly to the problem of who is the "subject" (though it would be better to call it "agent") controlling the filmic gaze. In the preceding chapter, we asked if on the screen we see facts in their immediacy or perceptions, reelaborations, and memories. The lure of the

machine leads us to consider the nature of what seems to "filter" our relationship with the world. Can it be said that what we see on the screen
is "someone's" perception, if it is a mechanical eye that does the perceiving? What is the relationship of this mechanical eye to that of man? Does
it exonerate his real participation, or does it embolden his decisions and
actions? Does it change the representation into a pure and simple copy,
or does it leave room for creativity? Does it contribute to the mechaniza-
tion of the world, or does it aid in its rehumanization? In other words, do
subjectivity and agency even exist in the age of the "machine"? Or do we
need to reformulate these concepts?

Three years after the publication of *Shoot!*, an article by Enrico Toddi
appeared in the film journal *In Penombra*, suggesting that the camera-eye
works at the mandate of the human one. "The viewfinder goes where the
spectator's gaze cannot directly go. Just as the agent was called the *longa
manus* of the mandant in the volumes of dusty university memory, the
cinema can call itself the *longus oculus* of the spectator."[18] Fifteen years
after Pirandello, Eugenio Giovannetti wrote a surprising book entitled *Cinema and the Mechanical Arts* (*Il cinema e le arti meccaniche*). In it, he reminds
us that the cinema is doubly tied to technology, both in its creative moment (in which the artist makes use of a machine that has "unconquer-
able likes and dislikes") and at the time of the work's distribution (the
mechanical reproduction of copies). Yet this double dependency does not
constitute a limitation: the cinema gives man back his gaze or, rather,
it restores it as a modern gaze. On the one hand, Giovannetti says, "the
world is becoming, thanks to the mechanical arts, a single immense artistic democracy."[19] This means that we cannot think of a social subject
in traditional terms. On the other hand, "the cinema admirably took care
of two antithetical necessities of modern life: seeing with scientific precision and placing itself in and broadening a vague medium."[20] We need
to think of the gaze in a different way as well. Between a mandate and a
modernization, a bond of faith and a step ahead: the camera-eye is suspended between these two fronts.

I will articulate these questions posed by the mechanical nature of
the cinematographic eye, going through some films that center on some
close relatives—if not actual brothers—of Serafino Gubbio: operators, or
operator-directors. Struggling with their "little device," they tell us how
the cinema reacts to the tensions that we have just illustrated.

THE MONKEY WITH THE CAMERA

The first among these relatives to Serafino Gubbio might be Luke, the protagonist of *The Cameraman* (E. Sedgwick, USA, 1928). The character played by Buster Keaton is, in fact, a newsreel operator. He has taken on this occupation for his love of Sally, the secretary of the production company, after quitting his former job as a roving photographer. The change is symptomatic, and refers to a profound shift in the field of images. Before, Luke made fixed photos; now, he takes snapshots. Then, he handled semi-rigid medium-tintypes, which were in some way the legacy of daguerreotypes; now he deals with the flexible medium of film. His work was once that of an artist-artisan; now, he works in an industrial environment, the MGM Newsreel production company.[21] First, his product was an object, the photo; today, it is an experience that consists in viewing or re-viewing current events on the screen. Last, at first the "receivers" were single individuals; now, it is an audience. Thus, from photographer to film operator, the material, the context, and the end of the work have changed. We are passing into a new era of the cinema.

These profound differences notwithstanding, there is a strong element of continuity. In both instances, the image produced must help in *identifying* a part of the world. In the case of photography, it is clear: Luke takes portraits, images in which the individual depicted must recognize him or herself, as well as be recognizable to others. His tintypes can also be used as ashtrays, as one man maliciously reminds him. Yet the fact remains that, in reproducing an individual's face, the tintypes put into play the identity of the person depicted. In this way, they are the direct descendants of both André Desderi's photographic "calling cards" and Alphonse Bertillon's photo-kits, two practices that highlighted the connection between the photograph and individual identity.[22] They respond to a need that Benjamin articulated so well around the time of *The Cameraman*'s release: in an age of profound political and social changes "coming from right or left, it will be necessary to get used to being looked in the face in order to know from where we come. On our part, it will be necessary to get used to looking others in the face for the same purpose."[23] Citing August Sander, Benjamin points out that the photograph helps in this task like "a training manual."[24]

This is the case of film, as well. MGM Newsreel asks its operators for reportages that allow us to "recognize" the depicted events. In order to do this, the takes must foreground two features, comparable in some way to the characteristics of a portrait: the event captured must appear to be something that has actually occurred in a determinate place and time; and it must also be significant with respect to everyday life. It is the "reality" and the "relevance" of an event that define "what happened." The newsreel can and must bring to light both of these elements: in doing so, it is able to carry out work on and about "identity."

The camera's ability to identify subjects and events makes it a medium that restores the real to us, instead of taking it away. In this light, *The Cameraman* continues and overthrows the analysis of *Shoot!* When the filmic image clarifies the "who is?" and the "what happened?" we are able to meet the world again on the screen. In Keaton's film, this conviction is attributed to the MGM Newsreel bosses, and explains their reaction to Luke's tests. He shoots three films with different results. The first is a work in which—through editing and seemingly casual superimposition—reality reveals a strange face: town streets plow through ships, the metropolis explodes into a thousand perspectives, unrelated actions find themselves in parallel. The work has a dazzling beauty worthy of the best of the artistic avant-garde, between constructivism and surrealism. Yet the MGM Newsreel managers ridicule and refuse the film, attributing it to Luke's inexperience. They cannot do any different. For them, the camera is not a magic eye that rewrites reality according to a personal map, changing its coordinate. It is, instead, an eye that recognizes reality and makes it recognizable, restoring it to us with its essential facts. Staying close to things is its goal, not transforming them into a fantasy. These managers do not know it, but the same dialectic had emerged some years before in a debate between the well-known director Marcel L'Herbier and the influential *Le Temps* critic, Émile Vuillermoz:[25] is the cinema a "machine that prints life," as the former maintained, or a "machine that prints dreams," as the latter believed? Can it simply gather the appearance of reality, or can it also push itself beyond these appearances into fantastic universes that reveal the manner in which artists approach the real? The MGM bosses, partisans of the first solution, need an impassive operator. (Serafino Gubbio could have been one. He would have done equally well for L'Herbier, who is also theoretically in the first camp. Perhaps for this reason, L'Herbier would honor Pirandello with an adaptation of *The Late Mattia Pascal*.[26] But here we are entering into Borgesian philology.) Luke/Keaton is impassive; but at his first audition, not enough so. He "manipulates" reality. Consequently, he is fired.

He makes up for it in his second film, however. His service on the Tong wars is perfectly in line with the criteria that render a current event "identifiable." The battle between the two Chinese gangs shines onscreen in all its reality and relevance. It is a shame that, in order to "perfectly" capture reality, Luke must intervene in a thousand little ways (but therein lies the episode's comedy): he puts himself in the middle to intensify the fire on both sides, allows the camera's tripod to be hit in order capture the events from a better visual angle, and finally ends up putting a knife in the hand of one of the rivals in order to heighten the drama of the clash. The operator is not really impassive: he takes part in the events and influences their unfolding. "I do not operate anything," Serafino Gubbio says. Luke becomes like Serafino in his second audition. He becomes an eye that is limited to verifying reality. He proves, however, that to be an operator, one must indeed *operate* a bit. What is important is that this manipulation does not show: it is enough to leave it implied, hidden under the depicted events. Reality can then reappear as it is (or at least as we believe it to be, since there is so much to say on these Tong wars—full of shots but lacking in deaths—which broke out during Carnival and are indeed carnivalesque themselves). The fact remains that the real returns. And the enthusiastic MGM Newsreel managers have Luke return as well. They hire him, this time for good.

There is also a third film by Luke that ends up in the company's hands. It is the report of a nautical accident involving Sally. Luke saves her from drowning, bringing her back to shore, but she thinks that someone else saved her. Seeing the rescue on the screen, she finally understands how things really took place. This third film corresponds to the rule of rendering an event identifiable: what happened is brought back with all its objective features. It is a shame that, this time, Luke is not the cameraman. When he dives in to save Sally, a monkey replaces him. The monkey turns the handle, and the camera-eye belongs to it. What does this substitution of the monkey for the man really mean? It brings us back to Serafino Gubbio's fear that one day the cinema will function on its own, without our hand (or eye).[27] Such a moment would represent the perfection of impassiveness, but also the end of humanity: the camera would be a pure machine. It would be out of our control, and man would lose all power. In turning the handle itself, the monkey in fact exonerates man from even being present. This happens, however, not under the auspices of a posthuman machine, but a prehuman beast. With this action, the monkey brings out primitive motivations that are decidedly primordial. Are monkeys not the emblem of the imitation of a gesture, its copy and replication? Luke's monkey not only replicates the action of her owner, but she also replicates an action that allows for the replication of the world. A pure game of reproduction emerges. In this game, there is a certain passiveness (if to film means to capture and reactivate the world, it is enough to let the real reveal itself), but there is also a reward (the world reappears, and the man is ready to be celebrated in a copy). It is not by chance that Luke—abandoning his role as operator—is now on the screen, carrying out an action that will immortalize him as a hero.

This cue leads us to Bazin's extraordinary insight: at the foundation of the cinema lies a need to reproduce appearances, in order to protect a part of life from the violence of death. This need does not pass through the artist's mediation. The filmic image is made by itself, automatically. In exchange, this need brings us back to something that is even more profoundly human—it is part of our intimate nature to try to keep with us an image of what is no more. From this point of view, "The Ontology of the Photographic Image"[28] could paradoxically function as a commentary on Luke's third film—there is an absent operator, the risk of death, the real and symbolic rescue, and the restitution of reality. Rather than insisting on Bazin, I will quote instead a piece dated one year before *The Cameraman*, which is written, however, in Bazinian tones. An Italian scholar, Alberto Luchini, writes: "The cinema satisfies an ancient and universal desire for reproduction and complete, exact representation; in other words, mechanical. . . . I want to call it . . . the *eternal cinema of the human soul*."[29]

Cinema is a machine that encourages impassivity, ready to exonerate man from responsibility. But it is also a machine that fulfills a profoundly anthropological desire, and is thus very human. The idea that emerges in Luke's third film represents a sort of ideal. The MGM bosses naturally appreciate this film, but they let it function as a seal on Luke and Sally's love. Perhaps they are a bit afraid of it: they preferred the second film, with its astute compromise between passivity and intervention, reproduction and subtle falsification. And perhaps the first film, refused by them, which spoke of a cinema able to re-create the real, would be accepted by another division of MGM.

Let us try then, to discuss these various faces of the cinematographic machine, with the help of some other films.

NOTEBOOKS OF M. K., OPERATOR

"An excerpt from the diary of a cameraman" is how Dziga Vertov defined his *The Man with the Movie Camera* (*Celovek s kinoapparatom*, USSR, 1929), as he introduced it before an audience of workers.[30] An operator and a diary once again: we are still in the Pirandellian wake with which we began. We are most certainly dealing with a different director and different intentions, yet there is something significant that returns. Beginning with an intersection that is so beautifully summarized in Dziga Vertov's introduction: "The material is interpreted and moves along the film according to three basic intersecting lines: 'life as it is' on the screen, 'life as it is' on the filmstrip, and simply 'life as it is.'" Cinema and life: Serafino Gubbio would have approved.

Let us get to the heart of this intersection, which brings to light three distinct conditions of life. Vertov begins with life on the screen. Unlike Pirandello's world, we are not dealing with only the semblance of life that is to be viewed with nostalgia with respect to an irreparably stolen "real" one. We are dealing with an existence parallel to the other two. It has an equal dignity, and enters into a fruitful dialectic with them.

In the first place, the "life as it is" on the screen registers and gathers both life itself and life on the filmstrip. It observes some recurrent moments in everyday life:

> Besides the theme of the cameraman, you'll see the theme of "labor and leisure," of "woman workers," of the "workers of club and the pub," of "cinema about cinema," and many other themes woven together. Negative moments of life are also shown in the film, which are necessary to achieve a more sharply accented emphasis upon the rest of the material.[31]

Yet the life on the screen recovers the life on (and in) the film as well. There are numerous passages in which we see onscreen frames of film alongside the things that they captured. There are even more moments in which we see the editor work on the spools, ordering, cutting, connecting the given materials. The editor's presence is featured alongside other forms of work, which are also moments of "intervention" in the real. Thus, the "life as it is" onscreen reflects both everyday existence and film existence: it puts the two in contact.

Yet life on the screen is also selective with respect to the other two. In fact, as Vertov writes, the film's attention for the world, "does not mean that all of life as it is is shown. In our experiment only those moments of life that coincide with the productive moments of the cameraman's work are displayed."[32] The activity that unfolds around the construction of the film becomes a kind of filter for the surrounding world: beginning with the presence of an operator and a camera, it is decided where the gaze will or will not look.

Finally, life on the screen gives everyday existence a new order and face. Vertov writes: "While showing and selecting these moments of life, we submitted in our assignment to one fundamental form: the diary of a cameraman or examples of a cameraman's work outside the studio."[33] Film therefore models the surrounding universe, literally giving it a form. It does so, once more, starting from its own abilities and efforts: the capacity of a machine, but also work guided by a profoundly human end.

This last point is decisive, and brings us to the heart of the problem. Which eye is that of the cinema? How does it behave? Whom does it make behave? Let us move some years back in time and read some passages from the manifesto "Kinoks: A Revolution," published by Vertov in *Lef* in 1923. Vertov writes: "The kino-eye lives and moves in time and space; it gathers and records impressions in a manner wholly different from that of the human eye."[34] This difference lies in the fact that the camera possesses a freedom of action, as well as an uncommon acuity:

> I am kino-eye, I am a mechanical eye. I, a machine, show you the world as only I can see it. Now and forever, I free myself from human immobility, I am in constant motion, I draw near, then away from objects, I crawl under, I climb onto them. I move apace with the muzzle of a galloping horse, I plunge full speed into a crowd, I outstrip running soldiers, I fall on my back, I ascend with an airplane, I plunge and soar together with plunging and soaring bodies.[35]

This capacity of the kino-eye can aspire to be something more than the simple recording of the real to which we are accustomed. "Until now, we have violated the movie camera and forced it to copy the work of our eye. And the better the copy, the better the shooting was thought to be. Starting today we are liberating the camera and making it work in the opposite direction—away from copying."[36] The world will be observed in a new way. It is always the camera-eye that "speaks": "Freed from the rule of sixteen-seventeen frames per second, free of the limits of time and space, I put together any given points in the universe, no matter where

I've recorded them." And it is always the camera-eye that explains its own intentions: "My path leads to the creation of a fresh perception of the world. I decipher in a new way a world unknown to you."[37] Thus, it is a matter of following reality in order to find within it "the chaos of visual phenomena that fills the space,"[38] the nexuses that hold it together. Better still, it is a matter of reconstructing reality, in order to understand it more clearly. ("I am kino-eye. From one person I take the hands, the strongest and most dexterous; from another I take the legs, the swiftest and most shapely; from a third, the most beautiful and expressive head—and through montage I create a new, perfect man.")[39] The camera is not alone in this mission: "Aiding the machine-eye is the kinok-pilot, who not only controls the camera's movements, but entrusts himself to it during experiments in space." The point of arrival cannot be anything but remarkable: "The result of this concerted action of the liberated and perfected camera and the strategic brain of man directing, observing, and gauging—the presentation of even the most ordinary things will take on an exceptionally fresh and interesting aspect."[40]

The Man with the Movie Camera applies these principles to all its different levels (perhaps with less radicalness than the *Kinoglaz* film series immediately before, but with a systematic nature that renders the operation even more didactic). It does so, for example, by putting forward a direct point of view of the world that makes the camera's presence "felt," countering the narrative tendencies that usually erase that presence.[41] It also constructs a series of visual associations that "rearticulate" the reality offered—in the divorce sequence, for example, the idea of separation finds new definitions and echoes. The basic principles are equally pursued by facing classic themes like life and death—filmed with insistence and without shame—but also by reinterpreting the camera's work, which is presented to us in the triple guise of a mechanical device in itself, an instrument of the operator's work, and as an almost human subject able to move and react by itself. In all this, Vertov never escapes the field of vision. His film must not be "read" but "seen." As he instructs, "It is impossible to *read* this film, and it is very desirable that, during a viewing of the film, the conceptual content of the visual phrases NOT be translated into words (as usually happens when watching theatrical-fictional films)."[42] Simply, to see is not only to observe. It is also to seek to enter into the logic and dynamic of reality.[43]

This basic assumption (which, I say jokingly, corrects and integrates the convictions of the MGM Newsreel managers and would force them to accept Luke's first film that they instead reject) clearly shows us how Dziga Vertov redefines the problem with which we began. The camera is able to restore the world to us, not because it simply establishes its appearance, but because it understands its mechanism. The camera's eye is associated with the presence of an operator (or, if you will, an operator-editor-director: it is not by chance that the first *manifesti* are signed by "The Council of Three," referring to Mikhail Kaufman, Elizaveta Svilova, and Dziga Vertov).[44] It explores the world in its apparent chaos, identifies its essential nexus, and reconstructs its functioning. In this sense, it is right to surprise things "in the act"; but the fact must be explained, not simply revealed. To do this, we must go beyond simple ascertainment: one's own impressions must be "retranscribed." One can then identify things completely, ascribing their place and role in the world.

Such a principle obviously leads us to the conviction, widespread in the period, that art (and cinema in particular) has an analytical value. Aesthetic work serves also to lay bare the functioning of things (and, in parallel, critical activity serves to lay bare the functioning of texts; I am thinking here of the formalists). The cinema embraces a similar vocation. We understand this, for example, in a 1927 article that appeared in the Italian journal *Solaria*. The author, Alberto Luchini, after underscoring the cinema's capacity to satisfy "an ancient and universal desire for reproduction and complete, exact representation," points out another feature: "The electric rapidity of the consecutive recordings gives the cinema, and the cinema only, the ability to surprise, repeat, demonstrate, exhibit, show that complexity and variety, and simultaneity, and separation, and reciprocal indifference of life, which art itself and poetry cannot but suggest the feeling."[45] Luchini ties the cinema's analytical capacity to a sort of profound need. Vertov instead connects it to the sociopolitical work established by communism: "The establishing of a class bond that is visual (kino-eye) and auditory (radio-ear) between the proletarians of all nations and all lands, based on the platform of the communist decoding of the world—that is our objective."[46] The difference is not insignificant, and it reflects the opposite leanings of the two authors. It does not, however, eliminate a certain way of looking at the machine and at the cinema-machine as an instrument for the understanding of things.

It is perhaps useful to recall that, in Vertov's 1929 presentation, he defined his film an experiment: "The workers of the Kino Eye group decided
to carry out a scientific experiment, an experiment in production, spe-
cially directed toward the improvement of [film] language, toward per-
fecting it."[47] Two ideas converge in the notion of an experiment: aesthetic
experimentation, aimed at enriching the filmic language, and scientific
research, aimed at an analysis of the world and an understanding of
its laws. For Vertov, both sides are essential, and must be kept together.
Within this perspective, the diary represents a point of juncture: on the
one hand, it refers to the notebook of a poet-operator in search of inspiration and, on the other, the protocol of observation of a scientist-operator
conducting a systematic investigation of a phenomenon. The cinema as
technology and the technology of the cinema favor this union of art and
science.

The experimental nature of the film certainly demands a particular
vision: "I would appeal to the audience with a request to watch our experiment with special attention, inasmuch as it conveys itself with sud-
denness and in uninhibited form. As a consequence, its unusualness
demands your full concentration."[48] From here, we can easily return to
the Benjaminian idea that the filmic image functions as a test, ready to
defy the spectator's perception.[49] To watch a film is not a satisfaction for
one's curiosity or a consolation for one's nostalgias (as it could have been
in Luke's films, and in Lumière before him). To watch a film is to challenge one's senses. Similarly, it does not entail finding evidence: it entails
facing a judicial process. The fact remains that it is film's experimental
nature that allows for the intersection of language, analysis, methodology, self-awareness, and finally education of the public. Presenting the
Kinoglaz film series in 1924, Vertov had understood this nexus: "Kino-eye
as the union of science with newsreel to further the battle for the communist decoding of the world, as an attempt to show the truth on the
screen—Film-truth."[50] Here is the cinema-eye, the eye of a machine: it
has a life of its own ("away from copying"),[51] but also a vocation: that of
the truth, a cine-truth.

KING KONG ON BROADWAY

If we tried to read *The Man with the Movie Camera* as a reversal (and a com-
pletion) of *The Cameraman*, why not read *King Kong* (M. C. Cooper and E. B.

Schoedsack, USA, 1933)[52] as a reversal of both? Why not reflect here as well on the relationship between the cinema and the machine—between cinema and the producing machine?

In order to foreground this topic, I must perform a small act of cruelty. For the moment, I will leave aside the film's two unforgettable sequences: the one in which the Great Ape kidnaps the White Virgin, brings her to the jungle, and tries to seduce her, and the one in which he breaks free from his restraints, escapes into the urban jungle, and climbs the Empire State Building, before being defeated for good. I will start at the beginning, at the moment in which a group of people gather in a ship's wardroom. They are getting ready to set sail for a mysterious island to film something never seen before, something extraordinary, "the eighth wonder of the world." Among them, there is the producer-director, Carl Denham, also an heir to Serafino Gubbio—though not at all "impassive." The skipper and the first mate express doubts and perplexity, to which he responds with confidence: their undertaking will be a certain success.

An undertaking. The trip is presented as such.[53] On second thought, it is an undertaking in the double sense of the term. The producer-director prepares himself to face an adventure that is significant, and also fascinating: he is like the Knight leaving in search of the Holy Grail, save the fact that his mission is motivated by ambition more than desire, and his Grail is a prehistoric beast—not a holy goblet. Yet the voyage on which he embarks has clear commercial implications: to film the never-before-seen assures precious material to offer up to theaters around the world, and the long journey will have a confirmation at the box office. The producer-director, besides being a Knight, is also an Entrepreneur.

The second face of the undertaking soon becomes dominant. The heroic and glorious deed gives prestige, but one must compete for the business activity. The gossip in the wardroom confirms it. All the foreseen conditions must be in place: in particular, the necessary resources must be available, and the much-researched project without holes. This is what lends confidence.

What emerges is a productive organization, with its instruments and ends. The instruments are the necessary tools and devices: the ship, the tenders, the gifts for the natives, the arms for protection, the cameras, the actors, the workmen, etc. The end is that of every industrial undertaking—to obtain the "raw materials" needed in order to transform them into "commodities" to be offered on the market.[54] For our knight-entrepreneur, unpredictable and unexpected realities make up the "natural resources," never before seen onscreen, which he will find on an unexplored island. Likewise, the "commodity" is the visual documentation of this reality. It is a collection of images that audiences around the world will run to see with curiosity and trepidation. The undertaking is set within this picture. A picture that explains with absolute certainty that to film the world is not only to copy it (as Luke believed), nor is it to simply reconstruct its underlying logic (as Dziga Vertov wanted to believe): it is also to produce, to produce a show.

Let us see more clearly what this final product—the spectacle—really is. As we said, it centers around a series of shots that the troupe will take on Skull Island. Through them, the spectator will be able to make an otherwise impossible journey, and witness events from which he or she would be otherwise barred. The cinema is a formidable witness that allows the person watching a film to become a witness as well. We are, once again, meeting up with some of the convictions that drove the MGM Newsreel bosses in their choice of news materials to offer the public: on the screen, what matters is an accurate record of the event. It is also clear that we are facing one of the most solid convictions accompanying the advent of cinema: the idea that it can assure us direct contact with what is distant, in terms of both space and time. A 1907 piece lyrically reminds us (with unspoken references to Jules Verne's science fictions):

> Though old and decrepit himself, every lover or husband who has for years visited his beloved at the cemetery will finally see her for himself, when he most wants or desires her before his eyes, alive and young, with words and a smile, intent on the housework. So it will be when someone dear crosses oceans, continents, and distant seas; we will be able to follow, to see, to move and act, to converse from afar as if we were there. So it will be that we will know of his or her needs in order to satisfy them, his or her joys to share them, the fulfillment of his or her dreams of riches and glory to exalt them.[55]

The cinema allows us to stay in touch with the world.

It is, however, a strange connection. If, thanks to the film image, the spectator can feel him or herself in the place and time of the event depicted onscreen, it is also true that this participation is neither complete nor total. He or she continues to be separated from what is onscreen. He or she is in a different place: a theater, a screening. Hence, there is one

important consequence: in order to shoot "the real" found on Skull Island, the producer-director will have to represent completely the amaze-
ment and fear that this mysterious reality provokes in the viewer. He
is there to capture emotion. Yet these shots, however fear-inducing, do
not risk the spectator's life like that mysterious reality might have: the
viewer is struck by the film, but remains safe.[56] We have emotion without danger. The Great Ape, once taken from his environment, is put in
chains precisely to ensure this sort of safety. Thus, we can say that what
the spectator is offered—the spectacle that he or she is sold—is, in good
part, a visual experience marked by attraction and protection, by pleasure and domination. In other words, it is a purely *voyeuristic experience*. It
is not by chance that, when the producer-director displays the enchained
Great Ape to the public, he affirms that "he comes to civilization, merely
a captive, a show, to gratify your curiosity." Nor is it a coincidence that a
contemporary review of *King Kong* commemorating its screening at Radio
City Music Hall notes the subtle contradiction of "an audience enjoying
all the sensations of primitive terror and fascination within the scien-
tifically air-cooled temple of baroque modernism that is Mr. Rockefeller's
contribution to contemporary culture."[57] The commodity of cinema is a
visual pleasure consumed in maximum comfort. It is the satisfaction of
spying from a safely adjoining room. In this light, the film's conclusion
seems almost more explosive: freeing himself from his chains, King Kong
(the actual living Great Ape, not the one that was thought to have been
brought in effigy: the director in the film is able to present his audience
with reality itself, fetishizing it) threatens this shameless voyeurism. The
living Kong forces the spectator to flee his refuge, to pour into the streets,
to go back to being a helpless citizen. He compels him—once a peeping
Tom—to become prey.

   If the voyeuristic situation constitutes the final product offered to the
consumer, the production process that is put into action remains to be
examined. Let us return to the beginning of the film. In the wardroom,
on the eve of the expedition, the captain and the officers check if all the
instruments for the undertaking are ready. Among them, there are arms.
The expedition, in fact, will not be peaceful. It will require the use of
force, precisely at the moment in which the crew will seize the "raw materials" from which the spectacle will be drawn—in which the men will
appropriate the "natural resources" that will be transformed into commodities. The production process involves a coerced submission. It is an

oppressive exploitation, something of a kidnapping. Such a manner of intervention has a dual effect: it changes the relationship to nature, and more precisely it breaks the sense of equilibrium with the environment from which the "raw materials" come (an equilibrium that, incomprehensible to the white men's mentality, seems instead to inspire offerings or rituals that are celebrated by the natives).[58] At the same time, it spurs resistance on the part of nature itself, which, once injured, must react in some way. This is what happens at the film's conclusion: King Kong's revolt represents a gesture of resistance to appropriation, in addition to an unmasking of voyeurism. The Beast rebels against his capture (for which the Beauty is used as bait). He summons all the energy of which he is capable, and that no chain is able to contain, and it pours out in the form of counterviolence toward those who, through violence, tried to cage him. In this sense, the film becomes a sort of disaster movie, not dissimilar to those about earthquakes or volcanoes, in which nature—damaged and exploited—reacts, breaking through shackles and reversing the power relationship with those who had unscrupulously thought to subdue it.

The violence connected to the production process has yet another face that is more subtle and seemingly innocuous. Let us return once again to the beginning of the film. The producer-director in the wardroom needs a last element for his undertaking: a young woman to entrust for a part in the film, that of the white woman who encounters a prehistoric animal. There will not only be shots of the "real" on Skull Island—they will also film a "story." This superimposition of the narrative and documentary dimensions makes at least two features emerge: on the one hand, the production is directed toward consumption; on the other, it requires significant manipulation.

Within the context of consumption, the story works as an attraction. In fact, it might appeal to the pleasure that great events offer, beyond a curiosity for what is remote in terms of space and time. And this will be a great event: it is nothing less than a story of love and death between the Beauty and the Beast. The audience will have a true myth that appeals to its imagination. At the same time, there is a reference to everyday reality, thanks to an actress who has nothing remarkable about her but a "pretty face to look at"; thus, it is easy to identify with her. Imagination and identification: as Alberto Abruzzese argued in his passionate study of the Great Ape,[59] these two elements render the "machine-story" in some way infallible. Better still, they orient the modern cultural product directly to its consumption. It is from this viewpoint that, in 1908, an Italian scholar justified the abandonment of reality for narration:

> The history of cinema has two paths that are distinct and quasi-antithetical. It was at first an ingenious and faithful mechanical reconstruction of reality in movement, a slightly tremulous reality . . . but one that is sincere, and as such pleasing to the cultured souls and artists, but not very much by the masses. The ardent love of the masses was born when cinema abandoned reality and became artificial, when with the help of imagination, scenic illusion, mime, disguising it imitated nature: it created farces and tragedies, idylls and comedies, visions and mysteries, when it positioned itself, in other words, on the same paths as art, when it became its cheaper facsimile.[60]

A narrative also implies a manipulation. To tell a story does not simply mean to adapt or reorganize facts, but to superimpose a fantasy onto them. In this sense, Carl Denham—knight, entrepreneur, but also a storyteller—has to go forward with respect to Luke/Keaton and Dziga Vertov. Luke/Keaton and Vertov influence the captured reality, in order to give a more vivid description, or to understand relationships between things. Carl Denham transforms the events in order to clear a space for imagination.[61]

Manipulation could have a justification in and of itself: we have already mentioned the polemic between L'Herbier and Vuillermoz on the reproductive nature of the cinema. The problem is recurrent between the first and third decades of the century: if film is a simple copy of the real (a *machine à imprimer la vie*, or "machine to print life," as L'Herbier said), then it cannot claim to be an art. Paul Souday, one year before in 1917, had called attention to this: "The cinema, like the photograph—of which it is a perfection—is limited to faithfully and mechanically following reality, while art is not a mechanical copy, but an intelligent interpretation of this reality."[62] Ten years before, in 1908, Canudo had already clarified the problem: "Now it is necessary to ask ourselves if the cinema is art. I say that it is not yet art, since it lacks the elements of characteristic choice, plastic interpretation, and not of a copy of a subject, which will always mean that photography will not be an art."[63] Many others would confirm the argument. Therefore, some manipulation is necessary to free the "mechanical eye" from its passivity and bring it into the aesthetic domain. With a story, though, this manipulation risks becoming excessive. There is the danger of altering real information, superimposing on it the elements that obey only the order of the narration. Reality would be caged in a preestablished and abstract mold, which is precisely what every story is. The semblances of a real world would appear on the screen, but it would only be a possible world, imaginable and imagined. Only the return to reality (or a story that becomes perfect mimesis, as Bazin hoped in his battle for realism, which began in the 1940s) can save the cinema from this risk.

The two features connected to narration—its orientation toward consumption and the presence of manipulation—make us fully understand how the picture has changed with respect to the two preceding films. Here, the camera no longer seems able to give back to us what its eye captures. On the contrary, it seems called to truly "devour" the world and transform it into a "semblance of reality," almost to confirm Pirandello's pessimistic preoccupations. In other words, the camera participates in a process (a production process, in which the reproduction is pressed into the production) that makes it impossible to ascertain the authenticity of what we see. The onscreen world has become an artificial universe, and we ourselves—immersed in a game of the frenetic satisfaction of our curiosity and imagination—become wheels in the economic mechanism of the circulation of a commodity. A machine-world for the machine-spectators, in which the cinema—machine among machines—exercises the power to cancel out nature. The latter—the one surrounding us, as well as the one still cherished in our hearts—seems to vanish. Swallowed up and voided out, Pirandello would say, canceled out in an existence that has by now become a "clamorous and dizzy machinery" that crushes us like a merciless machine. Nature is no longer around nor inside us. All that remain are "bits and morsels" of life on the screen, in the theater, on the streets. Here, the "mechanical eye" of cinema shows its ambiguous nature. Yet there is hope on the horizon. A story may respect the real, as Bazin would contend. A film may break its own "mechanism," especially in order to explore new possibilities. This is what unconventional works do, if for no reason other than to witness the dream of a utopia. This is what King Kong does in the film's final sequences.

Let us go back to these sequences, which were previously interpreted as an unmasking of the voyeurism carried out by the object of scopic desire, and nature's resistance to its own imprisonment. We can, in fact, see in them the anger of he who grows aware of having become prisoner of the machine, as well as the creation of a martyr who will make us regret the loss of nature. The Great Ape who crosses New York destroying every-thing in his wake and faces death clinging to the top of the Empire State Building illustrates both positions. King Kong behaves like a borderline subject who, suffocated by the established order, reverses his rage on the surrounding world by tearing it to pieces. If you will, he is a metropolitan hooligan who rebels against an environment that seems alien to him. He also behaves, in contrast, like a modern testimonial for ecological causes: he climbs the tallest skyscraper in the world as if it were a tropical peak. He faces the airplanes flying around him with the same determination he battles the pterodactyls of the island. He suffers what is, in the end, an unjust death, showing his valor to the end. In other words, he shows everyone what beings like him—who have lived in the heart of nature—are made of. Before the new triumph of the machine culture, he reminds us of what we have lost. Thanks to him, we have access once more to a dream. May he rest in peace—he has our regrets.

RESISTING THE LIGHT

But what if King Kong, instead of rebelling, had let himself be tamed? What if he had become a perfect dancer on the Broadway stage? If he had given up his primitive island and adapted to living in a Manhattan loft, eating hamburgers and drinking Coca Cola? And if he placed himself in the service of the processes of production and consumption, replicating to his best ability the actions of millions of machine-men? What would happen if the subtle operation of the cinema—that of taking possession of the world to make a spectacle—reached its conclusion? What if nature disappeared once and for all from our horizon, and we found ourselves moving about in an environment that is finally and happily artificial?

Let us imagine that there are no longer things to film, but only im-ages; there are no longer human bodies, only clones; no longer a primi-tive universe, but only copies. In other words, let us imagine that there is no longer any jungle to reach, but only a museum with beautiful works on display. It would be interesting to see how the cinema-eye behaves. Would it experience a Pirandellian pleasure at this eclipse of reality, this emptying of essence? Would it suspend its own inevitable violence (to shoot, to frame), since every violence has already been carried out? Or does it go down, with pride, some other path, and search for a Beauty, though this could end in martyrdom as it does for the Beast? Jean-Luc

Godard's *Passion* (France, 1982), forty-three years after *King Kong*, offers us both the opportunity to pose these questions, as well as some clues for possible answers.

This film too is centered around a direct descendant of Serafino Gubbio: Jerzi, a director involved in building and filming a complex and costly set. He is not, however, chasing after the capture of a never-before-seen reality, in order to transform it into images of mass appeal. What attracts him is the reconstruction of great artistic masterpieces of the past, in particular the paintings of Rubens, Goya, and Delacroix. He translates these paintings into *tableaux vivants*, which are featured in his film. Many surrounding events weigh on his personal and private life. The majority of his extras live around him, and bring their everyday problems to the set. In the adjoining village, a group of workers risks losing their jobs, and the matter has consequences for the making of the film. He finds himself drawn into a difficult relationship with a married woman, a fact that further complicates his life. But despite these demands, Jerzi shows an absolute dedication to his project. He works ceaselessly on the reconstruction of these masterpieces from the past, trying to reproduce every infinitesimal detail. His surrounding reality does not concern him. Yet the cinema is made of reality: of light, bodies, and objects. The material world can sometimes be put on hold, but it inevitably returns. And it is precisely the real that, resurfacing, places the director's efforts in jeopardy: the lighting that he tries to use does not work; the actors' bodies never fully adapt themselves; their postures and gestures always have some small imperfection. All of this renders useless his attempt to remake the masterpieces. The difficulties are evident, and the film is abandoned.

This is the story told in *Passion*, retold perhaps in a tendentious manner. It contains a reflection on the status of art in contemporary times: we find the obstinacy of an aesthetic search, the nostalgia for a inheritance that risks being lost, the frustration of an expressive accuracy never reached.[64] Yet there are other points that interest us, and that can help us bring this exploration to a conclusion.

The first is clearly an indifference for the real. The world around Jerzi is full of tension and turbulence, but the director ignores the everyday *petites Passions* for the *grandes Passions* staged by art. The fact that he is a film director does not seem to help him pay attention to the world around him. What is, in fact, the cinema? Or at least, what has it become? A voice-over at the beginning of the film explains, "It isn't a lie, but something imagined, which is never the exact truth, but neither is it its opposite . . . and that, in any case, is separated by the external real, by the deeply calculated 'approximations' of seeming." The cinema is something that must never call the external world to account; it seeks a center of interest beyond the real. In this light, the mechanical eye seems exonerated from the need to pursue and restore things: the camera is simply not taken up in order to capture the real.

The second point relates to images. If the cinema's task, as Jerzi interprets it, is an engagement with the tradition of visual representation in order to circulate some of its fundamental features, it must draw its materials and inspiration from this tradition. This carries an important consequence, however: the filmic images cannot be but reelaborations of something that is, in turn, a reelaboration of reality. They are second-degree representations, in which objects, bodies, and postures are mediated by the painter's treatment of them. We will have only images of images in a game of mirrors that can be extended *ad infinitum*. In this game, to shoot can only mean to replicate: to offer copies of copies. This is, moreover, precisely what Jerzi wants to do. For this reason, he paradoxically ignores the suggestion to follow Rembrandt and observe "human beings, carefully and at length, their lips and in their eyes"; for Jerzi, bodies are only masses to be rearranged as they had once been displayed, in either a given picture or its possible variants, real or imaginary. In this infinite repetition—in these images of images—it is obvious that it no longer makes sense to look for "an original," a source for everything[65] (least of all in the reality that provided the basis for the first representation). Man's Museum contains only pictures in dialogue with each other. Nature has vanished, once and for all, from its rooms.

And finally, once again, the real. This filming—like a continuous game of mirrors, this shooting without catching hold, ready only to offer a replica—runs up, in fact, against something belonging to the order of reality. Or better, with something that constitutes the basis of the real, before it is determined in any concrete way: light. "The camera is always there to witness the light. That's what I admire in painting: painters can create their own light." Jerzi could appropriate this assertion from Godard.[66] Perhaps this is why he tries to remake the great painted masterpieces: because he is envious of artists who could always have the light that they wanted. On his set, the lighting is never what he needs it to be. No matter how he works with his great *tableaux vivants*, there is always an area in which the chiaroscuro, colors, and refraction of the bodies leave him profoundly dissatisfied. He never has the "right" light. He does have, however, an authentic, concrete light. This is a light that does not let itself be adapted, subdued, or caged, precisely because it is what it is—a real element. In an otherwise completely artificial set, its presence reminds us how nature is ready to reappear, even within the folds of a machine. This resistance against a mechanical eye—the camera-eye—forces the latter to contend with the real, and to give in to its subtle presence. But Jerzi does not accept this concrete light, nor does he accept that reality enters into his copying of copies. For this reason, he gives up and abandons the film.

But while Jerzi carries out his defeat, beaten by the resistance of the light, the person making *Passion* (Serafino Godard?) offers us a lesson on how one could have gotten out of this jeopardy.[67] The film we have before us, which speaks of a film that cannot be realized, is presented as a most sensitive seismograph of the smallest details of life. It is not, in fact, a coincidence that the characters who cross Jerzi, even peripherally, are then pursued in their everyday hesitations, seemingly unrelated reflections, family confrontations, in their chatterings about themselves and their own lives. They are often filmed almost by surprise, as if to recover through them some *tranches de vie*. In telling the story of a director closed up in his museum, *Passion* wants to be a place in which the surrounding universe is itself a protagonist. So, the passing of existence becomes an essential factor; it is immediately recorded, it leaves its traces in the film. *Passion* is a film of the trace—often of pure trace. Let us think of the film's opening images of airplane tracks: these are nothing else but image-imprints. And let us contrast them with the complex figures orchestrated by Jerzi, which instead follow the law of the image-machine. If the film to be made is locked into theatrical devices, *Passion* opens itself to the real, pursuing it and submitting to it.

In this contested dialogue between a film and the film it recounts, *Passion* constructs an extraordinary reflection on a moment in film history almost one hundred years after cinema's birth. But it advances a response to some legitimate doubts. Nature still exists beyond the great museum, and it is still ready to come forward. We can see it because—in spite of everything—there is a mechanical eye sensitive to it, which gathers its progress and records its traces. Only traces, perhaps nothing more. Yet these traces leave a door open that might have already seemed closed. The cinema—the cinema-machine—still deals with the real.

THE BEAST AND THE MARIONETTE

With *Passion*, we complete the range of positions that the cinema articulates with regard to itself, the nature of the machine, its relationship to the person who handles it, and its rapport with the real that constitutes the filmed object. To film can mean to recover the world around us in order to bear witness (*The Cameraman*), to unravel it in order to explain it (*The Man with the Movie Camera*), to capture it for a spectacle (*King Kong*), to ignore it in favor of other images (Jerzi's film), or to perceive it in the viewfinder and feel compelled to record its traces (*Passion*). The cinema-eye is a symptom of the transformation of human existence into a great mechanism in which the artificial dimension erodes and even edges out the natural. It is also true that this eye is still able to relate to reality—including natural reality—and record its presence. On the screen, there is a continuous coming and going of the image-artifice and the image-imprint. And artifice will never completely conquer the field.

We clearly refer to the dialectic that began with the "civilization of the machines," previously touched upon by Pirandello, Guardini, and Mumford. Does technology, used almost constantly, continue to be at the service of a respectful acquisition of the world's resources, or does it carry with it a measure of violence with which it inflicts irreparable wounds on nature? And is this action exercised through technology still guided by man, or does it follow its own logic, which reverses traditional criteria? Finally, does the landscape that this technology makes up still contain natural elements, or has it become only an archive of signs, a warehouse of commodities, an artificial setting? The cinema, with its mechanical eye, seems to advance different responses embodying various positions. We have seen how the shot can be a recording of the real (*The Cameraman*) or a revisiting that brings hidden elements and nexuses to light (*The Man with the Movie Camera*), but also its violent conquest (*King Kong*), or a simple exercise in remaking (Jerzi's film in *Passion*). The cinema vacillates between having a grasp on the world, having too much of it, and not having any left at all. Similarly, we have seen how the operator can disappear (*The Cameraman*), or else hold the reins of the game in his hands (*The Man with the Movie Camera*). He can exploit technology and, through it, Nature (*King Kong*), or find himself defeated by an indefatigable Nature (Jerzi's film). The cinema vacillates between offering itself as a tool extending man's action, and becoming an automatic device that does not need any human intervention. Last, we have seen how the background world can reappear onscreen in all its density (*The Cameraman*); it can rewrite its underlying design (*The Man with the Movie Camera*); present itself as a "resource" to be captured and exploited (*King Kong*); and, once emptied, it cannot but vanish through a game of mirrors (Jerzi's film). The films vacillate between the recapturing of reality and its definitive loss. And yet, the final film of this analysis (*Passion*) speaks about the resistance of the light, and with it, the real. The cinema does not succeed in canceling out the real: perhaps it gives up. In any case, it marks this presence. Even the most artificial image—a *tableau vivant* that depicts only other images—is, in the end, crossed by the breath of things.

The cinema offers many responses, but primarily it looks for a negotiation. From film to film, we have discovered that the mechanical eye, in its status as our ocular prosthesis—a technical device, but also a sensory organ—constitutes an extraordinary point of juncture between man and machine, artifice (or artifact) and nature, filter and bridge for things. When the operator disappears, he is celebrated, and vice versa. When the machine dominates, it shows its weakness, and vice versa. When the real seems to vanish, it resurfaces, and vice versa. More than a vacillation, there is a continuous circularity between the different poles, which confirms, once again, the fact that the cinema offers itself as a point of convergence and compromise. In this sense, the mechanical eye is still a site in which various criteria converge and are superimposed.

I would like to conclude with an exciting sequence that fully demonstrates this sense of circularity. It is the famous moment in *Metropolis* (F. Lang, Germany, 1927), in which the device invented by Rotwang, the mad scientist, transfers the life of the Real Maria into the False Maria. We are given a young woman whose pureness represents the natural absolute (the Real Maria), and an automaton whose perfection represents the artificial absolute (the False Maria). We have a mechanical apparatus as well, Rotwang's invention, which allows the life force of one creature to pass into another. This machinery, not coincidentally, is run by electricity (that is, an element that moves devices and bodies, in some way giving them life, and in another, generating light and giving life to film images). We face two polar opposites (nature/artifice), as well as the possibility of their continuity. This continuity is assured by the absolute likeness between the Real Maria and the False Maria: the exact same body lends itself to both woman and automaton. What comes to mind are the words that Italian scholar Eugenio Giovannetti dedicated in 1930 to the bifurcated body and the actress playing the dual role:

> Brigit Helm is the demonical figure of the new metropolitan underworld, the flickering daughter of electricity and steel. . . . She has taken all that is feminine in the machine, and has given to the female an extreme mechanicity. She has no nerves: she has thin bands of steel; she has no heart: she has a fiery oven; she has no brain: she has a terrible electric lamp in her skull, perpetually running day and night. And with all this, she still has the flesh of a woman; here and there, her skin still shines with the iridescent freshness of primordial Eden.[68]

In this passage, Giovannetti gathers the full convergence of nature and artifice realized in the cinema. On the screen, we can have something that belongs both to the order of pure reality ("primordial Eden"), as well as the order of artificial reality (the bands, the oven, the lamp). We are able to stare an uncontaminated world in the face—which opens up to our eyes as if for the first time—as well as at a reconstructed and remade world, which has lost all connection to its origins. Cinema has a particular status. It is a machine, and thus it is able to enter into perfect harmony with all that is artificial. But, as a machine, it is also able to penetrate the heart of things, to understand them fully. According to Giovannetti, it is a "mechanical art": its eye has the power and exactitude of a technical device; but its eye is equally able to recover the intimate organic-ness still governing the modern world and exhibit the pantheistic richness of the real.

There is circularity and synthesis between nature and artifice. The negotiation changes the terms of the problem (Giovannetti's idea of cinema as mechanical art is exactly a rearticulation of both the concept of art and mechanism). At the same time, it assures the active presence of both sides. Each pole of the dialectic has something that has to be preserved. Let's go for a moment to Heinrich von Kleist and his *About the Marionette Theater* (*Über das Marionettentheater*).[69] Von Kleist speaks of two parallel and contrasting *graces*: on the one hand, that of the being uncorrupted by civilization and, on the other, that of being transformed into pure mechanical device. For him, the respective examples are the swordfighter bear with which the protagonist of his novel crosses lances, and the jointed marionette that arouses his most profound admiration. Analogies with our films are easy. In *Metropolis* there is the Real Maria, in whom the son of the city's founder sees what his father's invention destroyed, and the False Maria, who ignites everyone's passions dancing at the Folies Bergère dressed in Erté. In *King Kong* and *Passion*, respectively, there is the sublime Beast who knows what love is, even in times of danger, and Jerzi's scenic contrivances, which seduce the director to defeat. Yes, there is grace in all these extremes. Cinema is able to gather each kind, show it, compare it with its opposite, make it circulate, and infuse it with the others. It is able to take these extremes, give them value, and gather them into a single vision that, filled with pleasure, embraces them.

Machine, artifice, nature, human: film does not hide the contrast between these elements. But its eye—so mechanical, yet anthropomorphic—is able to promote a productive compromise.

Strong Sensations

INTENSIFICATION OF THE NERVOUS LIFE

In one of his most significant contributions of the 1920s, "Cult of Distraction: On Berlin's Picture Palaces,"[1] Siegfried Kracauer invites us to consider the cinema not only as the building in which films are projected, but as an actual place of worship. The religion practiced is that of entertainment. But what are the principles of this religion? And what are its collective rites? Kracauer's response is clear: "Elegant *surface splendor* is the hallmark of these mass theaters."[2] There is no search for intimacy, depth, or origins. The splendor of superficial appeal, immediate attraction, and appearances is majestically displayed. The style of these theaters says it all. As Kracauer remarks, "The architecture does perhaps bombard the patrons in its attempt to create an atmosphere."[3] The space, the furnishings, the "stylistic excesses" all serve to astonish those who enter, to stir the senses rather than offer symbols such as in traditional theaters. The performances that take place in the cinema are also indicative of this excess. They are characterized by a "well-wrought grandiosity," born from both the exasperation of the elements at play (all brought to their maximum splendor) and a complexity that places film alongside live performances and concerts. Both this richness of stimuli and well-constructed composition serve to create what Kracauer, in a parody of Wagner, defines as *the total artwork of effects*:

> This total artwork of effects assaults all the senses using every possible means. Spotlights shower their beams into the auditorium, sprinkling across festive drapes or rippling through colorful, organic-looking glass fixtures. The orchestra asserts itself as an independent power, its acoustic production buttressed by the responsory of the lighting. Every emotion is accorded its

own acoustic expression and its color value in the spectrum—a visual and acoustic kaleidoscope that provides the setting for the physical activity on stage: pantomime and ballet. Until finally the white surface descends and the events of the three-dimensional stage blend imperceptibly into two-dimensional illusion.[4]

If the cult of entertainment is consecrated for the sake of appearances, if its temples and rites focus on immediate effects, the rule governing all this remains to be understood. Why seek out a splendor that is based on a pure cascade of sensations? Why create a complex work, a Wagnerian *Gesamtkunstwerk*, and rob it of any mythic dimension? Why choose performances in which "the stimulations of the senses succeed each other with such rapidity that there is no room left for even the slightest contemplation"?[5] Kracauer is peremptory in response: "This emphasis on the external has the advantage of being *sincere*."[6] The picture palaces faithfully mirror a fragmented society, a confused and excited mass. The cinemas and the films they show—with their pursuit of accumulation, disintegration, and superficiality—directly evoke society's disorder.[7] It is not, then, a coincidence that Berlin audiences "increasingly shun art events . . . , preferring instead the surface glamour of the stars, films, revues and spectacular shows. Here, in pure externality, the audience encounters itself; its own reality is revealed in the fragmented sequence of splendid sense impressions."[8] Just as, when one tries to return to traditional performances, "amalgamating the wide range of the effects . . . into an 'artistic' unity,"[9] the film proves "inappropriate and hence remains unsuccessful."[10] It ceases to offer "distraction—which is meaningful only as improvisation, as a reflection of the uncontrolled anarchy of our world."[11] It ceases to be capable of "expos[ing] distintegration instead of masking it." It ceases to communicate with the masses, "who so easily allow themselves to be stupefied only because they are so close to the truth."[12]

And so we have outward appearance, an assault of impressions, the optical and acoustic kaleidoscope of the temples of entertainment. Conversely, there is the disorder, confusion, and stimulation of mass society. It is not difficult to jump backwards from Kracauer some twenty years, to the portrait that Simmel had then created of the new living conditions mirrored in the metropolis, living conditions centering around an "intensification of nervous stimulation."[13] Metropolitan inhabitants are subjected to a "swift and uninterrupted change of outer and inner stimuli." Their existence is marked by a constant exposure to stimuli coming from within and without. They become immersed in situations that are the source of infinite provocation. "With each crossing of the street, with the tempo and multiplicity of economic, occupational, and social life,"[14] they feel the pressure of all that surrounds them. Such an engagement requires some countermeasures: being drawn in with such violence, one risks, in fact, getting lost. Simmel indicates two remedies. The first is tied to the growing development of the intellect—that is, a practical and calculating reason that evaluates opportunities presented to the individual as something to be exploited.

> The metropolitan type of man (which, of course, exists in a thousand individual variants) develops an organ protecting him against the threatening currents and discrepancies of his external environment, which would uproot him. He reacts with his head instead of his heart. . . . Metropolitan life, thus, underlies a heightened awareness and a predominance of intelligence in metropolitan man.[15]

The second remedy is the inverse, and consists in adopting a careless attitude, with which one can adapt to the most complicated situations. This spirit is blasé:

> The essence of the blasé attitude consists in the blunting of discrimination. This does not mean that objects are not perceived, as is the case with the half-wit, but rather that the meaning and different values of things, and thereby the things themselves, are experienced as insubstantial. They appear to the blasé person in an evenly flat and gray tone; no one object deserves preference over any other.[16]

Here we have intellect and carelessness: the suspension of one's sensibility and its intentional dulling. Yet, if one can respond to the excess of stimuli, it must also be said that one cannot do without the excitement of the senses. For example, when the metropolitan man tries to break out of the anonymity into which the big city seems to drive him, he usually "is tempted to adopt the most tendentious peculiarities, that is, the specifically metropolitan extravagances of mannerism, caprice, and preciousness."[17] In fact, he feels like someone only when stimulating the interest of others. It is only by catching the attention of those around him that he can save "some modicum of self-esteem and the sense of filling a position."[18]

Simmel helps us to understand precisely how sensory excitement is a widespread phenomenon, and thus to gather together the origins of an entertainment based on strong external appeal. Indeed, everything seems to offer intense stimulation to us. Dwelling for a moment in the metropolis, let us think of how modern constructions are placed next to historical buildings, housing developments next to no-man's-land, churches next to factories, the bourgeoisie next to the *Lumpenproletariat* , the autochthon next to new immigrants. All are heaped together in a way that cannot be but striking.[19] Moreover, the various elements often tend to assume spectacular forms, becoming in this way the source of further wonder: such is the case of big department stores or shopping malls, windows that are ever more luxurious, seasonal displays, buildings rising up to skyscrapers, or streets that widen to become veritable set designs (as in the case of boulevards). The most characteristic element of every metropolis—the crowd—embodies this power of appeal. It is a concentration of the most diverse varieties of man, impressive for its composition and breadth, but having something picturesque about it, too. It envelops, frightens, and intrigues. More than the metropolis in itself, it is modernity as a whole that tends to surprise. We have only to think of how the continuous innovations represented by scientific discoveries and their application to industry open unexpected and unthinkable new scenarios; or how the profound transformations in production and social structures lead all people to probe themselves to find an identity or position; or how the extraordinary expansion of horizons, permitted by new methods of transportation and communication, establishes contact with previously inaccessible realities. In modernity, nothing remains in its place. Nothing is taken for granted. Nothing is unreachable any longer. Everyone is directly involved, and forced to hold his or her antennae up. Under these new demands, those who are endowed with an extreme sensitivity—such as those often described by Poe (Roderick Usher, or the anonymous murderer of "The Tell-Tale Heart," who begins his self-portrait with the words "TRUE! nervous, very, very dreadfully nervous I had been and am")[20]—are exemplary heroes.

But Simmel tells us something else as well. In the metropolis (and, more generally, in modern life), internal and especially external stimuli have an aggressive quality. They are not simple pieces of information presented to the consciousness; they function instead as true *provoca-*

tions. The "outer and inner stimuli," flowing intensely and uninterrupt-
edly, end up irritating and harming. From here comes a change in perceptual activity, which confronts a true shock. It was Benjamin (starting from
Baudelaire and recovering Freud) who pointed out the traumatic nature
of sensory stimuli:[21] whether walking at the center of a crowd or working
in a factory, it is like finding oneself on a battleground. Since the sensory
stimuli are shocks, they necessitate a defense. Simmel indicates two possible paths: recourse to the intellect or the indifference of the blasé. The
first brings with it a shrewd calculation of advantages, the second the
assumption of an outward separation from the world. Both permit the
reduction and weakening of the provocations with which one competes.
Other modes of defense exist, however. Benjamin reminds us of the "protective screen" formulated by Freud in *Beyond the Pleasure Principle*. Not
coincidentally, this essay ties the notion of pleasure and displeasure to
the respective decrease or increase of excitement present in the psychic
life. In it, Freud compares the living organism to an undifferentiated "vesicle" that, under the incessant impact of external stimuli, forms a kind of
"crust" able to resist and repel those very stimuli. The "enormous energies at work in the external world" must compete with this "crust": due
to its filter they can penetrate the living organism, yet they have "only a
fragment of their original intensity."[22] In this way, they do not put it in
danger, as they might have had their strength remained intact. When,
despite this "protective shield," the excitement opens a gap, we have a
trauma that can assume, for example, the form of a fright. But the "corti-
cal layer" tends to work: it reduces the quantity of excitement (and thus
avoids situations of displeasure), and at the same time allows the organism "to take small specimens of the external world."[23] Freud connects
the theory of the anti-stimulus shield to a series of other elements that
I must overlook right now. His work does, however, constitute an interesting suggestion for the shock/defense dynamic. I would add only that,
in the same essay, Freud suggests a second way to confront an excess
of excitement: play. Babies can, thanks to ludic activity, "repeat everything that has made a great impression on them in real life, and in doing
so they abreact the strength of the impression and, as one might put it,
make themselves master of the situation."[24] This second hypothesis is
interesting for the shock/defense dynamic. It reminds us that, in addition to what we can call "organic" responses (such as that offered by the

formation of a "crust"), there are other responses that humans develop at a behavioral level. Yet it also suggests that the various responses have a common basis, seeing that both game and the protective screen call for repetition (it is in replicating the strong impression that the baby learns to dominate it, and it is in sustaining blow after blow that the vesicle forms its own crust). Repetition foretells habit. Thus, we have many interconnected modes of coping with shock: the use of practical reason, the assuming of indifference, the formation of an anti-stimulus shield, and the ludic exercise.

Now let us return to film. It seems evident that the cinema finds itself entangled in a well-structured dialectic. We began by pointing out how the filmic spectacle is closely connected to sensory excitement. It offers a bombardment of impressions, a cascade of appeal. This is primarily true for early cinema, which according to Tom Gunning offers itself as precisely a "cinema of attractions."[25] Yet it extends to subsequent cinema as well, which is certainly not lacking in visual excitement. This crush of stimuli is not an end in itself: it gives us back a society characterized by the intensification of the nervous life, a society thus rendered suddenly more complicated and disordered. In such a society, to perceive means to expose oneself to shock while inevitably seeking protection from it. The cinema takes both elements into account, particularly in its "institutional" or "classical" form. In one way, it excites, and, in the process of excitement, it destabilizes. It is not by chance that, some years after Kracauer, Epstein speaks of possible spectator "strain" ("fatigue").[26] In another way, however, the cinema seeks forms of protection against provocations coming from the world that are too violent. It excites, but never in a way that makes the spectator feel truly, definitively lost. It is an excited gaze, a gaze open to risks, and a gaze that is perhaps reparative. The cinema is tuned in to its age on this frequency, as well.

We can pose some questions while keeping in mind film's capacity to follow this dialectic so consonant with its age. What is it about the cinema that stirs its gaze in particular? When it produces a vision with its heart in its throat? What risks are associated with an excited gaze? What is placed at risk? Finally, how does the cinema react to sensory excitement? How does it keep it under control? I will look for answers, starting once again with films that, though outwardly dissimilar, will hopefully prove revealing.

RUNNING AGAINST TIME

An automobile is zooming at top speed in pursuit of a train. The wife and friends of a condemned man have found proof of his innocence and must reach the governor to obtain a stay of execution. In ancient Babylon, the Child of the Mountains rushes in her carriage toward the city, followed by Cyrus's army. She must warn King Belshazzar that invaders are arriving. The car goes quickly, but so does the train. On the night of Saint Bartholomew, Queen Catherine's soldiers chase the Huguenots, looking to kill them one by one. Christ ascends Golgotha. The car overtakes the train and blocks its path. The massacre of the Huguenots continues in a gruesome twist of bodies. Cyrus's army reaches the city, and King Belshazzar faces death alongside the Princess. The governor orders a stay of execution, but the car must reach a telephone booth to communicate the news to the prison. The Passion of Christ is fulfilled. The condemned man is on the gallows; a jailer receives the telephone call, and runs to the executioner, who does not want to stop. The car has finally reached the prison, and the wife and friends rush to the scaffold. The executioner reads the injunction and suspends the execution. The wife and friends throw themselves on the condemned, who is freed.

The conclusion of David W. Griffith's *Intolerance* (USA, 1916) is characterized by feverish movement. It is a movement that implicates everyone and everything: it is reflected in the car chase and the acceleration of the carriages, in the train pursuit and the tumult of the crowds, in the frenzy of the executioners and the escape of the victims. It spreads from Babylon to Golgotha, and from Golgotha to the night of Saint Bartholomew, climaxing in the contemporary story. It is not undermined but intensified by the presence of a recurring image, that of a cradle rocking, this time slowly.[27] Such a movement, so accentuated and pervasive, is able to transmit a shock to the onscreen image. It reflects not only the drama of the stories recounted in the film but also celebrates the thrill of speed.

I will not spend time arguing how speed is a significant feature of nineteenth- and twentieth-century culture.[28] I will only say that it assumes different faces, as *Intolerance* (and the "Modern Story" in particular) attests. It is thanks to the speed of machines (and to ever more powerful engines) that faraway points are connected in ever-shorter periods of time. The very protagonists of the filmic episode are, in fact, a train and an automobile. Then there is the speed of men, who move ever more quickly—thanks to machines and in competition with them—as accelerating their "natural" motors makes their bodies ever quicker and more reactive. In the "Modern Story," we have the race of the condemned's wife and friends. Speed, moreover, is not only a transition of bodies in space but also rapidity in the execution of a task—a performance ability. The locomotive's velocity depicted on the screen refers us inevitably to the power of all mechanical devices: metonymically, it recalls their predisposition to produce ever more merchandise in ever less time, just as human speed refers us back to the idea of a body capable of extraordinary feats, ready for Olympic records. Finally, there is the speed of progress, the continuous changing of situations and overlapping of facts in an age in which the pendulum of human events seems to oscillate wildly. The "Modern Story," presenting us with an unstoppable chain of circumstances, also speaks of a History that advances in double time. Thus there is movement, and an ever-faster movement at that. "More quickly" becomes not only an invocation but also an imperative.

Speed, however, has something ambiguous about it as well.[29] It is profoundly engaging to us, and offers up a new and intense pleasure. We are undeniably reminded of this, for example, by the Futurist manifesto written by Marinetti in 1909: "We affirm that the world's magnificence has been enriched by a new beauty: the beauty of speed. A racing car whose hood is adorned with great pipes, like serpents of explosive breath—a roaring car that seems to ride on grapeshot is more beautiful than the *Victory of the Samothrace*."[30] Yet speed is also indicative of danger (in both the real and figurative senses). The acceleration of bodies and things directly threatens their safety: going fast, too fast, means putting oneself at risk. Modernity is dotted with tragedies as a result of speed: from train disasters, which Schivelbusch reminds us had an enormous resonance on growing public opinion,[31] to automobile and airplane crashes often stemming from races or sporting events, which give the victim the aura of martyrdom (to say nothing of the sinking of the Titanic, itself caused by the desire to arrive sooner).[32] In the second place, speed obscures the exact perception of things: it prevents the precise calculation of distances and time, and tends to make one lose one's way. It risks carrying us out of the world. Excitement alters the senses, and with altered senses, we can end up losing ourselves.

Thus, we are dealing with an intense pleasure, but also the risk of losing oneself. Let us return to *Intolerance*, where speed's two faces reflect
each other perfectly. On the one hand, we can apply to Griffith's film
what Hugo Münsterberg said in the same year: "The rhythm of the play
is marked by unnatural rapidity. . . . This heightens the feeling of vitality in the spectator. He feels as if he were passing through life with a
sharper accent which stirs his personal energies."[33] On the other hand, is
it not curious that two episodes out of four feature a race toward disaster
(or three, if you add Golgotha, setting aside the greater solemnity of the
mise-en-scène)? In *Intolerance*, the stories advance at breakneck speed.
We enjoy it, but we are flying toward tragedy. It is legitimate then to ask
ourselves, beginning with Griffith's film, in what way the cinema's gaze is
able to confront the vortex of the modern world. How does it respond to
the acceleration of things, deriving its advantages without exposing itself
to risks? How does it measure itself against speed: how does it appropriate the excitement that it transmits, yet avoid disappearing? In other
words, what form of vision seems to be necessary?

In the first place, it takes a gaze able to grasp the mobility of things,
to foresake all forms of fixity and contemplation. As Vachel Lindsay said,
one year before Griffith's film, speaking of the *Action Photoplay*, "Why does
the audience keep coming to this type of photoplay if neither lust, love,
hate, nor hunger is adequately conveyed? Simply because such specta-
cles gratify the incipient or rampant speed-mania in every American."[34]
Intolerance presents an extraordinary richness of camera movements, a
true catalogue of the ways in which the dynamics of bodies can be exalted. I have in mind the push in framing Belshazzar's palace under enemy
attack; the pans following the fighting on the palace steps; the cranes
accompanying the ritual dances at the Babylonian bacchanal; the camera
car shooting the frenetic race of the train and the chariots; and finally,
the backward camera car framed upon the condemned, followed by the
camera on the automobile, tying together the destinies of the two situations in a shared moment. The cinema-eye is always able to stay on objects and bodies without losing sight of them.

But a gaze measured by speed can never be content to follow one single event: it must be able to operate simultaneously upon a multiplicity of
backdrops. The crosscutting technique, previously tested by Griffith, finds
its apex in *Intolerance*: the camera frames a situation, moves to another,

then it returns to the first, and so on. Allowing us to witness different moments in real time, it transports us through space with such rapidity that we become ubiquitous without ever losing our sense of position.[35] This transfer does not only take place through space: *Intolerance* does not simply apply the crosscutting techniques within the single episodes that make up the film. These are also applied between various episodes. The "Babylonian Story," the "French Story," the "Judean Story," and the "Modern Story" are interwoven to form what Griffith himself called a "cinematic fugue." The effect created, besides one of being carried instantly from one place to another, is one of being transported from one age to another, achieving a spatial and temporal ubiquity, which nevertheless lets us retain our own position. As the film's reviews would point out immediately, its dizzying movement causes a veritable "mental exhaustion" in its spectator ("The universally-heard comment from the highbrow or nobrow who has tried to get it all in an evening: 'I'm so tired' ").[36] Yet this game of keeping up with the film never loses direction ("There is never a moment's lack of clarity").[37] The cinema-eye is granted movement beyond that of bodies and objects: it easily does away with the spaces to which such things are still bound. Without a doubt, this draws us into a kind of whirlwind—yet it prevents us from getting lost.

A truly fast gaze, however, must do even more. Besides moving quickly, besides taking away the spaces, it must be able to anticipate events. In *Intolerance* the structure of the suspense (mixed with and overlapping the process of crosscutting) serves to project us beyond the moment we are watching: we see someone in danger, but we also see that someone else is trying to save him. Fearing the worst, yet hoping that escape is around the corner, we also see in our mind's eye what is about to happen: the moment in which the dilemma between life and death will melt away.[38] In other words, suspense serves to make us see what is happening, as well as imagine what might happen. It forces us to keep up with the protagonists of the story, before the irrevocable happens. It also clarifies the fatal moment, as if it were already going on (in the hope, however, that it will not, or in the perverse pleasure that it may happen). In this way, the cinema-eye is a provident eye: it is so quick that it is a step ahead of things.

Thus, we have mobility, ubiquity, and foresight: the film eye is able to deal with speed. Eight years before *Intolerance*, Ricciotto Canudo wrote in "Triumph of Cinema" ("Trionfo del cinematografo") what might have served as a review of Griffith's film: "We have created a new goddess for our Olympus, and this goddess is Speed."[39] The cinema seems a celebration of this new divinity. In the "new temple" of the theater, "a marvelous movement made up of photographic images and light is realized, life is depicted at the height of action in a true convulsive burst."[40] We have only to think of the acts represented: "The most tumultuous and incredibly exciting scenes develop at a breakneck speed impossible in reality." Yet just as significant is the way in which it passes from one place to another: "No theater could ever offer such an astonishing speed in scene changes, no matter what marvelous machines it employed." And last, the spectator is even projected into the performance. The cinema offers "a vision of the most faraway countries, unknown men and human expressions, all moving, acting, and pulsating before the gaze of the contemplator, spellbound in the speed of the representation." Before the screen, our eye is compelled to take flight. According to Canudo, what we have is an "excess of movement of film in front and inside the light."[41]

The cinema takes on elements of speed, yet it is also able to avoid its dangers. I have already said that its processes allow the spectator to hold onto his sense of direction. He will always (as though he were a "motorist who witnesses a cinematographic spectacle coupled with a mad dash through spaces," once again in Canudo's words)[42] have the sense of being within the whirlwind of events without ever losing contact with them, finding himself caught unaware, or feeling late. This ability to face the challenge of speed—one of the typical obsessions of modernity—is exemplified in *Intolerance* by the race against time in which the condemned man's wife and friends engage. They are forced to compete with a situation that is coming to a head, and determined to arrive before the execution takes place. It is worthwhile to remember that the arbiter of this race is something that, while barely glimpsed in the film, constitutes a looming presence: the clock. It reduces temporality to an objective and common standard (the adoption of a universal time occurs contemporaneous to the birth of the cinema),[43] and it demonstrates the implacable advancing of time. There is no escape from the milimetrical progression of the second hand. Each instant is replaced by the next, in a never-ending succession. This unrelenting movement of the hands warns us that time does not flow—it runs. Events press on, and the appointment with death (the death of the condemned, and indeed our own) draws nearer. From this stream stems the fear of not having enough time: the sensation that things move more quickly than we do, that they irreparably leave us behind, and that, in the end, the mad dash is futile. Too late. But from this stream also stems the decision to speed up one's action: to adapt one's movement to that of the imagination—to floor the engine, accelerate the flight toward the gallows, and be able to arrive one moment before the execution. Just in time. Too late, or just in time. This formula, which has always been present in human stories, becomes a radical dilemma in modernity.[44] To be left behind by the course of events, or succeed in keeping pace with them? To let oneself be swept into the whirlwind, or remain inside its flow? To stay behind or resist from the get-go? The cinematic gaze, as *Intolerance* illustrates, assures a positive outcome: its capacity to keep pace with events, to jump between places, and to project itself toward the fatal moment, ensures that the eye (and thus, ideally, the observer) arrives at the place of the tragedy before it occurs—perhaps with a wildly beating heart, but certain of rescue.

In speaking of Griffith, Pudovkin recalled with admiration that "the whole aim of this method is to create in the spectator a maximum tension of excitement by the constant forcing of a question, such as, in this case: Will they be in time? Will they be in time?"[45] Victor O. Freeburg noted with irony: "There is not a chance in a thousand that the pardon will be too late, and yet we are at palpitant attention until the boy is safe."[46] These are precisely the emotional dynamics of *Intolerance*.

We must add that the cinema, and the "the last-minute rescue" film in particular (for which Griffith's contribution is so important), highlights other attitudes that are well worth discussing, at least in brief. The first is waiting. At the moment in which the drama's conclusion is prefigured, in a twist of hope and fear, one must wait. In *Intolerance* we wait as The Dear One is received by the Governor; when he signs the pardon; when the car arrives at the prison; when the executioner makes a decision. During this waiting the pace, which in actuality moves so quickly, seems paradoxically to go too slowly: the solution is at hand, but never arrives. From this tension springs a certain excitement. It is an anguish that eats away at the soul, and that will only dissolve with the final joy.[47] The last-minute rescue is precisely this: a peril, a possible salvation, an acceleration, and above all a wait before stillness can fall once again.

The race against time implies another attitude: the temptation to flee. If the world is rushing by, it does not necessarily need to be recaptured. On the contrary, it can be useful to evade its pursuit. One must simply reverse the direction of the race, and instead of swiftly speeding after the events, you have only to escape from them. The chase film—whose structure, as we have seen, underlies a part of *Intolerance*—can help in this regard. We can read it inversely, and see in it a game between guards and thieves that presents not so much the attempt (from the guards' point of view) to catch someone before he gets away, as the attempt (from the thief's point of view) to escape the clutches of the law. The "Babylonian Story" confirms this reading: a protagonist who flees before Cyrus's carriages, unlike in the "Modern Story," in which it is the protagonist who gives chase.[48] In the case of escape, we are dealing with anguish: even before avoiding danger, one escapes because the very speed with which things move generates fear. The fascination that lies in keeping up with events gives way to an even greater dizziness, this time marked by depression.

The last attitude elicited by speed is the temptation to stop. It is a question, once again, of the longing to escape the flow of things. This time, this desire is expressed through a sort of indifference that allows one to avoid dealing with the surrounding world. This means putting a stop to all forms of excitement and welcoming boredom. Boredom is a strange state of mind—it presents itself as a blank space in the vortex of existence, an emptiness and a renunciation that is nonetheless tinged with a certain pathos. In this sense, it can seem to be the awareness of death. Benjamin reminds us in a striking aphorism: "Boredom is the grating before which the courtesan teases death."[49] The state of boredom can seem just as much a refuge of consolation: "Boredom is a warm gray fabric lined on the inside with the most lustrous and colourful of silks."[50] And finally, it can seem like a stopping point from which one can always start over: "Boredom is the threshold of great deeds."[51] The cinema courts the arrest of movement, and thus challenges boredom. I am thinking of the suspension of narration represented by the presence of dead time. I am thinking of the deliberate slowing down of action. I am thinking of the photostop.[52] I am thinking of the recurring image of the cradle in *Intolerance*: a perfect interruption to the whirlpool of life, continuing without end.

Let us continue our exploration of the excited eye, aided by a new example: Sergei Eisenstein's *Old and New* (*Staroe i novoe*, USSR, 1926).

MARFA'S SEX

There is a violent conflict between the peasants of Marfa Lapkina's village: some fight, on the wave of USSR government reforms, for the creation of a kolkhoz, while others resist, carrying on with traditional production methods. The kolkhoz supporters send for a new machine—a cream separator—that will separate milk in a more efficient way. The machine is installed and turned on. Driven by the cogs, the central bowl begins to spin with mounting speed. The peasants watch, caught between perplexity and hope. Marfa is next to the machine, observing it with more intensity than the others. They begin to glimpse a single hesitant droplet of cream coming from the separator spouts. The gears step up their rhythm. A drop breaks free from the spout, then another, then still another. The cream begins to fall, at first in a weak trickle, then in a more decisive spurt. Marfa has drawn closer: the cream falls on her hands, on her face—it pours down her. The spurt becomes a jet, and the cream gushes like a fountain. On the screen, the jets become like a symphony. Numbers fill the screen, with figures that grow larger and characters that get bigger, indicating a rise in production. Marfa is enraptured. We see a plane with an abundant flock, and a calf superimposed upon the sky. Jets, clouds, whirling.

The "cream separator sequence" in *Old and New* is celebrated for its beauty, for its subtle craziness (the erotic inflection is clear, with cream that represents sperm), and for its programmatic nature (not coincidentally, the clip is used by Eisenstein himself as an example in his theoretical writings).[53] Here I would emphasize the pervasive excitement that finds its climax in Marfa's final ecstasy and in the almost oneiric images that act as a counterpoint. It is an excitement linked not so much to the growing speed of the creamer, as to the effect of its action. There is a mutation at play, first of milk into cream, but also against the backdrop of life itself in the village, which can (with the cream separator) offer better working conditions and a way of life that is less severe and unjust. The fever pervading the sequence is that which grants these transformations: the euphoria we see on the characters' faces and in the dance of images is the euphoria of change.

Let us take a closer look at the way the cream separator is the protagonist of this change. This device is the bearer of innovation: the centrifuge breaks old habits and opens an unexplored horizon. In particular, it replaces forms of production and consequently replaces social roles within the community and in the entire group of peasants: a fresh new world dawns, represented by the kolkhoz and its values and laws. We could say that the creamer has an authentic inaugural function. Second, the machine is the guarantor of progress. The new world it marks is, in fact, one that is characterized by greater availability of goods, greater rationality in behavior, and greater work satisfaction. The result is a total improvement in the life of the village and, metonymically, the USSR, the nation so committed to agricultural reform. In this sense, we can say that the creamer constitutes a step forward in the history of humanity. Finally, it is an object that references, and belongs to, the revolution. Everything is changing and improving. In order for this to happen, it is necessary to clean the slate, clear the past, open a new phase. The cream separator asks the peasants to choose sides: the priest or Marfa, the small business-owners or the kolkhoz, the old society or the new one. And it therefore asks all to overturn previous boundaries and to adopt both a different social organization and a different mentality. In this sense, it is almost unnecessary to keep in mind that the new world it marks is the one born in Russia in October 1917.

Change, and with it, innovation, progress, and revolution. These elements directly recall some of the grand themes that punctuate modernity. It is an age (or a form of experience, if you will) openly obsessed with the new. We have only to think of the role played by technical innovations, the re-sorting of merchandise, exchange of ideas, artistic avant-gardes, succession of trends, etc. This obsession is so pervasive that it ends up creating a paradox. As Antoine Compagnon points out, if one continues to seek out the new, this search no longer constitutes a novelty. It instead winds up being a true "tradition."[54] At any rate, the passion for renewal carries with it a constant opening to the possible: the existing and, in particular, the preexisting are no longer enough. What is needed is precisely what can be, but never has been, given. From here, there is both attention to the present (as the time in which the possible is occurring) and the tension toward the future (as the time in which the possible will find its full realization).[55]

But modernity is also the celebration of progress: the proof is in the great World Expositions and the success of the ballet "Excelsior,"[56] the positivistic faith in scientific discovery and the pride marking advertising, the institution of the Nobel Prize, and the introduction of new social and political behaviors. With progress, attention to the possible also becomes faith in reason. Innovations are not enough: they must render the world fairer and more efficient, closer to the one that humans desire. In this light, progress seems connected to some preexisting plan—perhaps only abstract or ideal—and presents itself as its realization. There is one plan guiding history, and it guarantees that innovation constitutes improvement.

Modernity is also a time of revolutions. There is upheaval on a variety of levels: the economic-productive ("the industrial revolution"), the aesthetic-expressive ("the surrealist revolution"), the ethical-cultural ("the revolution of customs"), in addition to the sociopolitical (the October revolution, the twentieth century's most celebrated revolution, would begin and end within the century). The defining characteristic of revolution is its dialectic component: the appearance of the new is tied to the negation of the old; only by overturning the "what is" can the "what might be" emerge. It follows that revolutionary change is never bloodless: killing must occur for life to emerge. As Benjamin suggested, fashion—the locus par excellence for continued renewal—plays hide-and-seek with death.[57] More radically, in revolution death is promoted to principal agent. After change—change guided by reason—a history emerges that requires violence to move forward.

This picture undoubtedly demands a much more extensive analysis: I simply hope to point out that we are dealing with some of modernity's most essential junctures. I would add that the idea of *change*—with its connotations of innovation, progress, and revolution—puts into play a temporality that is different, though complementary, from that temporality which is nourished by the idea of speed. Time is not a current, advancing unstoppable second after second. Here, it is a point of passage, which divides heterogeneous and antagonistic phases. It is not a succession of moments overlapping and merging in continuity; here, a radical distinction emerges between a "before" and an "after." It is not an accumulation of lined-up instants; here, there is a jump. From this point of view, the cream separator of *Old and New* represents the exact opposite of the clock appearing in *Intolerance*. The one embodies the image of time passing, while the other incarnates time flipping through the pages of history, meeting a different chapter at every turn.[58]

Let us return once again to the cinema. What is its response to the change and the excitement that it generates? What limits does its eye adopt? In order to respond, it might be useful to continue with *Old and New* and examine Marfa's gaze. It is a curious gaze—Marfa repeatedly assumes the initiative and goes in search of what the kolkhoz needs; she identifies first the centrifuge, then the bull, and finally the tractor as necessary purchases for the village. In this sense, her gaze proves perfectly able to deal with the new: it recognizes, grasps, and finally forsakes it in the name of something else. Moreover, it is a utopian gaze: Marfa dreams of a world that is wonderful, orderly, and rich, only to discover that all this indeed does exist, that the land of plenty is no other than the Central Cooperative. In this sense, her gaze has made the logic of progress its own: it foresees what will then be realized. Finally, it is a discriminating gaze. We need only to think of the force with which Marfa opposes the selfish peasants (and in particular her anger toward the bureaucrats) to understand that she does not perceive everything in the same way. On the contrary, she is able to allow for conflict and violence. Her gaze is imbued with the spirit of the revolution: for her, seeing also means subduing, canceling out.

Old and New also presents the opposite of Marfa's gaze. The larger part of the village rejects change. The traditional peasants are not able to understand the approach of the new. They do not accept the path to progress and refuse all revolution. They are dominated by fear of the unknown—a fear in some ways justified, considering the individual's risk of becoming lost in a totally new world. Continual transformation dissolves what had seemed to be well established, and it prohibits a full understanding of what is going on. From here stems an anxiety that attacks one's sense of orientation. The abandonment of the old forms leaves one exposed. A world dies, and the new one is no longer familiar. The response is then inevitable. The people seek refuge within the gates of nostalgia, represented in the film by the renewal of traditional religious rites. They dream of a return, as seen in the killing of the young bull on which the kolkhoz had placed so much hope. They express skepticism in the face of the new, in the conviction that history knows the game of the eternal return, rather than the leap forward.[59]

In addition to celebrating change, *Old and New* effectively poses the problem of the "catastrophe of forms" connected with all radical transformation. It affirms the necessity of change, on the social, political, and aesthetic levels, but it also questions the risks of this change. How can we assimilate the unfamiliarity of the new and accept it? Does the new not become unrecognizable and thus non-recognized? The response rests on the implementation of a practice of *refiguration*. Eisenstein put forward formal structures in a nascent state,[60] and at the same time he attempted to recover well-established materials and give them new meaning. This is the case for all those moments that trigger the erotic isotopy appearing in the creamer sequence. There, the cream that comes from the machine spouts brings ejaculation to mind. This visual metaphor enables the film to represent the act of impregnating a new society. The following sequence presents a similar dynamic. The peasants attempt to regain the money collected by the kolkhoz; Marfa is opposed, and is surrounded by some suspicious characters, cornered, and thrown to the ground. We see a rape—the violence we see perpetrated, however, is not against her body, but a budding idea. Later on, the young bull mates with a heifer: the encounter is transformed, in an ironic shift, into a marriage celebration, the two animals dressed as bride and groom. What is at stake is the idea of a new family. Even further along, the kolkhoz's precious tractor breaks down. To repair it, the driver reclines on the hood and reaches into the motor, all the while leaning on one side toward the machine and assuming positions worthy of the Kama Sutra. Marfa offers her skirt to the driver, who needs a rag (and is tempted to use the Red flag). The skirt is ripped piece by piece, in a kind of striptease. Eisenstein was never a particularly reserved director, but here we are getting to the bottom of his game: it consists in creating new forms from the old, exploiting them, getting their substance, changing their orientation, but also letting them support the new meaning that emerges. In this way, the new sends the old to its death, but only after having used it to the fullest (and precisely because the old has been used up completely, it is able to change and support the new). Marfa's "adventures" become the destiny of communism, and the latter becomes clear precisely by means of the former.

This process of refiguration (or transfiguration) finds a perfect illustration also in Eisenstein the theorist. I am thinking in particular of his last great theoretical work, *Nonindifferent Nature*, which centers on the relationship between organic-ness and pathos. A work of art (a film, a picture, a poem) is organic when it presents a coherent and perfect composition. To rephrase this in terms used later by structuralism, when all of its elements "hold tightly," it gives us a "sense of sutured whole." Yet organicness does not mean closure: such a work also knows how to grow and tends to become something else. In fact, a particularly "solid" composition can open itself to mutation: it is typical for all "mature" organisms to be ready to pass to a superior stage. From here, it follows that all organic works have true "qualitative leaps." Their system of representation sees ruptures intervene, particularly at points of suture, which push them toward a more advanced system of representation. From this comes the creation of an authentic state of ecstasy. At the moment in which the work reaches the height of its intensity, it seems to go outside itself and transform its own features (ecstasy is precisely going out of the self). This provokes a state of extraordinary emotional intensity, a moment of absolute pathos.[61] The cinema is able to negotiate this dynamic between organic-ness and pathos superbly. When an image or a sequence reaches structural perfection on the screen, it always says more than it shows. In these cases, the camera-eye, together with the eye of the spectator, cease to "fix" reality before them. They no longer contemplate it, nor do they lock it in. On the contrary, they find its lines of tension, follow its development, get hold of its transformation. The gaze opens onto a world that is transfigured, transfiguring it in turn.

In his *Nonindifferent Nature*, Eisenstein gave many examples of a similar dynamic. He analyzed El Greco's paintings, as well as Loyola's spiritual exercises. In some pages, he went back to the cream separator sequence in *Old and New*. He notices that as Marfa reaches ecstasy at the episode's climax, the film "goes out of itself," and passes from "realistic" images to entirely "abstract" ones. What I would like to suggest is that the entire "erotic" sequence functions in the same way. Owing precisely to its systematic nature, which lives within the organic-ness of the film, the sequence ends up functioning as a point of passage: the images go beyond their apparent meaning (we are not speaking of Marfa's "adventures," but of the revolution), yet they allow the meaning of these "materials of departure" to reverberate (the revolution is, in the end, an "adventure"). The result is a representation in a continuous state of becoming, characterized by the constant comings and goings on different levels of meaning. It is also a representation that fails to put the spectator into check, making sure to accompany him toward the shores of the new, while staying entirely legible.

In this light, if I had to choose an image that best exemplifies *Old and New*'s capacity to work with refiguration (and more generally, the cinema's capacity to give us the ecstasy of change without making us feel lost), I would choose the final scene. We see a driver on a tractor, with pants and a leather jacket, a helmet and goggles, as well as lipstick and a smooth face. It is Marfa, and she is finally in the driver's seat of the machine for which she struggled so long. It is Marfa, whom we suddenly recognize now that she has taken off the goggles and smiles with her usual candor. It is Marfa, and yet it is no longer Marfa. Woman, but no longer just a woman. She is also a man, even a machine. She is even more ecstatic than she was in front of the cream separator. Marfa, and more than Marfa. She is "beside herself," in the dizziness of transformation, re-figuring what she was and what she will be. Woman-man-machine. Here is Marfa's sex.

REASON AND SENSATION

Gold Diggers of 1933 (M. LeRoy, USA, 1933) recounts the quasi-canonical experience of the backstage musical. A theatrical show is cancelled owing to lack of funds; a romance blossoms between a singer and a dancer; some money flows in by surprise; and the new staging becomes a hit.[62] What is interesting, however, is that the film begins and ends with two diametrically opposed musical numbers. The first ("We're in the Money") sees the singer and dancers in line—in dresses made of coins and a back-drop of blown-up dollars—singing an ode to riches and abundance. The thread of the last ("Remember My Forgotten Man") is a long song—almost a lament—which evokes the sorrow of the war and the poverty stemming from the economic crash of 1929 and the Great Depression, while imag-es pass in succession from a lost woman singing the melody, to soldiers at the front marching toward battle, then to a bread line of the unem-ployed, and ending with the crowd advancing on and closing in around the singer.

There is not only a contrast in contents: the first number celebrates the abundance of money (that is, apparent abundance, seeing as the song and dance are interrupted by the onstage intrusion of the police, who an-nounce that the soon-to-open show is drowning in debt), while the sec-ond exposes the misery of the times (creating a great success for the new show put on by the company). Nor is it simply an opposition of modes: the first number is, in its own way, linear (the song and dance develop in continuity), while the second seems much more complex ("Remem-ber My Forgotten Man" is constructed by accumulation, progression, and leaps). I have always thought that Eisenstein would have liked its essentially "pathetic" quality, which allows it not only to be a Hollywood version of Giuseppe Pellizza da Volpedo's *Fourth State* (*Il Quarto Stato*)[63] but also a spin on the theme of pain and redemption. The contrast is more subtle, but in some way decisive.

Let's take "We're in the Money": the number's title expresses a physical sense of immersion in money (indeed, the chorus girls are "showered" by dollars, like the cartoon Scrooge McDuck). There is the idea of direct contact with the sparkling coins of the material, and thus the reference to pleasure connected to the presence of strong and immediate sensations. In fact, the musical number presents a richness of perceptive stimuli, on the levels of visuals as well as sound. Choreography, scenography, and melody run into each other and overlap, making up a whole that overflows. The cadence that permeates the performance gives this whole an additional intensity. A *sensory thrill*—or really, a rhythmic one—comes from this: the onscreen world pulsates, and we go along with it. "We're in the Money" is a good example of Kracauer's "total artwork of effects": everything catches our attention, and it is the provocation of attention that is truly at stake.

"Remember My Forgotten Man" seems to work on another level. The sensory intensity is no lower here than in the preceding example. Again, we have choreography, scenography, and melody which intermingle, creating a decisive whole. In addition, the variety of situations renders the whole even more charged. However, as the title of the number suggests, we are dealing not only with a great wealth of sensory stimuli but also with memory, and thus with commemoration and consciousness. Remember my forgotten man. Remember and understand him. It is no longer just a cascade of *sensations* coming into close-up (let's say the presence of an extreme "sensoriality"), but also the need to give *meaning* to what surrounds us (in a word, the need for good *sense*).

Sensations and sense, sensoriality and meanings. This contrast brings us back to one of the essential nodes of twentieth-century modernity. On the one hand, we have a growing excitement of the senses (it is the Simmelian "intensification of nervous stimulation"),[64] and with it, the desire to open ourselves to all the stimuli coming from the outside world. Such a desire expresses the need "to be there," in the heart of things, in order to "feel" them fully. Only when we notice the uproar of reality can we say that we are in contact with it. And if the "being there" cannot actually come to pass, we ask that the stimuli be reproduced artificially, in order to have the impression of an "almost" real contact. Here, what emerges is an equation between having our senses touched and having a full experience. On the other hand, we have the indistinct fear of not understanding what is happening, of not grasping its logic and meanings. In that case, then, "being there," in the heart of things, becomes counterproductive. To understand reality, a certain physical and mental detachment is necessary, which is tied to the possibility of reworking the information. In other words, a critical distance is needed. Stimuli that are too vivid render such distance difficult: they involve, seize, and overwhelm. It becomes crucial to defend oneself from it, at the cost of breaking the equation between sensation and experience, making the latter (contrary to the preceding case) the place of a strong reflexivity. Thus, there are two poles, two options, and consequently a dilemma. To be overcome by the fullness of sensations or to try to regain meaning? To expose oneself to the world in all its chaos or pass through language with its meanings? To think of experience as direct contact with things, as *Erlebnis*, or a slow personal recovery, as *Erfahrung*? To see in order to feel, or to see in order to understand?

Gold Diggers of 1933 offers a response to this dilemma with the passage from its first musical number to its last. Let us go over the film, starting once more from the beginning. The rhythmic thrill of "We're in the Money" possesses an internal fragility, despite the euphoria it induces: at the same moment in which it expresses a physical contact with the material, it also seems to make us lose an actual understanding of the facts. "The Depression, dearie": so says one of the chorus girls regarding the forced interruption of the rehearsals. In doing so, she implicitly recognizes that the performance in which she was just involved was not dealing with the concrete social situation outside the theater. This reality is not avoidable, not even by the most escapist of performances: it imposes both its presence and its purposes. Here, the film will try to make room for this presence and these purposes. It will have to move on two parallel paths, which will lead us to add the persistence of meaning to sensory density.

The first path consists in the weaving of an "external" situation, which reflects and explains the developments of an "internal" situation, centered on the realization of a theatrical show. In *Gold Diggers*, the external situation is that of the love between the singer and the dancer: it unravels through a series of events that find an echo in those of the internal situation.[65] The two lovers court, and begin to dance the number "Petting in the Park." This frame is enough for the dance to cease being a moment of simple delight. It reveals its connections to social rituals and, by analogy, its subtle nature as an act of seduction in regard to the spectator. Let us add that this overlapping of levels is quite familiar in the backstage musical, a genre in which the presentation of a show is accompanied by the illustration of its staging. Yet the formula is always productive: through it, moments of pure perceptive excitement—the song and dance numbers— find their motivation and, more generally, lead the film to open itself to a sort of self-awareness.

The second path is somehow more radical. It consists in putting on-stage the reality that led to the interruption of the opening number, transforming it from forgotten presence to clear information. Here the Great Depression rises again to the stage, this time as a theme of the show itself. It is precisely what happens with "Remember My Forgotten Man": Joan Blondell sings all the unease of a woman who has lost her love as well as herself, while the chorus recalls the causes that led to such defeat, and the choreography illustrates what the song's verses tell us. The effect is that of giving an even deeper dimension to perceptive excitement. It acquires not only a self-reflexive component but also some chance to cognitively grasp the world. The situation offered by "We're in the Money" is thus redeemed: the film's subsequent numbers now have an explanation. The closing in particular shows how the thrill of rhythm does not necessarily preclude an understanding of the real. Sensations and meanings can be joined, and the pleasure of the senses can also become a moment of consciousness.

Both these paths implicate the recovery of a narrative: on the one hand, it is a story (that of the two lovers and the theater company), and on the other history (that of a nation).[66] If the sensations assume significance, it is because there is a narration that moves forward. The narration indeed has an extraordinary capacity to bring out the "logic" that moves the reality it touches. It draws attention to the connections between events, and thus brings the plot to light. It also brings back the single event to similar and recurrent situations, and thus helps to generalize and abstract. Finally, it defines what is relevant and what has to be focused upon, and in this way it helps in making a choice. Narration is thus an instrument that foregrounds the meaning of events. Although it works with meanings, the narration never disregards sensations. Its strength, in fact, rests on the presence of a series of *provocations* directed at the receiver's senses. Let us think of the key scenes, those in which the characters' various destinies come to the surface, clarifying the substance and forms of all their behaviors. They are often scenes of great perceptive intensity as well, in which the action and musical tracks seem quite literally to explode. Here, meaning does not obliterate sensation—if anything, it integrates it.

This point is an important one. There is, indeed, a widespread historical-critical approach that holds filmic narration to be a moment of deprivation.[67] The adoption of such an approach by the cinema of the late 'teens and early 1920s would have spawned a renunciation of the variety of references directed at the spectator so typical of early film, in which the presence of genuine "attractions" was what counted.[68] Its centrality in mainstream cinema would have undermined the visual dimension, which is only enriched in experimental cinema, where pure image functions as the focus. Concentrating on the "logic" of the facts, narration would not have left space for other types of signs that do not serve to clarify the string of events. Such a historical-critical approach has some merits. It is, in fact, true that narrative does not involve the spectator as the "attractions" did: it implicates him more than strikes him. Still, it is true that narrative operated a monopoly, impeding the adoption of paths that might have been more attentive to the perceptive dimension (film theory would play host to these countercurrents, such as the "cinemelografia" invoked by Pirandello).[69] Finally, it is true that narrative often offered schematic solutions, which justifies a poverty of originality. Yet, I repeat, narration has never ignored sensoriality. We have only to think of the use of the close-up or the detail, which undoubtedly serve to fix the spectator's attention in narrative film, but do not lose all their primitive function of visual shock. I am also thinking of certain elementary symbols such as the turning of calendar pages, which serves to transmit a narrative idea but constitutes nevertheless another small perceptive provocation. These moments of surprise are not always "tucked away" in the story's motivations. They are often occasions to call into question the diegetic dimension. The close-up serves to make one see and understand better, but it also changes the objects' familiar features. The turning pages of the calendar give us an idea of passing time, but it tells us also that the world may always surprise us. Sensation often interrogates meaning.[70] Thus, the narrative is a point of convergence of the sensitive and the sensible. It is a locus of circularity between two poles, in light of both a refunctioning of the sensorial components and a requestioning of their significance. Beyond the example of *Gold Diggers*, the musical genre is particularly indicative in this regard. The musical numbers scattered throughout appeal to sensoriality, yet they are also posed to circulate within a narration that gives them meaning. This narration, on its part, obeys a logic, but thanks to the numbers, it maintains an extraordinary air of excess, freedom, and subversion.[71] The parade, which often brings musicals to a close (the number that closes *Gold Diggers* is, in part, a parade), might be the emblem of this unstable equilibrium. It celebrates the pomp of the nation, but with dancing, fanfare, masks, and costumes. It unites the taste for attraction with a lesson in history. It provokes and teaches, admonishes and excites. It presents itself as the runway on which the sensitive and sensible can go hand in hand: "National Reconciliation."

CONSTRUCTING EMOTIONS

Let us try to join the threads of this issue. The three films analyzed revolve around one of modernity's most essential junctures, what Simmel called the "intensification of nervous stimulation." The world becomes richer in provocations, and the sensitivity of its inhabitants increases. Each film has shed some light on a particular form of sensory excitement: the thrill of movement, the thrill of change, and the thrill of rhythm, respectively. The dangers associated with such sensory excitement have likewise emerged: the risk of losing one's way (the world is moving forward, and I don't know where I am); the risk of not understanding the new forms (the world is changing, and I do not recognize it, nor do I recognize myself); and the risk of losing the meaning of things (the world is following a rhythm, and I do not understand why). In such a situation, the cinema develops a dual line of behavior. It puts into play an excited gaze that gathers stimuli and boosts them, yet it also gives this gaze adequate defenses, which protect it from possible dangers. It is here, in front of a fast-moving reality, that the filmic gaze reveals itself just as fast: it moves, it jumps between different scenarios, it anticipates the next step. At the same time, it does not get lost: the observer knows where he or she is and goes along with the flow of events, instead of being overwhelmed by or excluded from them. The race against time is the key image of this challenge to speed, but the cinema registers and appropriates attitudes such as the wait, the escape, or immobility. The filmic gaze is also able to open up to the new, to dream it as well, and finally to separate it from the old. At the same time, it prepares itself against the fear of the unknown: the process of figuration and refiguration carried out by the films allows the new to appear as the effect of a regeneration, and on this basis, as something acceptable and accepted. The cinema adopts a similar behavior with the world as pure rhythmic pulsation. On the one hand, its gaze is able to gather all provocation (it can "dance" in rhythm to the material and bodies). On the other, it can also put itself back on the path to meaning (that meaning that seems lost in the stupefaction of impressions, and that narration is able to reconquer). In short, the cinema is able to compete with the excited world. Better still, it gives an image of this excitement and thus contributes to making it perceptible: it enjoys the thrill that it brings, but it is also able to face the catastrophe that hangs over all excitement. The dialectic between the intensification of the nervous life and a defense from sensory excess finds a point of equilibrium in the cinema.

There is clearly a dynamic of negotiation, directed at finding convergences among different stimuli and needs. This dynamic intersects with a process of putting in form, of shaping, keeping in mind that this excitement without risks has the ability to establish itself in exact images or procedures, even at different levels (crosscutting; suspense; iconographic contamination; the parade). Among these negotiations, the most interesting is undoubtedly the one that takes place between the fullness of sensations and a recapturing of meaning, for at least three reasons.

The first is that the convergence of the sensitive and the sensible makes it clear that cinema has a dual relationship: it belongs to two "families." On one hand, cinema is a relative of the devices that worked on sensory stimuli. I am thinking, for example, of the machines that create an "excited" experience between the nineteenth and twentieth centuries: amusement park attractions like the roller coaster or the Ferris wheel, the tunnel of love or the funhouse, the haunted house or the merry-go-round. Yet the cinema is also connected to devices in which perception is transformed into knowledge: instruments of scientific observation, such as the microscope, the telescope, microphotography, etc. The references go on and on. In the early twentieth century, there was experimentation in the field of painting directed more toward stimulating the observer's senses than capturing the world. The canvases were mere surfaces to be perceived in their materiality. Yet we also have experimentation, particularly in the field of literature, directed at understanding uncertain regions of reality, through a systematic extension of one's own expressive instruments. The cinema can make reference to one side as well as the other. Sometimes it is a merry-go-round, sometimes it is a telescope, sometimes it is an experimental painting, sometimes a self-reflexive novel. It is each of these things, in forms that are often extreme, and it is a place in which the opposite poles meet, until they are finally fit.

Second, cinema's attention to both sensation and meaning allows it to create a double story. It is not a coincidence that the cinema was able to follow the path of the "attractions," especially at the beginning, and then to veer toward the methods of narration characteristic of mainstream cinema. Its destiny could have gone either way. The technical innovations that have punctuated its life offer one final confirmation. Let us take, for example, sound. The adoption of sound allowed us to acquire a new sensory channel, and thus to induce an additional source of perceptive excitement. It also represented the entry of a new expressive dimension into the field, thanks to which a discourse on reality altogether more complete and complex is created.[72] Film approached the Wagnerian ideal of a "total artwork" in which perceptual intensity and symbolic density may converge.[73] Or, let us take color. Color further stimulated sight and often created a state of stupor. Yet it mobilized a new semantic code, thanks to which themes otherwise hidden and meanings otherwise submerged came into view. The "yellow rhapsody," Eisenstein's extraordinary description appearing in one of his most famous essays,[74] is a perfect example of rereading reality through the colors with which it is depicted.

Third, the convergence of the sensitive and the sensible, beyond bringing to light the dual threads tying the cinema together, helps us understand how the essential problem consists in the organization of sensory excitement. Narrative order is one of these ways. The story organizes, connects, and renders reciprocally functional sensory stimuli: its gives them a meaning. But we can also extend and perhaps shift our attention, and take into consideration the problem of the organization of "sensoriality" in general. In a somewhat heretical move, I would yoke together two theoretical texts from the 1920s, which are quite different in importance and quality. The first, almost forgotten (and perhaps not wrongly), has a meaningful title and placement: Léon Pierre-Quint's "Meaning of Film" ("Signification du cinema") appeared in the splendid collection *The Art of Cinematography* (*L'art cinématographique*).[75] Pierre-Quint, after a brief digression, makes a rather decisive reference: he calls into question the "scientific inventions that extend the range of our senses," whose distinctiveness consists in creating "an excitation previously unknown to our consciousness."[76] The cinema is directly connected to these inventions: "Through changes of field, close-ups, dissolves, superimposition, the slow motion and high speed motion shots, tricks and distortions, the cinema brings new sensations to our senses." It is precisely these impressions that constitute the general material of film art. If a film expresses something, it does so departing "not from an idea, but from an immediate emotion." For such an expressive capacity to be affirmed, it is necessary that these impressions be "multiplied, organized, and take on a rhythmic progression that they wind up evoking great human feeling." Only proceeding from this fact can the cinema find its own path and become a form of original art. Only in this way can it redeem its first uncertain steps. Thus, what we have is a technology that stresses the senses, a set of impressions, and an orchestration of stimuli that orchestrates meaning. Pierre-Quint's formula is, all things considered, precisely this.

We find almost the same terms in the second text, published two years earlier. In his famous essay "The Montage of Film Attractions,"[77] Eisenstein takes up a path already experimented in the theater, and sees in it the perfect applicability to the cinema. At the heart of every film there is always a series of sensory provocations, a series of attractions. Action is not, however, an end in itself, but instead serves to orient the spectator within the facts being represented. To achieve this orientation, it is necessary to connect these attractions with the other elements at play, arriving in this way at a complete reorganization. Eisenstein writes:

> An attraction is in our understanding any demonstrable fact (an action, an object, a phenomenon, a conscious combination, and so on) that is known and proven to exercise a definite effect on the attention and emotions of the audience and that, combined with others, possesses the characteristics of concentrating the audience's emotions in any direction dictated by the production's purpose.[78]

Three observations will clarify the picture. First, Eisenstein thinks that the organization of attractions can engage, and rests on an accurate calculation of the pressures exerted upon the spectator. It is only such a calculation that can guarantee a film's effective action. Second, the organization of attractions orients the spectator's emotion. Here, a "psychological modeling" is at play, more than the creation of a concept as in Eisenstein's later writings. Yet this emotion is not separate from meaning. On the contrary, it is precisely because the stimuli sent to the spectator are structured, directed, and translated into a precise attitude that a set of perceptive shocks becomes an emotional whole. This means that the emotion must be created, and this must happen through the same process with which the meaning is elaborated. Only an orchestration of the excitement allows the spectator to be both moved and touched.[79] Third, for Eisenstein, the keystone for the organization of attractions is clearly editing. The editing process is what assures the possibility of tying together the discrete cues offered to the spectator.[80]

Here is not the place to run through the history of this idea, nor to compare Eisenstein's concept with others. I will only say that the Eisensteinian notion of editing in particular—which emphasizes not so much the technical procedure (the cut-and-paste of the pieces of film), as that of the structural principle of film (the foundation of its formal organization)—is precisely what reveals how editing is the instrument par excellence for negotiating the presence of an excited perception, with its risks and benefits. In the editing, in fact, all elements retain their specific quality as "attractions": each shot can continue to be put forth as a shock, and thus "strike" the spectator. More specifically, a sequence of shots in particular editing styles such as "flash cutting" further accentuates the "aggressive" value of each segment.[81] Editing also gives order to the sequence of shots, and thus reorganizes the sensations as a coordinated whole. In structuring a film, editing can follow different criteria. We have already seen, by analyzing *Intolerance* and *Old and New*, how it can distribute different images of reality maintaining a stable reference to the spatial-temporal parameters (Griffith) or, on the contrary, merge these images in a synthesis which exceeds its own limits (Eisenstein). Let us say, more generally, that editing can offer itself as locus of the conflict between shots (the early Eisenstein); as a means for realizing a sequence of takes (Pudovkin); as an instrument for constructing an ideal reality (Balázs); as a simulation of the optical journey of an observer (classic découpage). Whatever the case, it remains that a coordination of shots permits us to take the shocks in hand, to channel them, and to make them functional. Editing (even the least "disciplined") is in some way the other face of narrative order: it works so that a diversity of cues can be reorganized around a "logic."

This power of editing recalls the solutions sketched by Simmel in order to resist the "intensification of the nervous life." On one hand, editing recalls the Simmelian "intellect." In a situation characterized by the excitement of the senses, stimuli can be measured according to their utility. They will not be let free to strike at any place or time, but they can be chosen and combined on the basis of a calculation (as Eisenstein does). On the other hand, editing may also evoke a Simmelian "blasé." To seize the stimuli in a structure means to "smooth" them, creating a certain capacity to dull the senses, not keeping them always tense. Editing also leads to a rhetoric of easily recognizable conventions, resulting in habitual attitudes of perception.

I will end here. The cinema is a place of perceptive exaltation. To see a film is to fill the eyes as well as to have the heart in one's throat. Moreover, this "aggressivity" of the cinema can be related to its inclination toward reality. As André Bazin showed, and Serge Daney after him, at the same moment in which a film investigates the folds of the world and brings them to us without pity, it becomes sometimes "cruel," sometimes "violent."[82] All film is in part pornographic: it exhibits the body of things and its own body as "wounded" by reality.[83] Its perceptive excess finds a justification and a confirmation precisely in this basis. Yet the cinema is also a place in which perceptive shock does not constitute a threat for the equilibrium of the spectator, who can get carried away without necessarily losing him or herself. Film is a construction, and like every construction, it "gives order" to its founding elements, including the provocations directed at its receiver. Stimuli are thus coordinated among themselves, they assume a function, they bend to a design. They complement each other in a story, and in so doing, they get back their coordinates, their recognition, their meaning. The cinema is exactly this: an experience that vacillates between the possibility of an excitement beyond measure, and an adherence to measures that avoid all risk. It is the space between, in which the comings and goings serve to recover a balanced turmoil in order to arrive at what modern man needs: good emotion.

The Place of the Observer

IN THE HEART OF THINGS

"Sicily! The night was an eye full of gaze": *The Cinema Seen from Etna* (*Le cinématographe vue de l'Etna*), one of Jean Epstein's most fascinating essays, starts with this evocative image.[1] The essay describes, in a sort of diptych, an ascent and a descent. The ascent is the one to the volcano, "the great actor that explodes his show two or three times a century" and of which Epstein came to film "the tragic fantasy."[2] On this journey—both physical and moral—the filmmaker finds himself crossing a threshold: the carabineers have set roadblocks, but the "colored leaflet of the aspirins' bottle" has on it "more effect than the genuine signature of the prefect of Catania," and allows the troupe to penetrate the forbidden land. In front of their eyes a grand and terrible scenery bursts open. "The fire had covered up everything in the same tintless color, gray, opaque, livid, dead. Every leaf on every tree, as far as the eye could see, went through all the shades and crackles of the autumn, and, in the end, twisted, burnt, fell to the breath of fire. And the tree, naked, black, stood up for an instant in its burning winter."[3] The effect is one of authentic revelation: things suddenly reveal a soul. Indeed, they come to life, and they seem to talk to whoever is watching them. "The earth had a human and stubborn face. We felt in the presence of someone and awaiting him."[4] Thus, Epstein is amidst a vivid landscape openly involving him. This situation, made of chance, closeness, and complicity, brings us back to the very core of cinema. Films also offer revelations "to unexpectedly discover, as for the first time, all things in their aspect divine, with their symbolic profile and their greatest sense of analogy, with an air of individuality, this is the joy of cinema."[5] In films even landscapes come to life. Epstein goes on: "One of cinema's greatest powers is its animism.

Objects have their attitudes. Trees gesticulate. The mountains, as the Etna, signify."[6] In the film reality is literally born again before our eyes. We are captured and included in this world: "In the end, when man appears in his entirety, it is the first time that he is seen through an eye—an eye that is not human."

The descent, symmetrical to the ascent, takes place, however, in a closed-in space.

> Two days before, in the morning, I was leaving the hotel for that expedition and the elevator was stuck since half past six between the third and fourth floors. . . . To go down I had to take the main staircase, still with no banisters, where some workmen were singing insults against Mussolini. That huge spiral of steps gave me vertigo. All the walls were covered in mirrors. I descended, surrounded by many selves, by reflections, by the images of my gestures, by the cinematographic projections.[7]

It is thus a descent that is as terrible and revealing as the ascent. Epstein, step by step, ends up facing himself. "Those mirrors forced me to look at myself," he writes, "with their indifference, with their truth."[8] He finds himself naked, stripped of all former self-conceptions: "I thought of myself in one way and saw myself in another; that spectacle was destroying all the usual lies I had been building around myself." Naked and manifold at once: "I moved my head and to the right I saw only a root of the gesture, while to the left that gesture was raised to the fourth power. Looking at one side and then the other, I started to have a different awareness of my prominence." Manifold and ephemeral at once: "Each of these images lived but an instant, just the time to grasp it and it was gone out of sight, different already"[9]. Epstein is naked, manifold, ephemeral, surrounded by his own reflection, and uncertain of himself. Obviously a sense of authentic bewilderment takes over:

> I saw myself void of illusions, astonished, denuded, eradicated, arid, veritable, net weight. I wanted to run away from that spiral movement in which I felt I was swirling down toward a terrible center of my self. Such a lesson of egoism is merciless. An upbringing, an education, a religion, had patiently consoled me of the fact of existing. Now everything had to be started all over again."[10]

In this journey of initiation, what emerges once more is the call to the cinema. "The cinématographe provokes such unexpected encounters with oneself, more than a play of reflecting mirrors," Epstein concludes. The camera lens is "an eye of inhuman analytical abilities."[11] It displays individuals in their bare truth, forces them to look at themselves with no excuses; reveals to each person the self that was theretofore unknown. From this, of course, comes a sense of unease: "the restlessness in front of one's own cinematographic image is utter and sudden";[12] moreover, "the first reaction to the cinematographic reproduction of ourselves is a sort of horror." To the point that the person filmed quite often does not recognize himself in his own portrait. What he sees is a stranger. The moment after finding himself, he has literally lost it.

Epstein's essay is a parable. The ascent that he describes is a voyage to the core of things: we may discover that things are alive, and we may participate in their existence. But as we are in the middle of the spectacle, we also become the object of our own gaze. As the descent shows, we perceive ourselves as such and as other, and we feel a sense of bewilderment. In short, Epstein's parable speaks of plunging into what surrounds us, and finding it difficult to get ourselves back. Cinema repeats this double movement. The camera is indeed inevitably implicated in what it is being filmed. In chasing things, it somehow shares their destiny. In exchange, it cannot hide its presence. Its action, laid bare by its object of interest, ends up being expropriated, so to speak. A similar dynamic applies to the spectator as well. The spectator before the screen tends to connect with what he is watching. He projects himself onto and at the same time identifies with the shown reality. He feels it as living and feels himself living it. In the very moment that he achieves this intimacy, though, he finds himself suspended between different worlds—the one from which he is watching and the one from which he is watched. The risk is the uncertainty of his position, indeed of his identity.

Such a situation refers directly to the new status that modernity seems to assign to the relationship of observer and observed. Instead of an opposition between two poles, what emerges is a mutual interdependence. The observer partakes in the destiny of the observed. He moves on its same ground, but intertwines his existence with the object of his gaze. He also ends up losing his privileged position, such that he blends in with what he observes, or what surrounds him.

Hans Blumenberg, going over the metaphor of the shipwreck from Lucretius to Otto Neurath, skillfully shows how this new pattern imposes itself.[13] His starting point is Lucretius' *On the Nature of Things* (*De rerum*

natura), in which a person on shore watches a ship in a storm and is very
pleased to be on solid ground. Beginning with Pascal, however, the situation changes: the ship somehow takes us on board ("vous êtes embarqué"),
and we share its struggle. From here on, the implication of spectator and
spectacle goes further. There are no more safe places to seek shelter. Life
itself is a big tempest, and he who thinks that he is merely watching the
sea's surging waves actually does so from its throes. We are wrecked, and
we have always been, so much so that the only thing we can do is build
ourselves a raft with the debris from earlier shipwrecks.[13]

Away from dry land, we are in the midst of waves and winds, cast away
in the middle of the eruption, rebuilding ourselves from the fragments of a
mirror. It is not difficult to see a parallel between Epstein's metaphors and
the ones explored by Blumenberg. In both cases, there is the idea that what
modernity brings to light is an ever-closer intimacy with the surrounding
universe and, at the same time, the progressive loss of all certainty. All distance is wiped out. Complicities are created. Coordinates are lost. We enter
into an unstable world, and we feel unstable as well. The observer is "inside" the observed world, yet with no precise place. He is situated amidst
the sea, on the mountain of fire, on the glass stairs. He is at risk, exposed
to winds and waves, exposed to the lava, exposed to himself.

The lesson of *The Cinematograph View from Etna* becomes clear: what
Epstein discovers along the paths of a volcano and the mirrored hotel
staircase is a more general condition of which cinema is an excellent
witness, and, as we will see, interlocutor. It is a condition marked by an
overlapping of presences (rather than a strict division of roles) and by an
interweaving of gazes (rather than the dominance of one). It is the condition of an observer with apparently no safety net, who finds himself immersed in the landscape he observes, compelled to share his destiny with
that of the object of his gaze, and at the same time to *himself* become the
object of a gaze. This is the condition with which we must finally come to
terms, perhaps with some unease, but in the unyielding spirit of truth.

JOSH'S LESSON

Let me now attempt to clarify this general idea in my own way (winding,
as it were, a path for myself up and down a magic mountain). I would like
to consider some films that, though highly dissimilar, seem to thematize
this new position of the observer; this way of being inside and on top of

things; this living side by side the object of one's own gaze; between losing and finding oneself.

I will begin with a work from the early cinema, *Uncle Josh at the Moving Picture Show* (E. Porter, USA, 1902). This film develops a theme already examined and destined, in turn, for further adaptations: the fool who goes to the cinema and mistakes its illusion for reality. We find the same theme, for example, in *The Countryman's First Sight of the Animated Pictures* (R. W. Paul, Great Britain, 1901),[14] which was decidedly the basis for Porter's film, or in Godard's *Les Carabiniers* (France, 1960), which gives this situation a subtly tragic hue. Beyond these references, *Uncle Josh* is a film that seems to offer a direct illustration of what Epstein evokes in metaphorical form: it is a "live" description of the spectatorial experience.[15] Let us follow the images one by one.[16]

Josh is at the cinema, sitting next to the screen, apparently alone. The Kinetoscope Edison program presents its first piece, "Parisian Danger," in which a woman dances the cancan. Josh jumps down from the platform and gets closer to the screen, clumsily miming the dance. "The Black Diamond express" follows; in it, a train approaches until it appears in the foreground, and Josh becomes afraid, returning once more to his seat. The third piece is "The Country Couple." A beautiful peasant girl goes to the water pump. A boy approaches her, but is hit by the bar of the pump. He gets up and hugs the girl, finding in her a sort of consolation. Josh, who has descended once again from the stands, becomes even more agitated at the sight of their embrace. He takes off his jacket, throws it to the ground, and finally hurls himself at the screen in an attempt to enter into the scene. Instead, he makes the curtain fall, revealing the operator projecting the film and his equipment. Josh and the operator come to blows, and both end up tumbling to the ground.

Through this amusing story, *Uncle Josh* offers us a definition of the cinematic apparatus, its characteristics and dynamics. We have a spectator placed before a screen. A spectacle draws him in, ultimately provoking his reaction. He confuses the spectacle for a real scene and wants to participate in the situation he sees. Finally, an interference upsets the show, putting an end to the filmic experience. The spectator lets himself get involved in the spectacle, but he goes too far in his desire to take part in it. Having placed himself in the middle, he ends up destroying the conditions upon which the spectacle itself operates, such that he loses his own status as spectator. Game over.

Let us analyze more closely the journey illustrated by *Uncle Josh*, beginning with the *attraction* that images exercise. This is an attraction in the
literal sense: images are striking. We cannot be indifferent to them. But
our attraction is also an ambiguous one that can incite fear. The spectacle
he sees on the screen causes Josh to flee (the train episode) as well as to
penetrate deeper (the other two episodes in which Josh attempts to participate). Moreover, it is an attraction that leads to action. The performative
force of these images is evident, as they provoke Josh's continuous reaction. What is an attraction like this based on, and to what does it appeal?

Little more than fifteen years after *Uncle Josh at the Moving Picture Show*,
Victor Freeburg offered one of the first concise studies of the audience
in his book *The Art of Photoplay Making*.[17] Filmic images attract, and they
do so through three forms of appeal—the sensory appeal to the eye, the
emotional appeal, and the intellectual appeal. There are many factors at
play in this attraction: the beauty of the filmed subject (for example, "a
moon-lit lake, a surf-swept beach, spruce-covered foothills"),[18] the presence of certain movements that only film is able to convey (as, for example, "the rhythmic undulations of the sea, the fan-like spreading of a
sky rocket, the slow curling of smoke from a factory tunnel, the varying
balance of a bird in flight"), and finally, above all, the movement of the
human body "individually, as in the case of a dancer, and *en masse* as
the case of a regiment on parade."[19] But the decisive factor is the spectator's sense of *contact* with what appears on the screen. "In the motion
picture theatre this illusion of personal contact with the characters is especially strong,"[20] Freeburg states. The contact is almost physical, and it
is immediately transformed into a moral intimacy. "We select our friends
from among the heroes and heroines, but we scorn the villainous, the
stupid, and the low."[21] In particular, this sense of contact with the characters is what allows the feeling of participation in the narrated events.
"By a law of psychology," Freeburg explains, "we project our very selves
into the characters on the screen. Thus, every spectator in the audience
may get by proxy the experiences and emotions of the character he is
observing."[22] This need for contact operates on the intellectual level as
well, in the form of a curiosity. "We constantly desire new material to add
to our store of knowledge," Freeburg remarks. "We crave novelty."[23] It is
here that the cowboy from South Dakota finds satisfaction "in the story
which is laid in a Cape Cod fishing village," just as the fisherman finds

satisfaction "in the spacious drama of the South Dakota ranches."[24] They enter into a relationship with another reality, and this allows them to acquire a real knowledge, though it is through the onscreen illusion.[25]

Though Freeburg speaks of film already in its "classical" phase, he helps us to better understand the film we are analyzing here, putting it into perspective. The Kinetoscope images attract Josh because they have some essential qualities. They possess a beauty of their own, however naive; they show movement both human (the dancer) and mechanical (the train); they present bodies caught in movement (seduction, dance); they depict "exotic" situations that stimulate the curiosity (the Parisian cancan). In short, they excite the vision and feelings of the naive spectator. Most of all, they create contact between the spectator and what is depicted on the screen: observer and observed are brought side by side. They interact, as shown on the one hand by the various situations that "jump out" at Josh—the train that advances on him, the dancer who offers her favors, and the two lovers who let him in on their intimacy—and on the other, by Josh's continuous movement, culminating in his seizing and pulling down the curtain.

So there is contact, and with it, a nearness and an interaction. This inevitably compels us to talk about the *close-up*. Let us put aside *Uncle Josh at the Moving Picture Show* for the moment, given that the naive spectator witnesses Kinetoscope pieces filmed as long shots.[26] Beyond its various functions in the passage from early to classical cinema—in the former, to exalt the observed reality, in the latter to direct observation—the close-up primarily celebrates drawing the object of the gaze near in such a way that, occupying the entire visual field, this object establishes a quasi-exclusive relationship with the spectator. On the screen, a face, body, or thing suddenly grows. These enlarged images might evoke surprise or focus the attention: the face, the thing, the body have come out of their most intimate sphere. They turn themselves over to their observer, enter into close communion with him or her, and create a new union together.

Epstein examined this dynamic with great intensity in "Enlargment" ("Grossissement"),[27] written in 1921:

> The close-up changes the drama thanks to its impression of nearness. Pain is within one's reach. Extending my arm, I touch you; intimacy. I count the lashes of that suffering. I could feel the taste of its tears. I have never had a

face so close to mine. It follows me from so near, and I seek it face to face.
Nothing comes between us: I devour the air that separates us. It is like a sac-
rament in me. Maximum visual acuity.[28]

With his usual lyric prose, Epstein establishes how the blown-up close-up
compels the observer to get closer to the object of his or her vision, ultimately fusing (and perhaps also confusing oneself) with it. We are certainly dealing with a process of amplification ("The close-up adds force,
if only for its dimensions").[29] It brings about a true explosion on an emotional level ("this enlargement works on emotion"), and consequently,
the need to regulate the sensory flux ("The close-up limits and directs
the attention").[30] Yet what counts most is really its ability to create a
nearness that directly involves the observer and implicates him or her
in the observed world: "I can't say how much I like American close-ups.
Neat. Suddenly the screen shows a visage and the drama, in a face-to-
face, speaks directly to me, growing with an unexpected intensity. Hyp-
nosis. Now Tragedy is anatomical."[31] Nearness, interpellation, union with
the object, transformation of landscape: these are the axes on which the
close-up revolves.

   These measures recall a more general process that materialized between the nineteenth and twentieth centuries: a progressive narrowing
of distances, through which the world seemed to diminish in size, finally
handing itself over into the possession of its subjects. We have only to
think of the geographic explorations that reminded us that nothing was
truly "elsewhere." From the discovery of the Nile's sources to the conquest of the Poles and beyond (Everest, the Mariana Trench, the Moon),
each step let us know that distances had been shattered, and that nothing was beyond man's reach. On a day-to-day level, we have only to think
of the transportation system, the waves of immigration, mass tourism.
The world no longer possessed insuperable barriers. Everything could be
put into contact with everything else. Even the most protected recesses
were reachable. The close-up (and with it the detail) shapes this general-
ized *accessibility* on a visual plane: things are now "reachable by gaze." Or
rather, they offer themselves up to my gaze in their entirety—I no longer
have to go look for them. They are not *prey* to conquer, but *gifts* borne to
me. The world has condensed itself, it has thrust itself forward, made itself mine. In offering itself up in this way, it in turn captivates me.

Let us return to *Uncle Josh*. It is precisely the realization of a "contact"—along with the sensations of absolute proximity and close interaction that accompany it—that characterizes the experience of the naive character. At this point, Josh feels entitled to act. He can advance upon the world before him. He can respond to the gift that he is offered, seeking to grasp it and thus transform it into his prey. He can try to overcome the barrier between himself and the spectacle, descending into the universe that has opened itself up before his eyes. If the world no longer has barriers—if the "there" has become "here" and vice versa, if there is no longer an "outside" to watch from and look at, but everything is now an "inside," hosting both seer and seen—the step that Josh prepares to make should be almost obvious. And indeed, Josh advances, strong in this initiative. But in the cinema nearness is only an illusion, as Freeburg, as well as Epstein, reminded us *en passant*. It is true that the stimuli coming from the screen lead to the creation of images having many characteristics of reality.[32] Yet the impression of reality does not correspond to factual reality. The other world within reach is definitively a *different* world. Thus, the barrier that seemed to have dissolved instead remains; it has only rendered itself impalpable, here as elsewhere.[33] All spectators should know this.[34] Yet Josh advances: he is now so close to this reality that he is ready to take part in it. He runs up against the screen, and it gives way. Falling to the ground, it reveals the apparatus in action.

That is Porter's film. It gives an overt "reading" of the spectatorial situation. It shows us what a cinematographic séance is and elucidates its qualifying criteria; it offers a spectator type, though ironic, and puts forth an idea of what is typical of a spectator; and, finally, it adds a prescription to the description, warning us not to be naive spectators. However, as in every "reading," there are blind spots. In order to see them, we need to move on to a new film.

JOHN SIMS IN THE AUDIENCE

King Vidor's *The Crowd* (USA, 1928) concludes with a memorable sequence. Husband and wife are watching a vaudeville performance. It is the first moment of relaxation they share after a long series of misfortunes: the death of their daughter that made the husband forget the enthusiasm of his arrival in the big city, the excitement tied to a social life filled with friends, and his minor work ambitions. What follows is a period of de-pression and a series of mutual misunderstandings that almost push him to suicide. Now the spouses enjoy themselves, together again in a public space. The camera frames the two in a close-up. Next, with a movement drawing backwards and up,[35] it shifts to frame the whole theater, where dozens and dozens of other men and women are watching the same performance, having the same reactions and expressing the same feel-ings. John Sims and his wife Mary are lost in the crowd—a crowd made of many Johns and Marys, each couple with its own story, perhaps not so dissimilar from that of the two protagonists.

The sequence stands out for at least two reasons. First of all, it has a clear metalinguistic value. The film leaves the spectator with the image of two spectators in the hall, surrounded by a multitude of other specta-tors. It almost seals the narrated story with a dedication such as, "I am speaking to you, about you." We have, once again, a work that reflects upon the very experience that it offers, representing it on the screen. Second, the sequence is significant because it not only constitutes a ded-ication, but it posits a moral as well. Its magnificent camera movement—essentially a crane movement—serves to unite an individual to the mass of individuals surrounding him, to plunge him into an audience, to transform him into one of the many, until we finally lose him. Through-out the narrative, John Sims resists the idea of melting into the masses, yet this is what happens. Thus, we are once again dealing with the prob-lem of proximity and participation. This time, however, the question is perpendicular, so to speak, to the one illustrated by *Uncle Josh*. That is, the character in the hall finds himself relating to those at his side, rather than to the screen itself. In fact, this is an axis that *Uncle Josh* chooses to omit. In Porter's film, rather paradoxically, the protagonist enjoys the performance alone, and only through Freeburg might we see the black hole there, the something "unseen." "It must never be forgotten that the theatre audience is a crowd."[36] Vidor's film invites us to reflect on the individual and the mass—spectator and audience—a single position and its surroundings.

The Crowd explores, in a systematic way, the relationship between John Sims and his environment. For example, John's arrival in New York, full of hope, is accompanied by a real portrait of the big city, with a series of shots dedicated to the cars on the street, the crowds on the sidewalks, the subway, the boats, the skyscrapers. Even his daughter's accident and subsequent funeral reveal the urban context. This time it is hostile, with neighbors who curiously congregate at the site of the tragedy along with cars that—indifferent to the drama—block the procession. Among these narrative poles, other moments produce the same connection. One has only to think of John and Mary's courting, which takes place in a dazzling amusement park full of wonders. This narrative strategy holds a gesture typical of film, with its tendency to "set" the events it recounts. It isn't by chance that the discipline of the *master shot*—fundamental to classic editing—rests on the idea that next to the shots detailing the protagonist's actions, it is necessary to have shots that contextualize the action that occurs. In fact, the classic sequence often begins with one full shot (the *establishing shot*) and closes with another (the *re-establishing shot*) in such a way that this context and its evolution are clear. This is then proof that they merit just as much attention as the hero's behavior. We can even say that the character's insertion into his or her setting is, after all, achieved by every filmic shot. It is enough that the character be surrounded by a bit of "air," so that his or her environment makes itself felt at once. Film, unlike literature, which can only say one thing at a time, can include in the same frame not only the he or she who is acting but also the fragments or effects of his or her field of action.[37] Thus, film expresses a marked tendency to offer us the character and the environment. The two terms tend to turn up on the screen together.

Yet *The Crowd* brings to light a second element as well: the difficulty John Sims experiences in adapting to his setting. Relating to one's context is never easy, but for our protagonist it seems almost impossible. John Sims suffers from boundless ambition, which leads him to obsess over his very destiny as an individual. This conviction is instilled in him by a father who had always expected extraordinary things from his son—expectations initially confirmed by his serendipitous birthday, the Fourth of July. Waiting for the right occasion to show everyone his true worth, John refuses to adapt to his surroundings. Yet the world does not wait for him. It moves on its own, proving itself not only indifferent, but even hostile. This becomes clear in the sequence that constitutes the climax of this situation. His daughter's death, his wife's detachment, and his difficulties at work drive John to attempt suicide. Precisely at the moment in which he needs others, he finds himself terrifyingly alone. He is not a part of his metropolis. All that is left for him is his obsession and disappointment. There is, therefore, no connection between character and environment, but only a dysphoric or adversarial relationship: this is no *character-environment* but, if anything, *character/environment*.

Only in the last two sequences does *The Crowd* present a journey in reverse, which will lead John to reintegrate himself into the social body. It begins at the moment in which Mary leaves the family house and John tries to stop her. He has brought her presents: a bouquet of flowers, three tickets for a show, purchased with the little money he has earned as a clown. Suddenly, he chooses a record and puts it on the gramophone. He takes his wife in his arms and dances with her. In this moment, only John and Mary exist in the small room and a true intimacy is created between them. They act in a true unity, as in a world unto themselves, if you will. Immediately after, in the immense vaudeville theater, John is able—with Mary at his side, surrounded by dozens and dozens of others like him—to fully connect to the environment in which he lives, to see himself alongside others, laugh in unison with them, and to become part of a whole. He finds himself, all told, by losing himself in the crowd.

Going over the film, we understand why the final sequence is so crucial. The complex crane shot, carrying John Sims to the public that he will join, fulfills the contact with his surroundings that he had so long refused, despite the occasions that film paradoxically seemed to offer him. More than a contact, it carries out a true *fusion*. In the last shot of *The Crowd*, John is not only inserted into the context of his action, he is organically joined with this context, almost as though one and only one shot can completely embrace both of them.

But why this fusion? What makes it somehow necessary? A symptomatic reading of *The Crowd* allows us to suggest at least three answers. In the first place, against the backdrop of modernity, there is a new perception of space to which the cinema is not extraneous. We are immersed in not only a compressed space (thanks to the apparent elimination of distance) but also a full and active one.[38] In one way, the things that take up this space thoroughly determine it, modeling its shapes and fields of energy. This space in turn acts on what is contained in it; it inserts it within a complex environment, it declines it according to this accent or that, it defines its weight and role. In this sense, we are not before a simple container, but something that dictates and responds. In a word, we are in front of a world.[39] The manner in which the cinema outlines the relationships between character and environment reflects the modern sensibility for space: if the two are tightly correlated in the cinema, it is precisely because the one finds itself immersed in a space that it must take into account, to which it gives and from which it receives, in which it acts and by which it is acted upon, in a game of reciprocity that leads precisely to a kind of reciprocal fusion.

This is true particularly when the environment in which the character moves is the human one. Here, the exchange and interdependence are even more evident, and the necessity of a reciprocal fusion is imposed, seeing that an individual can end up as part of the *social body*. Certainly, this is neither easy nor simple. As *The Crowd* shows, the individual has his own motives, and when he becomes part of the mass, he risks losing his individuality. The confrontation between John Sims and his friend Bert is exemplary. The latter adapts himself too readily to his environment. He makes a career for himself, yet he betrays himself in some way, too. John Sims, on the contrary, does not accept becoming like others at all. Consequently, at a certain point in his life, he finds himself adrift, wandering alone in the metropolis that moves of its own accord.[40] Here, we face a crucial problem in modernity:[41] how to conform to others without losing oneself? Or better, how to immerse oneself in the surrounding world and still maintain one's own status? The cinema's obsession with representing the crowd while conserving the individual features of its components is indicative. Spottiswoode, who in his mid-1930s *Grammar of the Film* attempted to standardize the forms of filmic representation, called a sequence exemplary in which "the camera, flashing from one part of it to another, discovers one man expectant, another already assured, a third confident or disappointed; the film, running in perfect silence, catches the tension of all."[42] The important thing is to seize the individuality of each member of the crowd. Then he or she can be integrated into the whole.

In this picture, the fact that John Sims is finally rejoined with his setting, finally melding with it inside a theater (or perhaps a cinema),[43] is significant as well. The cinema hall is a perfect mirror of the social context within which an individual moves. In particular, as Freeburg reminded us, "it must be never forgotten that the theatre audience is a crowd."[44] This means that we are dealing here with "a compact mass of people held together by a single purpose," and with "various units [that] are in close contact with each other."[45] Here, too, we find a reality characterized by an actual closeness and sharing. Identifying with the masses and identifying with an audience is therefore the same thing. If anything, the reasons for which one needs to join the masses become clearer in a movie theater. It is a question of creating a new and denser *community*, in the Wagnerian sense of the term, as Ricciotto Canudo emphasized in 1908. In the cinema hall emerges "the will for a new party, a new joyful humanity in a spectacle, in a party, in a meeting place in which the oblivion of one's own isolated individuality is dispensed, in small and large doses."[46] It is, too, a question of creating a group of individuals capable of a *collective dream*, as Jules Romains pointed out in 1911: "They sleep; their eyes no longer see. They are no longer conscious of their bodies. Instead, they are only passing images, a gliding and rusting of dreams."[47] And finally, it is a question of arriving at a sort of *elementary life*, which does not mean one that is less rich or intense. As Matilde Serao emphasized in 1916, in the audience "a single simple soul" is formed, which "becomes annoyed and irritated at complications," but is nonetheless "sensitive, tender," recognizes "true affection, sincere affection," and responds "to the great sentimental calls of love and pain."[48]

Above all, it is a question of creating a real and modern *public opinion*. Let us return to Freeburg. He writes: "Close contact is spiritual as well as physical. You not only touch elbows with your neighbour and live in his atmosphere but you are infected by his emotions and share his desires, purposes, reactions."[49] Yet this does not lead to a cancellation of individuality. "While the crowd is single-minded, the public is many-minded," Freeburg continues. "It may be looked upon as a vast web-like association of unified groups, families, cliques, coteries, leagues, clubs and crowds. . . . Its groups come in contact, though not simultaneously; views are exchanged, discussions are carried on, letters are written, until as a result of all this reflection a deliberate expression is arrived at. This deliberate expression is called public opinion."[50]

Here then are the reasons underlying an authentic fusion between an individual and his environment: we move in a full and active space, we must contend with the masses, and we must become part of a *social body* (of public opinion, for example), in which our individuality, instead of being sacrificed, finds a wider representation.[51]

This last observation lets us conclude by returning to *Uncle Josh at the Moving Picture Show* and comparing it with *The Crowd*. In Porter's film, we have the spectator's desire to give himself up to the spectacle, a desire frustrated in the end by the illusory nature of the onscreen world; in King Vidor's film, we have instead the individual's resistance to giving himself up to the social body, resistance that is conquered in the end when the individual becomes spectator and his environment is a theater hall. Thus, we find ourselves dealing with two paths that put a "fusion" into play. We can see here the two fundamental traits of all spectatorship: the relationship of those who follow a film with the world that the film represents, and his or her relationship with the surrounding world, beginning with the audience of which he or she is part, respectively. These two relational axes coexist in the frame of the spectatorial experience. Those who follow a film are just as much scopic subjects as social ones.[52] Quite simply, it is a scopic subject who relaxes his or her own social constraints when the house lights go down, while it is the social subject waiting for or leaving his or her scopic state when the lights are on or when they go back up.[53] But the comparison between the two films reveals something else as well. They are characterized by two attitudes that are in some way contradictory: one underscores that becoming immersed in the performance is fascinating, yet silly. The other stresses how giving oneself up to the social body is difficult, yet necessary. To put it in another way, one illustrates the force of the call of the fictional world, but also the risk of identifying oneself fully with it. The other shows the difficulty of establishing social relationships that limit one's subjectivity, but also the usefulness of doing so. From here a sort of chiasmus emerges. In one case we have a "fusion" that is desired yet feared, while in the other a "fusion" that is feared yet proper. Why then can we not imagine that the fulfillment of the latter is the subtle effect of the difficulty of realizing the former? That, in other words, one occurs because the other does not fully occur, and better still, that the one does not occur so that the other may occur? There is a world in which one would like to take part, and that is taken away. It is taken away by the apparatus, which offers only representations (that is, substitutions of a reality destined to remain absent) and taken away by common social sense that derides those who desire what they cannot have. And there is a world in which one can take part—rather, in which one must take part in order to be social subjects—but it takes some prodding to identify with it. Then an imperfect relationship with the represented world perhaps serves precisely to improve one's relationship with the surrounding world. Removing an object of desire conceivably makes one desire an object within reach. These two components of spectatorship—the scopic and the social—can therefore put internal adjustments into effect. The impossibility of a unity with the fiction finds release in a unity with the audience.[54]

In conclusion, we have a *spectator-spectacle* manqué in order to arrive at a *spectator-public*. And we have a *spectator-public* as a positive answer to an impossible *spectator-spectacle*. A 1925 review by the surrealist critic Robert Desnos offers paradoxical evidence of this exchange:

> The other night at the Marivaux I wasn't particularly enjoying the long French film when a white light irresistibly attracted my gaze: it was the bare arm of my neighbor. For an instant, it was enough to stare at the luminous white shade; then I rested my hand on the apparition. The woman didn't retract her arm. Meanwhile, some imbecilic heroes clamor around on the screen. Benign darkness propitiates illusions.[55]

The terms used emphasize the equivalence of the two objects with which it meets. The whiteness and the luminosity refer to the screen and the arm of the woman. The progression of the action shows the change of objective: the interest in the (bad) film makes way for the interest in his neighbor. The surroundings, with their "benign darkness," favor this blurring between one "illusion" and another. "Her hand squeezes mine. My knee presses against hers, without either saying a word. I became aware of her slightly agitated breathing," Desnos writes. Desnos obeys a personal impulse (and goes further than what is allowed in a cinema). The John Sims of the day obeys a social obligation instead (he must fall into a collective to feel a part of it, to integrate with it). Yet the path is analogous from one observed object to another, from one unity to another. The being inside of things, in the field of our own gaze, in the world, can become reality.

As for Desnos and his adventure with the beautiful neighbor, I'll skip how that story ended.

THOMAS, WATCHING

If the shift from *Uncle Josh at the Moving Picture Show* to *The Crowd* involves a leap in perspective, our third film involves a greater leap still. We find ourselves in another time, in another stylistic and historical environment. Yet we encounter again a strongly reflexive film, one that is able to convey the spectator's experience.

Michelangelo Antonioni's *Blowup* (Italy/Great Britain, 1966) contains a rather tense sequence, though nothing important seems to happen in it. The film's protagonist, Thomas, a trendy fashion photographer, takes some pictures in a park. He then develops them and hangs them on the walls of his studio. He is collecting images of London for a book of his work. When Thomas gets closer to one of the photographs, going over its surface with a large magnifying glass—he notices a detail. The detail is enlarged and placed next to other images. The camera passes smoothly from one photograph to the next, before resting on the photographer who goes over the various images, looking for a connection between them. The photographer works feverishly in the dark room. He hangs the newly printed photographs on the walls. Once again, the camera passes over the different images, and at the end of the uninterrupted pan it captures the photographer intent on examining the results of his work. This final shot contains a surprising element: it begins with a scene that seems to be seen by someone (the movement of the camera on the photographs simulates, in fact, the gaze of the photographer who inspects them), but instead of cutting to that person who is watching, it ends with the discovery that the observer has always been in the scene, inside what was thought to be his field of vision. Thus, we are no longer dealing with a *point-of-view shot*—that is, with the image of what is seen, followed by an image of the person seeing.[56] We have here what has traditionally been called a *semi-point-of-view shot* (or *semi-subjective shot*), or a single shot that incorporates both the object seen and the subject seeing in the same field of vision.[57] The two elements could not coexist in the same image, since if someone is seen, that someone cannot be inside his or her own field of vision (that is, the person looking ahead cannot frame him or herself as well). Yet here object and subject coexist as equal parts inside one single gaze. This is the small paradox that renders the shift surprising: what is usually divided, and should remain as such, is instead reassembled. Thus, a unity—conspirational and a bit disturbing—emerges.

Taking this semi-subjective shot as a point of departure, let us try to expand on what it can teach us. It is hardly necessary to say that this is not the first time that Antonioni has employed such a process. He uses it in other films, always in order to mark moments in which the character's capacity to understand a situation on both perceptive and cognitive levels seems to deteriorate and rupture.[58] But the semi-subjective shot seems to assume an even greater significance in *Blowup*. The definitive elimination of the barrier between observer and observed (the two share the same shot; there is no editing cut that separates them) appears both intentional and expected in this film in particular. The story begins, in fact, with Thomas dressed as a lower-class, blue-collar worker, photographing London's lost humanity. His clothing shows not only how he wants and needs to camouflage himself, but also that he chooses to make himself into the object of his own gaze. Unlike when he works in his studio, where he behaves as absolute master of his environment, here he is conforming to what is before his camera.

In the second instance, Thomas is looking at landscape photos. In one way they constitute for him a sort of spectacle, particularly because they are born from a (possible) crime and thus function as a small story unfolding in perfect mystery style that must be carefully analyzed. In another way, however, these photos represent nothing more than the environment. Thomas had photographed a couple in the park, just as he had previously photographed some vagrants. He has London's complex humanity—and therefore the social milieu in which he lives—in his viewfinder. Here, spectacle and environment are superimposed. The environment is presented as a true spectacle, and the spectacle has moved into everyday life (e.g., the procession of clowning street revelers-protesters-panhandlers and, some sequences later, the same group, more or less, who improvise a tennis match show). This blending of spectacle and environment means that the unity realized between the observer and the observed is also a unity between the individual and the surrounding world. Thomas, next to the photos and inside his own field of vision, is both a scopic subject that has been connected to his object, and a social subject that has been united with the physical and human universe.

Thomas is undoubtedly in position of observer, yet this is not the only scopic role that he knows how to fill. We shouldn't forget that, before beginning to look at his photos, he shot a series of viewpoints, printed them, then chose details to enlarge. He then printed the new images and arranged them in his studio in careful order. In other words, he "put together" his own show. Previously in his studio, Thomas had lined up a group of models and made them assume stylish unnatural poses. Scolding them, he finally orders them to close their eyes and to stay still. In this way, he reaffirms his role as "boss of the set." He is the one individual able to "manipulate" a scene. As producer and director, Thomas, in addition to being the *subject who sees*, is also the *subject who shows*. He is, furthermore, a *seen subject*. At the very moment in which he begins to think that he has photographed a crime, he also suspects that he is being spied on by someone. He discovers, after returning home, that all the films have been stolen, giving him proof of this fear. The killers are watching him, and he is not able to identify them. Thomas is a scopic subject in various ways who, in turn, faces other scopic subjects, ready to cross their action with his. The semi-subjective shot puts us on the alert: in it, the character saw and was seen at the same time, seen in his own gaze, which inevitably becomes our own as well. Let us say, in other words, that the protagonist of *Blowup* has always moved on a terrain with a dense network of gazes running through it. Glances follow each other, they mix and overlap. They outline rich trajectories, in which seeing, making others see, making oneself be seen and being seen are positions that somehow seem to blur into each other.[59]

Finally, in this game of crossed gazes, Thomas ends up losing both himself and the reality he seeks to observe. Once again, the semi-subjective shot should have aroused our suspicions. By giving us an observer who inside his own field of vision, both the source of the gaze (aligned to seen objects) and the substance of the vision (characterized by ambiguity) seem lost. *Blowup* continues in this direction. Thomas enlarges his photos one by one, in search of a detail that can confirm the crime. The images develop, however, as simple dotted surfaces, not very different from his neighbor's abstract paintings. He returns to the park, where he discovers a body. He doesn't have his camera with him, and as a result he will never have evidence of what he has seen. He throws himself into a crowd at a rock concert, where concertgoers come to blows over a piece of the guitar smashed by the bassist. Thomas grabs it, only to throw it away, as if it had suddenly lost all value. Finally, at the end of his nighttime wanderings, Thomas crosses a group of revelers—the same group that appeared at the beginning of the film—playing tennis without a ball. Asked to pick up an invisible ball that has apparently gone out of bounds, he complies. Witness to a reality that fully draws him in, Thomas is no longer sure of his gaze or the reality that he is observing. Perhaps too close, too much a part, too involved, he is left nothing but a game that takes from him both his role as scopic subject and the object of his vision.

Here we have *Blowup*, reread in the light of a significant sequence. At least three issues emerge: first, the fusion of an observer, what he watches, and the context in which he operates; second, the creation of a terrain in which multiple gazes intersect; and third, the loss of all certainty due to an intimacy and interdependence that is perhaps excessive. Here we recognize a series of themes that we have already encountered, but

expressed in an even more radical way. We have a "spectator" who measures himself against both a performance and an environment to which
he is drawn. Only, in this film, he is no longer made to choose between
reality and its representation. He can literally immerse himself in both,
making himself part of them in every possible way. This is possible since
the worlds (the depicted and the surrounding ones), not only share many
characteristics but also form a single large field of vision, in which many
gazes intersect and overlap. Entering into these two worlds means finding oneself in a web of gazes that envelops and perhaps even imprisons.
In this web, a spectator in fact experiences the changeability of his or her
own position. If for an instant he or she is a seeing subject, he or she can
become a subject that makes one see, and then move on to becoming a
subject who is, in turn, seen. Similarly, in this network a spectator experiences reciprocity. If it is true that he or she sees, it is also true that he
or she can be seen, and seen by those whom he himself tries to see. The
spectator experiences the reification of his or her own view: the world is
no longer sustained only by his or her gaze, but by a gaze that circulates
and unifies independent of that from which it comes (in other words,
a gaze without a source, a gaze in some way in and of itself). Finally, in
this network, the spectator experiences defeat: he/she loses both him or
herself and the surrounding world. On one hand, he or she experiences
the loss of function as observer. Though moving in a world permeated by
his or her gaze as well, the spectator no longer has either the exclusiv-
ity or the certainty of this role. On the other, he or she lives the loss of
the observed world. However literally placed in view, this world no longer
knows to which view to respond, pervaded as it is by a gaze that can no
longer reveal anything but its own pervasiveness.

If this reading is correct, *Blowup* offers itself as a great celebration of
modern spectatorship. It embodies its themes and brings them to their
extreme. In fact, the film seems to take up the crucial points that we have
encountered in the preceding analyses and leads them to their logical
conclusion. In proposing the intersection of the scopic subject and what
surrounds it, contact becomes total immersion, interaction becomes complicity, domination becomes dispossession, and certainty becomes loss of
self and the other. In other words, it is as if the path whose steps we first
traced speaking of Etna and Catania, ends here, with the "modern cinema" represented by *Blowup* (though this "modern cinema" is no less modern than "classical cinema"). Perhaps it would then be helpful to place

alongside the film a text that is one of the manifestos of the modern gaze. Remembering that extra leap I alluded to in the beginning of this section, let us look at Jean-Paul Sartre's *Being and Nothingness*.[60] I will not go through it in detail, but refer to only some of its most important pages.

The chapter "The Look" begins with the observation that a person entering into a visual field assumes the status of an object: "This woman I see coming toward me, this man who is passing by in the street, this beggar whom I hear calling before my window, all are for me *objects*—of that there is no doubt."[61] It is enough, however, that we realize that these objects are human for the organization of the visual field to change. Placing themselves at the true epicenter of the scene, they have the capacity to make everything turn in relation to them. Thus, the reality before my eyes suddenly reveals itself in its totality (as it is structured around these human objects), yet in its totality it escapes me (as it converges toward them). Consequently, "there is now an orientation *which flees from me*."[62] In front of me there is not something that I am simply framing, but something that conditions me entirely: "An object has appeared which has stolen the world from me."[63] Now let us imagine that I am, in turn, observed: "But all of a sudden I hear footsteps in the hall. Someone is looking at me!"[64] The situation changes further: in discovering that I am seen, I discover that I am myself in turn the object of another's gaze. I am a rather special object, capable of structuring the surrounding world for the other, and at the same time capable of taking it away from him or her (and of taking myself from him). Now, in this game of crossed purposes and assumptions, some important information emerges. First of all, I discover the reversibility between myself and the other. I discover the possibility that the other I see watching me is the subject, as well as object, of my gaze. I also discover the possibility that I, seeing myself watched, am an object, in addition to being the subject of a gaze. Second, my objectification is also the objectification of my gaze itself. In the eyes of the other, I not only see myself seen, but I also see the seeing (his/hers, mine, *the* seeing). Finally, I discover my rootedness, my being in the world. The world that I formerly observed, and that was organized around the other, now turns around me, even flowing away in a sort of "internal hemorrhage." In this sense, entering into the gaze of others leads to a moment of self-reflexivity ("The look which the eyes manifest, no matter what kind of eyes they are, is a pure reference to myself").[65] Primarily, however, it leads to an immersion in reality ("To apprehend myself as seen is, in fact, to apprehend myself as seen *in the world* and from the standpoint of the world").[66] Let us add that the gaze on me is not necessarily linked to the presence of an eye, and therefore a person: "the look will be given just as well on occasion when there is a rustling of branches, or a sound of a footstep followed by silence, or the slight opening of a shutter, or a light movement of a curtain."[67] One can be observed not only by another but also by a natural element. Any object can be the source of a gaze; it is the world that watches me, that world that I myself watch, which swallows me up, yet escapes me completely.

I have certainly gone over Sartre's work too quickly. The scenario that emerges is, however, clear enough. Sartre offers a phenomenological description of what now seems to be the *visual experience*, an experience characterized by the reversibility of subject and object, the taking root in a world that simultaneously disappears, the reification of the gaze, which detaches itself from the sight organ and from concrete vision, in order to act in some way by itself. This description will resurface in Merleau-Ponty and Lacan.[68] But these pages of Sartre's that go over the visual experience essentially describe *a spectatorial experience*, or rather, a *filmic experience*. It is not, in fact, a coincidence that these pages contain numerous resonances with the crucial points that we came across in a self-reflexive film like *Blowup*. The observer in the modern consciousness finds the spectator of the cinema to be something more than its simple extension. He or she is, instead, the realization of the idea of the observer. Moreover, it is precisely in front of a screen that we best feel the observed observing, that we feel ourselves inside a gaze that is no longer ours alone, in communion with a world that carries us away. In front of the screen we experience the comings and goings of subject and object, possession and loss, vision and gaze. Applying Sartre's philosophies to film is not an unjust act. It confirms that the latter is able to insert itself into the processes of modernity, to make them its own, and to reinvent them in a way that becomes canonical. "This woman I see coming toward me, this man who is passing by in the street": why not imagine that, as I am living my ordinary day, I can also be seeing a film?

THE LOST POSITION

We began with a voyage up Etna. Epstein gave us a way of understanding how the problem of the film spectator is that of feeling him or herself implicated in the spectacle that is occurring, finally losing him or herself in the moment of shared experience. He clarified how there is at play the breaking of the boundary between the scopic subject and the object of his or her gaze, the creating of a close intimacy, and, at the same time, the loss of all privileged positions. On this terrain, film echoes the more general condition of the modern observer. We were able to put such a picture to the test with three films reflecting on the spectatorial experience. *Uncle Josh at the Moving Picture Show* gave us an ironic illustration of the attraction that a film exercises over its viewers, and consequently the sense of closeness and interaction that is established between theatergoers and what is onscreen: the represented world is within reach; it offers itself up directly and demands our participation. The desire that it ignites cannot, however, have a reciprocal response. *The Crowd* shifted our attention to a different axis, that of the relationship between the spectator and his or her fellow audience members. Here as well, however, we deal with a sense of unity: the spectator is called to be a part of his or her own environment. He or she must recognize him or her self not only as scopic subject but also as social subject. If he or she reaches this status, it is also because the impossible unity with the fictitious world enacts some kind of compensation: we immerse ourselves in the surrounding world because we are not able to completely enter the represented one. *Blowup* seemed to close the circle: we can "merge" with both the spectacle and the environment, insofar as both are permeated by a network of gazes. In this network, the spectator experiences an uncertain position (he or she is both subject and object) and the reification of his or her gaze (the act of seeing becomes independent from any agent). This intimate unity with the spectacle and the environment makes him or her feel lost. This has been our path. It was marked by three devices: the *close-up*, with the sense of nearness that it conveys; the *crane shot*, with its capacity to immerse the character in his or her environment; and the *semi-subjective shot*, in which the character who observes is captured together with the seen objects, reduced to their same status, and perhaps also deprived of his or her own gaze. This journey has been facilitated by a series of theoretical texts, starting from Epstein's narration of an ascent and a descent and concluding with Sartre's description of the act of seeing.

The complex situation that has come to emerge, and that precisely marks the experience of the spectator as well as the condition of the modern observer, leads us to some additional considerations. First of all, it is evident how this condition corresponds to a farewell to that sort of "theater of vision" that had long worked as a model for scopic activity. Such a "theater" was based on the presence of a seeing subject and a seen object. They were conceived as well separated—one faced the other, with the former seizing and keeping hold of the latter through its own look, and the latter one entrusting itself to the former, revealing itself in a direct and exclusive relationship. Blumenberg, with his shipwreck metaphor, gave us the basic elements for such a model, as well as the more general paths of its crisis. We might recall some crucial passages of this path. For example, among the factors that strongly undermine this model, there is the awareness that things do not show themselves; reality becomes a perceived reality only thanks to a series of mental processes that makes it perceivable, but which also inevitably act as a filter. Jonathan Crary, in *Techniques of the Observer*, highlights this passage, reconsidering physiological studies from the first half of the eighteenth century as well as the discovery of phenomena such as the afterimage or perceptive adaptation. Max Milner, in *The Phantasmagoria* (*La Phantasmagorie*), reminds us that this new orientation originates in the Kantian revolution.[70] Similarly, there is also the awareness that the observer does not operate innocently: he or she approaches reality with the sometimes heavy burden of mental assumptions, almost forced orientations. In this regard, it will serve us to recall Marx and his notion of "ideology." The complex network of social and productive relationships creates an "environment" in which the social subject finds himself inserted, and that deeply conditions his or her thought processes. We could go on and on: the fact remains that, from some point on, the relationship between the scopic subject and the object seen can no longer present itself as direct and exclusive. It is not direct: there are mediations that intervene on both sides. It is not exclusive: the context in which subject and object find themselves also plays a decisive role. Most of all, it is not a face-to-face confrontation. It is a two-player game based on a common belonging, intertwined with mutual determinations, and therefore sustained by a strong complicity. Along these lines, we must begin to think of scopic activity as leading to confrontation with and immersion into what one sees, as well as into one's own environment.

Film then seizes on this ongoing transformation and makes it its own. If, as Crary reminds us, what I have called the "theater of vision" found its emblem in the fifteenth century's *camera obscura*—then film and its stereoscopic vision can posit itself as the emblem of this new pattern of vision. Its position is sealed by its capacity to offer itself as a field of cross-gazes that include and embrace the observer, the observed and the situation. Yet if it is true that film can intercept and give form to the turning points that agitate modernity, offering itself as an exemplar, it is also true that it does so by negotiating between innovation and resistance. There is a subtle sort of wariness that accompanies its desire for what is new, almost allowing the old to leave its mark. And so it happens that cinema incarnates the need for a deep relationship between subject, object, and environment, but it does so by offering a fusion that is partly *imaginary* and temporally *delimited*.

An imaginary fusion. *Uncle Josh* has already suggested how the relationship between spectator and spectacle is based on illusion. The observer watching a film faces not reality itself, but images that "look like" reality. This status undoubtedly depends on their photographic nature. It is reinforced, however, owing to the fact that the spectator reelaborates and perceptively integrates the filmic stimuli,[71] and at the same time he or she deliberately suspends his or her disbelief.[72] We must add to this the mechanism of projection and identification.[73] If the spectator participates in the onscreen adventures, it is because he/she is placed in the hero's shoes, and in this way he/she lives firsthand what the character is experiencing. At the theater, spectator and spectacle are tied together, but through a bond that is essentially imaginary.

A temporally limited fusion. When the house lights go up once again, the spectator's relationship with the spectacle is interrupted. When a member of the audience begins to leave the theater, his or her relationship with the audience is broken. The lightness of an experience that transported him or her to a different world, however, remains. But along with this fleeting wonder is the sticky closeness of the rest of the audience, the subtle thrill of having fully been part of some collective body. Roland Barthes, in his "Leaving the Movie Theater," describes the moment in which a spectator departs from a cinema.[74] What he or she leaves is a darkness that is "the very substance of the reverie [and] also the 'color' of a diffused eroticism."[75] Barthes adds: "In this darkness of the cinema (anonymous, populated, numerous—oh, the boredom, the frustration of so-called private showings!) lies the very fascination of the film (any film)."[76] The spectator leaves as well "that dancing cone which pierces the darkness like a beamer" and "whose imperious jet brushes our skulls, glancing off someone's hair, someone's face."[77] Moreover, the spectator leaves a state of immersion. "The image captivates me, captures me; I am *glued* to the representation, and it is this glue which established the *naturalness* (the pseudo nature) of the filmed scene."[78] This "glue" involves the image, but it also induces the spectator to "be fascinated *twice over*, by the image and by its surroundings—as if [he/she] had two bodies at the same time: a narcissistic body which gazes, lost, into the engulfing mirror, and a perverse body, ready to fetishize not the image but precisely what exceeds it."[79] In this way, when the spectator moves away from the movie theater, he/she abandons both a relation with the images and a situation in which he/she enjoyed the ambience. Outside the hall, he or she loses the possibility of taking part of a represented world and of a public. Now "he walks in silence, . . . a little dazed, wrapped up in himself, feeling the cold . . . "[80]

The viewer is immersed in the spectacle and the environment, though only in a partial and momentary way. The cinematographic apparatus plays an important role in this interplay. It encourages a fusion between subject and object and between subject and environment. It also lays the conditions that prevent this fusion from ever totally being realized, once and for all. The illusion of reality is supported by the specific physical and mental conditions brought about in the spectator during the screening (representations that can be taken for direct perceptions of the world,[81] and a suspension of the flow of life that permits this belief). Meanwhile, thanks to the simultaneity of the spectators' reactions, a veritable community is created in which each can feel a part of a whole. The structure of the theater results instead in a double segregation: the spectator cannot physically touch the screen and what is on it. Neither can he or she share intimacy with the other spectators, for they are separated. In this sense, the setting partially reverses the mental and social attitudes. This ambiguity of the apparatus is not an innocent one, but functions to keep alive a practice that would otherwise be interrupted, as demonstrated with *Uncle Josh*. It is only the preservation of an intangible boundary that permits the spectator to enjoy the show and enjoy it as spectator. But this non-innocence goes even further. In fact, in preserving this boundary, the apparatus allows the spectator to keep believing that he or she has some sort of *control* over what is observed and what surrounds him or her. The spectator not only "takes part" in the show; he or she also "dominates" it. On this basis, some scholars have made the connection between the cinema and Jeremy Bentham's *panopticon*.[82] In both structures, we are dealing with a situation in which a subject "oversees" all that is happening from the center of the scene. This connection is useful. It illustrates an important side of the spectatorial experience. In fact, if the spectator were to be completely immersed in the represented and surrounding worlds, he or she would not be able to control anything at all. Only the slightest distance from the action (that is, a single seat) is enough, however, to make him or her look at things "from the outside," and thus allows the spectator to seize and master them. Cinema provides this distance. It is a partial detachment: the spectator may always feel at the mercy of winds and waves—in a wreck, though a happy one ("And sweet to me is shipwreck in this sea": Italian poet Giacomo Leopardi, not Blumenberg)—but it is not a real wreck. The spectator is at sea, yet within safety's reach. In this virtual state, he or she can go as far as to orchestrate the storm.

Thus, film is precisely an occasion to "confuse" oneself with the performance and the environment, while keeping some form of distance, if only for safety. The boundary is quite useful—indeed, it is necessary. Nonetheless, the dream of its complete elimination remains alive, and it has always haunted film. From *Sherlock Jr.* (Buster Keaton, USA, 1924) to *The Purple Rose of Cairo* (Woody Allen, USA, 1985), films that enact the dissolution of all film's boundaries and the perfect fusion of fiction and reality are numerous. They depict the desire of an immersion in the spectacle which could be no less than absolute—come hell or high water. How sweet the shipwreck.

Glosses, Oxymorons, and Discipline

I have examined a number of films in order to recon-
struct the gaze elaborated by the cinema, as well as to understand these
films' departures from and intersections with twentieth-century modernity. The selection might seem obvious to some and slightly random to
others: too many well-known works, and too many loose reciprocal ties.
I have never, however, been tempted to construct an ideal pantheon of
great works. What interests me is the possibility of gathering together a
series of proofs in the cinema that are able to show its collective work, in
particular the broad assumptions and consequences upon which such
diverse works are based. The selected films all possess this feature. In
fact, they seem able to put their own mode of functioning into discussion; they offer an excellent point of observation for what the cinema is
or what it could be. Searching their depths, even if with a certain levity,
we find that these films reveal provocations, problems, and choices characteristic of the medium. If we reflect on what it means to take a world
and give it back to the spectator on the screen, these films lay bare the
conditions of existence—both symbolic and social—for all films. From
this point of view, we have dealt not so much with "works of art" (the artistic value of some is openly problematic), but with "theoretical works"[1]
able to develop a general *notion of cinema*.

In parallel, I have discussed a number of critical works dating from
the 1910s to the 1930s, taken from far-ranging twentieth-century cultural
debates. Here as well, some combinations might seem random in their
abrupt jumps from one geographical or chronological setting to another.
And yet these texts were chosen with a precise intent. Though in very
different ways, they all represent moments in which questions regard-

ing the cinema were being posed—what it is, what it brings with it, and to what it responds. In other words, these texts questioned what kind of experience film constitutes and, at the same time, how it influences our experience of the world. Thus, we are dealing with an idea of the cinema that echoes, while not necessarily conforming to, the idea expressed by the films themselves.

This dual approach represents a desire to work on the cinema, in its intersections with modernity, beginning with the *network of social discourses* that extend within and around it.[2] This network, as we have been able to sketch it, leads to several questions. It covers reviews, analyses, essays, prophecies, political speeches, ironic reporting, drafts of laws, literary pieces, and so on. It matches up discourses made of words with those of images and sounds. Yet the problem does not lie in the form or in the status of the discourses which made up this network: in the years taken into consideration, what would later be called "film theory" evolved in ways and situations that were not always canonical. The question really lies elsewhere: in privileging "theoretical works" and "theoretical interventions," what probationary value can we anticipate from these networked discourses? What authority can they express? To whose authority do they give voice? My answer is that they have hardly any authoritativeness or authority save one that is small yet decisive: that of creating *glosses* for the cinematographic phenomenon that help, if not directly determine, its intelligence and understanding.[3]

The discourses that we have tried to interconnect may represent many small moments through which the cinema developed a direct or indirect commentary on itself—not for the pleasure of speaking about itself, but to find its own definition and render it shareable and shared. Through these glosses the cinema was able not only to formulate a certain idea of itself but also make it recognizable in the larger public arena. Thanks to them, it became clearer what film was and what it could have been. Through these glosses, in particular, the cinema "returned" to itself, in order to understand what it was doing, in what way, from which perspectives, and in the name of what hypotheses. In other words, the cinema built the framework through which to be perceived and realized. Glosses helped the cinema to "describe" itself; they also "prescribed" how to take cinema for what it professed to be. The description of these glosses became an "official" definition of the cinema. From this point of view, glosses, overlapping descriptions and prescriptions, helped cinema to find its social "institutionalization" (including the institutionalization of its own ways of observing things).

We therefore have a definition of cinema that gives meaning to its own function, together with a definition of cinema that tries to operate on a collective plane. What characterizes every social discourse is both its self-reflexive capacity and its performative effects. It sees itself and brings about action. The choice of analyzing films and texts which operate as glosses might help us to value both features. The often brief analyses carried out here prevent us from understanding as thoroughly as I might have liked the depth of the self-definition and the path it took to assert itself. In particular, I was unable to give proper emphasis to the element of event, in the Foucauldian sense of the term, which characterizes each of these discourses. The event roots itself in history, creating echoes, establishing points of reference. And yet the often adventurous intersections I have attempted are directed precisely to reveal how the cinema—with its own arms (the films) or with those it acquired (theory)—was able to elaborate an image of itself, and ratify it as well. In this way, I repeat, the filmic or verbal texts analyzed here possesses hardly any authoritativeness, hardly any authority, save the fact that in their role as glosses they have decisively helped along such a process. In "thinking" the cinema, they make the medium both thoughtful and thought-provoking.

TO GIVE A FORM, TO NEGOTIATE

If it is in fact true that theoretical works and interventions give shape to the cinema, it is also true that the cinema in turn gives form to the demands that circulate around it. There is a game of subtle complicity between the two forces. The glosses make a certain image of the cinema emerge and impose it on a collective audience; on the other hand, the cinema gives an image (and sound) to its surrounding reality—both actual and possible. The cinema is modeled on the world, but it in turn models that world. Its capacity to construct a gaze of its age is played out primarily within this dual intersection.

Let us briefly run through the process through which the cinema gives form to a series of demands that circulate within a cultural and social space. It is a process that we saw at work in all the films analyzed, which is realized through an "interception" of cues offered by the context, a re-

working based on the possibilities of the medium, and finally their restitution in a form that is in some way exemplary.

As for the "interception," analyses have consistently emphasized the
cinema's capacity to gather various stances—among them fragmentation, the increasing role of subjectivity, the excited perception, etc. All
the ideas borne on the wave of the profound transformations imposed by
modernity found a precise "echo" on the screen. Yet we are not dealing
with a passive recording. First, the very presence of the cinema contributes to nurturing the processes from which these ideas come out. Film
is a pivotal element of the modern landscape. Its strength, vivacity, and
capacity for provocation let the attitudes of the time emerge and reveal
themselves. Second, the cinema reworks the surrounding cues, giving
them a particular form and synthesizing them. Cinema embodies the
idea that reality cannot be gathered if not in pieces, insofar as the onscreen image is limited by four borders. The shot becomes an emblem of
the fragmentation of the world. Cinema embodies the idea that the real
is no longer offered in its fullness and immediacy, giving us (particularly
on the narrative level) the possibility of seeing things not so much as
they are, but as they are perceived by a series of sources for the gaze:
the point-of-view shot, the flashback, the flash-forward, the representation of dream or hallucination then become emblematic of the existence
of a personal filter of reality. Cinema embodies the idea that machines
will end up substituting for man, since its eye moves with an uncommon
agility and coldness: the camera, with its extraordinary possibilities, but
also with its peculiar sensibility, then becomes the emblem of a prosthesis that begins to move of its own accord. Thus, the preoccupations of the
era take shape onscreen, and with them the ways of observing things; it
has the effect of anchoring a series of widespread sensations to precise
symbols, which allow those sensations to become largely recognizable
and recognized.

The cinema's capacity to construct emblems manifests itself through
some exemplary themes, as well as through certain devices of language
and apparatus. In my analyses, we have encountered numerous examples of key themes. *King Kong* concentrates the idea of nature caged and
injured by technology; in *Old and New* the cream separator causes abrupt
changes of state that bring with them a profound excitement; the behavior of the spectator in *Uncle Josh* reflects the imaginative imprudence of
a daydreamer; the theatrical audience of *The Crowd* mirrors a mass that

becomes a social body, etc. But the strongest emblems are those that concern either language or the apparatus: it is in these instances that we see how the cinema is literally able to "incarnate" in its own way of enacting the cues that it has intercepted and reformulated. The shot, the camera movements, and then the editing, découpage, flashback, crosscutting, or the semi-point of view—some with their insistence on fragmentation, others on mechanicalness, still others on excitement, others finally on the implication of observer and observed—directly recall questions already circulating in the ambiance of their era. In this sense, we can say that the cinema is a witness of its time. It fine-tunes processes that synthesize a pervasive feeling, and places them at the foundation of its own action.

Yet this is only one part of the game. In elaborating its own emblems, the cinema does not limit itself in giving a proper form to the provocations that it receives or that its own presence provokes. Its work goes beyond, and consists also in gathering the subtle contrasts that accompany these provocations, as well as finding a solution for them. The great demands of modernity briefly outlined here are, in fact, internally contradictory. The world offers itself only in fragments, but the desire for totality continues to press. Reality is always filtered by someone's perception, but this does not exonerate us from distinguishing between perceptions and facts. The machine offers us a gaze that is extraordinarily sharp, but humans want to continue to feel in some way a part of it. Sensory excitement makes us feel alive and present, but we also must not lose control of our surroundings or ourselves. Spectator and performance are, by now, one and the same, but it is often necessary to establish distance. The counterforces that emerge are not only vestiges of the past; they also constitute elements of modernity. They are the other side of the same coin. The cinema tries to move between these forces and counterforces, negotiating them. It tries to confront the elements concerned, to clarify their different positions, to bring their discordances and concordances to light, and finally to elicit solutions accepted by all; or rather, in which everyone (or almost everyone) can, in the end, recognize him or herself.

Thus, in the process of giving form, the cinema negotiates. In negotiating, it looks for a compromise in which conflicts are not eliminated, but are in some way rewritten.[4] It is in the light of this convergence, among these contrasting impulses, that we can fully appreciate the value of the emblems that the cinema constructs. Let us take the shot. Because it is framing, it undoubtedly reminds us how the gaze cannot gather anything but fragments of the world; yet the fact that it endures in time and can be moved in space gives it a sense of "openness" to reality. Let us take camera action. Its mobility and flexibility are a celebration of the machine, but the fact that it almost always tries to reproduce human movements in space gives its presence an anthropomorphic value. Let us take the flashback or the point-of-view shot. These two conventions indicate that the gaze is always filtered, but they also give a strong objectivization to an outcome that is purposefully personal. Let us take editing. Editing offers a great variety of viewpoints, it stimulates our perception to the maximum. By regulating the shot sequence, however, it manages and orders the shocks that it offers. Finally, let us take the close-up. The close-up seems to invite us into a close communion with the object represented, and yet precisely because of its structure it includes the observer only in an imaginary way. In the cinema, modernity's forces and counter-counterforces find a possible meeting point.

Confronting these drives and counterdrives, the cinema inevitably ends up redefining them in some way. The negotiation has a second face that cannot be forgotten: in putting modernity's different exigencies in contrast, it *rearticulates* them if, for nothing else, to find a compromise. Let us take once more the shot: in its "permeable" borders (the camera can always move laterally, and the reality next to that shot can always encroach upon the shot itself), it marks the presence of both an "in" space and an "off" space while trying to connect them. On the screen, I see only a portion of the world, but I am aware of the presence of the rest. I can slip from what I am offered to what I am denied. The shot, creating an "on-screen" and an "off-screen," places them in opposition and at the same time makes them meet up. In other words, it operates a mediation: the fragment can dialogue with the whole, the visible with the invisible. What the shot does not succeed in doing with its duration and mobility, editing does. The practice of shot/reverse-shot shows us that what stays outside a shot can be "had" in the next one. But if it is true that the shot (and editing) seem(s) to offer a remedy to an otherwise unsolvable conflict, it is also true that they rearticulate this conflict just the same. Let us take visibility and invisibility. Brought back to an exercise of framing, the two terms lose the ontological value that they have long had in cultural history. Their dialectic is reduced to a mere question of spaces, the one "in" the frame and the other "off." In this dialectic, there are no longer different realities at play—the human and the godly—neither is there a knowledge and a non-knowledge that wants to be fulfilled, but simply a "here" and a "there," a piece of world and another piece of world. The comparison between visibility and invisibility becomes a simple problem of topography. Certainly, as I have said, the "off-screen" can present itself as the space of the possible, and in this sense makes its value grow. There is a "can be" that does not become saturated with the simple restitution of further fragments. Yet the fact remains that the cinema, negotiating between two exigencies of modernity, not only individuates a point of compromise, but it also offers their reformulation (and a reformulation directed at compromise). In this sense, it demonstrates how it is able to become an optimal interpreter of a latent tension, but it is nonetheless a non-neutral witness. It "rewrites" contrasts.[5] It is under this aspect that the cinema can be considered as a "form of thought":[6] historically, it has been able to give "flexion" to the categories of its time, when it has not actually reworked them on its own.

I would add that the cinema's capacity to "think"—thanks to the reformulation of problems and its search for compromise—realizes one of modernity's other great intentions. As Georg Simmel perceived at the beginning of the twentieth century, we live in an age in which the greatest amount of knowledge is located in technological devices and in social institutions. Simmel writes: "In language as well in law, in the technique of production as well as in art, in science as well as in the objects of the domestic environment, there is embodied a sum of spirit. The individual in his intellectual development follows the growth of this spirit very imperfectly and at an ever increasing distance."[7] The elaboration of knowledge is no longer in the hands of the individual: institutions and devices know more than he does. From here, we have a twofold effect. On the one hand, stimulations and consciousnesses offered to an individual "from all sides . . . carry the person as if in a stream, and one needs hardly to swim for oneself." On the other hand, knowledge becomes largely impersonal. As Simmel points out, the individual "can cope less and less with the overgrowth of the objective culture."[8] In this sense, if the cinema "thinks," it does so for mankind, but also beyond it.

In any case, it remains true that the cinema presents itself as an extraordinary place to redefine circulating social demands. In giving a form to them, it necessarily negotiates. It does this in search of compromises, but in doing so it also provokes a reworking of preexisting concepts. It is precisely this that makes the cinema a crucial presence, a protagonist of its time.

DISCIPLINE OF THE EYE

What is more, this intense world of negotiated redefinitions makes the cinema an ambivalent presence: beyond being an active witness, it also promises to be a site in which the various solutions offered may become models to which one must conform. Let us think, in fact, of what a redefinition might mean, as well as a rewriting of the different demands running through modernity. It is not difficult to see in these demands a way of keeping under control a situation that is otherwise too complicated. What emerges is a question of *maîtrise*: the problem lies in mastering a series of elements that seem to exceed all sides. Compromise (and rearticulation) seem(s) to assure manageability. The solutions offered seem like formulas ready to be adopted.

In recent times, it has become almost obligatory, on the wave of studies such as those from Jonathan Crary,[9] to analyze the cinema as one vast discipline. The term *discipline* clearly recalls Foucault,[10] and designates a series of practices typical of modernity intended to render the subjects—particularly their bodies—"docile," in a historical phase in which a progressive "liberation" of previously strict bonds can represent a risk in the light of social order. Discipline assures this order not through repression, but the organization of activities on the spatial, temporal, categorical, and logical levels. It dictates the norms that subjects in some way interiorize, and that render their behaviors functional and productive. I will not try to see if and to what extent the practices brought to light by Foucault are found in the cinema. I will only observe that a film organizes it own gaze (and that of its spectator) on principles not dissimilar to those Foucault theorizes. In the cinema, we also find processes of spatial localization, temporal articulation, segment structure, and construction of a compact organism. We have only to think, for example, of how a film defines points of view that situate who sees and what is seen (the spectator, the character, the implied observer, etc.); how it connects these points of view through recursive principles such as the match-on-gaze (of the character acting as observer) or the match-on-action (of the observed character); how it places these points of view along a cogent

line, fixed by the advancing of the action and the progress of an exploration; and finally how it integrates these points of view into a complex
plan that gives us back as much the meaning of the situation depicted
as an understanding of its ideal observer. The four great dimensions that
Foucault recognized in all disciplines—the cellular, organic, genetic, and
combinatory, respectively—return here. Yet, more than expanding upon
the possible analogies, I would like to take up a contribution that was
influential both in Europe and America, in which the idea of the cinema
as a machine directed at framing the gaze emerges with extreme clarity.
I am referring to the writings that Pudovkin dedicated in the late 1920s to
filmmaking and filmscript, whose influence on scholars and professionals was notable.[11]

Pudovkin outlines a discussion that might seem exemplary. He equates
the camera-eye and the eye of the spectator: "The lens of the camera is
the eye of the spectator," or "The lens of the camera replaces the eye of
the observer."[12] Now if this eye intends to be truly efficient, it must understand what is and is not essential: the filmmaker, in order to obtain
the clearness and the evidence of the scene, has to "concentrate the attention of the spectator on only that element important to the action."[13]
Here, a true work of selection is thus needed—with the resulting elimination of some pieces of the world and the conservation of others—that
is able to return to us what counts. "The camera assumes the task of
removing every superfluity and directing the attention of the spectator in
such a way that he shall see only that which is significant and characteristic." Pudovkin continues: "The film is exceptionally precise in its work.
There is, and must be, in it no superfluous element."[14] This allows for the
realization of what we might call a true *economy of attention*: "The film, by
showing [the spectator] the detail without its background, releases [him]
from the unnecessary task of eliminating superfluities from his view-field.
By eliminating distraction it spares the spectator's energy, and reaches
thereby the clearest and most marked effect."[15] The film spectator can
then operate better than he or she could in following other performances,
such as the theater, or even better than he or she could in everyday life.
"The film spares this work of stopping and downward-gliding. Thus the
spectator spends no superfluous energy. By elimination of the points of
interval the director endows the spectator with the energy preserved, he
charges him, and thus the appearance assembled from a series of significant details is stronger in force of expression from the screen than is the

appearance in actuality."[16] In other words, the spectator becomes a truly optimal observer. All this certainly has a consequence, which becomes clearer when one thinks, in addition to the shots, of their editing: "editing is not merely a method of the junction of separate scenes or pieces, but is a method that controls the 'psychological guidance' of the spectator." Moreover, "The guidance of the attention of the spectator to different elements of the developing action in succession is, in general, characteristic of the film. It is its basic method."[17] The cinema in some way takes the eye of the spectator by the hand, so to speak; it directs it toward what is essential, accompanies all its movements, takes away its unnecessary strain. In exchange, it offers it a better point of view. It disciplines it, because the act of seeing becomes a functional and productive activity.

Here is Pudovkin, albeit drastically summarized. It is not hard to see in his discourse a reference to the practices that Foucault would then bring to light. The cinema fragments the world; it makes a selection, connects the chosen pieces, and finally integrates them into an organic vision. The cinema rests its observation of reality on a structured and replicable schema. More importantly, the cinema organizes this process in order to assure maximum efficacy. Through these acts, it makes functional and productive elements emerge. And at the same time, organizing this process in this way, it gives an order to its vision that it can then impose on the spectator. In this sense, the cinema is totally *disciplinary*.

Of course, Pudovkin certainly presents only *one* of the possible disciplines of the gaze: the one that circulates around the *découpage*, or analytical editing. The cinema also knows other forms of discipline. I am thinking, for example, of the regulation of perceptive shock in the early period (in Pudovkin, we are dealing with a modulation of attention more than a modulation of attractions); or, beginning in the 1940s, of the construction of visual paths that no longer pass through the forced splintering of reality by the camera (Pudovkin does not yet contemplate cases like the sequence shot, depth of field, the unfocused shot, and so on, that would become common in modern cinema). There are, therefore, many ways of regulating scopic activity—many disciplinary styles, if you will.[18] But if the modalities with which the discipline works can change, the end result is unique: the cinema's gaze as well as that of the spectator must compete with patterns of action. In the name of a principle of efficiency, they find an internal order of their own. In this way, the eye becomes *docile*.

I would add some observations necessary to complete the picture. I have underlined how Pudovkin speaks of the preservation of perceptive energy, as well as the efficiency of the filmic gaze, and thus creates a criterion of "economy." This criterion is often evoked in regard to the cinema. I am thinking, for example, of Münsterberg and his request to "adapt" filmic procedures to the cognitive processes of the spectator.[19] But I am also thinking of Eisenstein and his hypothesis of "calculating" the effects provoked by visual shock.[20] Such a reference to "economy" brings us directly back to one of the underlying characteristics of modernity. As Simmel reminds us, this is an age in which the logic of money permeates the whole of social behaviors.[21] This idea emerges in many commentaries on film. I will limit myself to a passage from 1907 that is certainly indicative. The Italian essayist Giovanni Papini writes:

> One of the characteristics in our life that is becoming evermore accentuated is the tendency toward economy, not for tiredness or avarice—on the contrary, modern men make more things and are richer—but to obtain, with the same quantity of time, exertion, and money, more things. The cinema satisfies all these tendencies toward savings at the same time. It is a brief phantasmagoria, only twenty minutes, in which everyone can take part for only 20 or 30 cents. It does not demand a great culture, too much attention, a lot of effort to follow. It has the advantage of holding only one sense, the sight . . . and this one sense is artificially deprived of distractions by the Wagnerian darkness of the cinema hall, which prevents distractions to attention, those signs and gazes that so often are observed in well-lit theaters.[22]

His words not only offer a weighty portrait of the cinema but, in explaining the reasons for its success and the modes of its operation, they confirm what I am saying. There is a need for functionality and efficiency reflected in it, and it is for this reason that it is presented as discipline.

A second observation. If it is true that the cinema regulates the eye, it does not however regulate bodies in the same way. Without a doubt, in fact, the cinema shapes both the gaze and postures of social subjects. In particular, the rise of the traditional movie theater leads to a series of rituals connected to the consumption of films and, consequently, to a category to which a "good spectator" must conform. Yet these rituals are not rigidly restrictive: on the contrary, they break old social divisions, encourage promiscuity, allow immediate reactions to the onscreen performance, etc. Once more, I will limit myself to testimony from the first decade of the twentieth century. An anonymous Italian journalist writes in 1908:

> Those who enter a movie theater are suddenly struck by the variety of the audience, blended better than at any other performance. In general, there are few who occupy the reserved seats. Most rush to occupy the general seats, where you find the worker rubbing elbows with the elegant young lady, the restless middle-class youth next to some bundled-up elderly gentleman, some from one class mixed with those of another.[23]

In the audience, bodies obey some basic rules, yet they are also set free.

Moreover, their filmic representation confirms this freedom. Onscreen, bodies move challenging the laws of physics and morality. They run, jump, react continually, openly express sentiments; they undress, they meet up, they exhibit themselves, they transform themselves, they move toward the animal dimension or reveal features of the divine. In other words, they assume an extraordinary agility and flexibility, and at the same time they disclose their intimacy almost without shame. It is not a coincidence then that in 1912 an anonymous reporter characterized a group of French criminals known as the Bonnot band in this way: "Its morality is resoluteness, its rhythm vertigo. . . . They have learned something from film: organic speediness. They have a filmic style that is becoming the manner of our existence."[24] The reference to the cinema shows us how the agility and the effrontery of onscreen bodies can end up serving as a sign of anarchy.

A third observation. The freedom enjoyed by bodies, though subject to discipline, also shows us how the eye has space in which to move. The cinema renders the whole world available to see. It adds to it fantasies and desires, hypotheses and dreams, nightmares and perfections. The camera is independent from a single observer and may move everywhere. Its gaze challenges the laws of physics and morality. Thus, it is true that the cinema works toward a docile eye, but this docility does not signify submissiveness. Let us say, in other words, that at the very moment in which the cinema tries to gives order to the scopic activity, it defies sight as well, provoking it, putting it to the test, bringing it to its limits. In other words, film fills and surprises the human gaze. For this reason as well (indeed, especially for this reason), discipline is needed. But it is an open discipline, one that measures itself against an enlargement of traditionally connected possibilities, and that unites the need to regulate the excesses and the desire of exploring the limits of the given order. We have, then, a discipline in search of liberty. Here lies another paradox for a cinema that continually struggles to negotiate and fuse apparently irreconcilable fronts, allowing for otherwise impossible convergences to be realized onscreen and in the movie theater.

DECALOGUE

I have insisted on how negotiation effects a rearticulation of positions at stake and, at the same time, reaches for a compromise. The different stances of modernity are brought together, redefined and rematched via cinema. In the end, they find positions that are entirely practicable—and in some way inevitably practiced.

Let us remember now the major points of comparison discussed here. The first is the one that sees fragment and totality at play. The cinematographic image, defined by its four borders, seems to confirm what modernity brings to the surface. Tied to a point of view, every glimpse is always partial and therefore gives us the world back only in fragments. Yet this does not mean a rejection of a larger vision. The machine movement allows for the systematic widening of the visual field; the shot/reverse-shot for the integration of one portion of space in another; the superimposition or the split screen for offering many glimpses in the same frame; the close-up for concentrating us on what summarizes the entire situation; the "off-screen" finally for perceiving that something escapes, at the same time staying aware of it. A gaze is born that, penetrating fragmentation and totality, witnesses and rewards both.

The second point of comparison concerns subjectivity and objectivity. The point of view loads every glimpse with a strong subjectivity as well; the "what" always unfolds in relationship to the "who." The filmic image exemplifies this situation; more than an image of reality, it is an image of a *perception* of reality; the real is brought back to us filtered by an eye. And yet the evidence that things assume on the screen gives them an absolute consistency of the real; the world is there, in its immediacy and its actuality. From here, there is the necessity of identifying what seems to appear in itself and what instead represents someone's vision or imagination. The cinema distinguishes between the two levels through stylistic devices such as the impersonal shot or the point-of-view shot, the direct presentation or the flashback. Nevertheless, it rotates the real and the mental, or the real and the possible, so that one dimension nurtures the other and vice versa.

The third point relates to the tension between man and machine. The advances of technology change not only the surrounding landscape but also the very conditions of existence. Man risks becoming machine, and his environment risks falling into artificiality. The cinema is granted a mechanical eye, which directly competes with the human one: its mobility, precision, and indifference are qualities that only technology can assure (and moreover, they are qualities that only modern means of transport and observation can succeed in making emerge). Yet we also find in the cinema ways of observing the world that are typically human: the foci of attention are traditional (the body, the face, the landscape), just as are its forms and developments (exploration, witness). Thus, the cinema-eye is mechanical as well as anthropomorphic. It unites both virtues, without nurturing their conflict.

The fourth point involves the tension between excitement and order. The world around us is in chaos, and bombards us with continuous stimuli. The cinema reproposes the features of an excited perception. The way in which bodies move onscreen, situations transform, and events overlap is the source of continual surprise and often potential displacement. To follow a film is to test our senses. But the cinema also causes the spectator—though subject to authentic visual shock—to have the sensation of being in control of what he or she sees: methods such as crosscutting, shot/reverse-shot, refiguration, and, more generally, editing allow us to orient ourselves with respect to the world represented onscreen, as well as to the forms of its representation.

The last point, finally, includes immersion and detachment. The modern experience tends to cancel all distance between observer and observed reality: the former is implicated in the latter, and the latter includes the former. The extraordinary participation that the cinema provokes seems to move in the same direction. The spectator is immersed in the spectacle. Similarly, the immersion also takes place in the surrounding crowd at the movie theater. Such a state can make us lose sense of our own position and role. To avoid this, the cinema creates a communion between spectator and spectacle only on an imaginary level and in a transitory form, while it favors its connection with the audience in the name of the establishment of a social body. From this experience derives a participation that allows distance and with it a true control over the situation.

These are the essential problems we have discussed, which show how the cinema is able to gather the demands of modernity, reread, and mediate them. Its work is that of negotiation, which leads the cinema to unite opposites in order to make practicable and practiced solutions emerge. This has the effect of constructing a gaze that takes various exigencies into account and tries to reconcile them. In this sense, we deal with an *oxymoronic gaze*. Let us conclude by going over the features of this gaze, which emerge from the analysis explored here.

1 **Visibility and evidence.** Reality is openly revealed on the screen, thanks to an eye that becomes its explorer and witness. According to Balázs, the world becomes visible once again and in its totality. Indifference to the surrounding world is defeated, just as the uncertainty of our senses finds solid anchors. Things are "out there," and we can grasp them. And yet, on the screen there are only images.

2 **Visibility and completeness.** The filmic image, defined by four borders, gives us back only fragments of the world. We see in pieces. But thanks to editing, the pieces can be joined, giving us in some way a sense of the whole. Thanks to the movement of the camera, we may grasp more and more reality. Thanks to the imagination, we can go beyond in the "off-screen" space, prefiguring what we have not yet seen. We become ubiquitous: our gaze can move anywhere, at any moment. It can reach what is only a possibility. The "limits" of the image are never barriers.

3 **Visibility and immediacy.** The camera works as a filter on the world. Yet the camera is a subject-object, as Epstein reminds us: this status renders its filter devoid of all traditional psychological dimensions. It seems to see without human prejudice, hindsight, or mental schema. The mediation thus assumes a paradoxical character: we depart from a gaze, but we arrive straight at the heart of things. The world becomes a kind of gift that is personally delivered.

4 **Visibility and intensity.** The cinema challenges perception: it forces a constant attention, and it holds continual surprises. Yet editing, especially when it assumes the form of découpage, regulates the intensity of sensorial stimuli; it

highlights only what counts, and prefigures what arrives. Also, the presence of recurrent figurative schema is directed toward the same aim. In this way, excitement and order are joined in the same gaze.

5 *Visibility and intelligibility*. At the cinema, we live things even before we understand them. Moreover, films are able to restore to us first and foremost ordinary moments, fleeting seconds, the small areas of existence unrelated to the unraveling of a destiny. Yet, thanks primarily to the narrative, the on-screen world reveals a plot and events . . . a logic. Reality, more than simply visible, also becomes intelligible. We see and decipher, in one single glimpse.

6 *Visibility and collectivity*. The cinema gives the right to see to everyone. Each of us sees how everyone else sees. In this sense, it is a perfectly democratic instrument, as scholars such as Delluc and Giovannetti emphasized. The scopic experience becomes a mass experience. The "I see" is declined as "we see," remaining however always in the first person singular.

7 *Visibility and prosthesis*. The cinema's gaze rests on a technological device; at its source, there is a glass eye. Though the latter offers performances that go beyond human possibility, it is offered as an extension of our sight organ. Or rather, as a point of conjunction of the physical eye and the mental one. Machine and man can renew the alliance.

8 *Visibility and immersion*. At the cinema, the spectator is immersed in the performance. More than simply in front of the events, the spectator finds him or herself in the heart of them, in communion with the world. And yet, the separation between observer and observed persists; the universe of the one is never completely confused with that of the other. This allows one to live what one sees, but also, in seeing it, to be able to subtly dominate it.

9 *Visibility and cost*. At the cinema, seeing has a price. Shooting the real world has a cost; it costs even more to construct a possible one; finally, it costs to follow the one or the other on the screen. The scopic experience becomes a commodity whose value is determined by an entrance ticket.

10 *Visibility and security*. The cinema guarantees a vision that is protected from risk. On the screen, the most dangerous situations can be faced, without however enduring the consequences. The cost of your ticket covers this as well. The world is then turned from a possibly poisonous gift to a treasure with which to fill one's pockets.

The ten characteristics that I have just listed, taken from the analyses of the preceding pages, demonstrate the intersections around which the cinema works. They define points of compromise and paths that are navigable, around which the cinema has woven a dialogue with its time, offering an interpretation and an original contribution. Ten characteristics, a small decalogue, though one without precepts. A decalogue of the cinema. A decalogue of modernity.

Remains of the Day

What remains of the cinema as "the eye of the twentieth century," at a moment in which the old century has ended and a new millennium begun? What remains of a gaze that once sought to rearticulate and reconstruct the tensions of its age—setting itself as its witness and guide—now that the age seems to have succumbed to the triumph of new industrial models, social forms, and conceptual configurations? What remains of the splendid challenge that the cinema posed to late modernity, in an age that is so fond of calling itself postmodern?

We are, in fact, facing a profound transformation within the context in which the cinema operates. Limiting ourselves to the topics we have touched on here, we have only to think of how globalization redraws the tensions between fragment and totality. This contrast is reduced to a blurred mixture of local and global. Since we live both "here" and "anywhere," what we face is a "glocalism." Think of how a new self-consciousness refigures the tension between subject and object. In the explosion of points of view and voices, what emerges is no longer a common meaning that nevertheless attaches us to things, but a simple collection of lived moments. The miniaturization of technologies changes the relationships between man and machine. The human body, more than extending itself through a series of devices, absorbs them directly into itself; the notion of prosthesis gives way to that of hybridization, and the man-machine no longer seems shocking. We might think also about the creation of how new forms of passion—all extremely physical—redraw the contrast between excitement and meaning. What emerges is a "feeling" which operates beyond a full understanding. And, finally, we have a cancellation of both geographical and mental limits, making us not only witnesses implicated in the world's performance but also accomplices in every respect to what happens, and thus active combatants.

The cinema no longer manages all the conflicting stances that it used to control so well (or at least not in the same way). It can no longer effect the same mediations. These are instead entrusted to other media. Television, for example, works best as a mediation of geopolitical space, giving us simultaneously a sense of extreme localization and the awareness of a world scene. The Internet, in addition, creates networks of contact in which the relationship between the self and the other is best balanced, and from which new forms of collectivity can be born. The cellular phone, in contrast, seems the medium most driven to integrate an element of technology in the human body, rivaling only internal medical prostheses such as the pacemaker. The palm device, finally, delivers readily available memory and constantly developing action.

The task of negotiating between the different drives of the age touches other media—supposing that it is still a question of negotiation. The present time is apparently far from any process that allows opposites to be summoned and, through a series of internal redefinitions, synthesis to be reached. The emblem of the epoch is the slippery morphing image, more than actual comparison and reciprocal influence. In other words, it is no longer a time of productive and revelatory compromises, as in the modern age (and, less than ever, of models that are mirrored in antimodels, such as in the classical). We are in a liquid age, to recall a perhaps overused expression of Bauman's.[1]

Losing its capacity for negotiation, the cinema loses its role as guide to scopic exercise, too (again, supposing that vision is still a sense that matters, and that hearing and touch do not reign supreme). Film no longer dictates a discipline of the eye. Cinema no more does that—if anything, the job falls to others (specifically, the computer or television). Moreover, cinema does not want to do that. What emerges in films is rather violent wonder, the desire to astonish and displace, the exploration of unexpected paths, and obscenity without redemption.

I refer here to the cinema, but perhaps I am speaking of an object that is no longer the same thing I have handled in the preceding pages. The time and scene have changed, and with them, the cinema has as well. Indeed, and to such a degree that it is no longer the same, but something else entirely. A *Cinema* 2.0, if you will.

The transformation derives from three important challenges. The first concerns the presence of new modes of producing filmic images without passing through the photographic device. I am clearly speaking of the digital image:[2] it not only permits the realization of extraordinary special effects, and thus the presentation of realities that do not exist in nature, but it also allows filmmakers to do without any preexisting reality, even that of a model. We see on the screen things that have not necessarily passed before a camera, but are born from mathematical algorithms. What we follow are no longer *traces* but *inventions*. This means that the cinema ceases to be a tributary of the actual world. Before, film needed reality to create even possible worlds, while now it is not held accountable to the real world at all. The filmic image therefore no longer bears witness to anything: it stops being an *index* and becomes a *simulacrum*.[3]

The second challenge regards the emergence of new ways of consuming films without going to the movie theater. The spectator gains access to cinematic products in many new ways: on videocassette or DVD, by cable or satellite, through free access, pay-per-view or on-demand, on the computer screen, by CD-ROM, on the Internet, or the cellphone. The movie theater has changed as well. From the multiplex to IMAX, it no longer has the features it once did and, if anything, it often represents an extension of other general situations such as the mall or the theme park. In this widespread transformation, not only do the old rituals of going to the cinema die out but also the very idea of a collective performance, able to address a concrete group of people intent on the same purpose. The cinema is consumed more and more individually, or in small groups. It is consumed in an ever more personal way, though—at least ideally— the activity still connects us to others. In other words, the public—i.e., a crowd gathered in a space—progressively gives way to an audience—as with television, radio, newspapers, and albums or compact disks.

The third challenge, which situates the first two, is tied to the advent of a new media landscape, thanks to the explosion of ITC, or Information and Communication Technology. What we are facing is the general adoption of a digital signal (as opposed to an analog one) and the expansion of networks, from the telephone to wireless systems. The effect of such a changeover is twofold. In the first place, a series of media previously operating in isolation can connect in a systematic and intensive way, since they share the same signal and there is a network to put them in touch.

In the second place, media products can model themselves directly on their consumer, responding to his or her needs, in a sort of direct conversation. What then emerges are the successful features of multimediality and interactivity. The cinema is trying to adapt itself within this picture: it dialogues with other media, both carrying on its action and giving to them motives to be developed (the intersection with comics or videogames is, in this sense, pertinent). The cinema enlarges the scope of its own offering, putting alongside films an ample array of related merchandise; it continues its life on the Net, becoming the object of discussion and, often, cult status in forums and blogs (when it is not borne directly from the Net itself, as in the case of some products destined for a "peer to peer" circulation, in which an author offers his or her own works via the Internet to many single spectators, in an almost interpersonal exchange). To a great degree, film certainly continues to be a typical format (an hour and a half of fiction) and an object to be consumed (something that is attended, not with which one dialogues), but the referential territory becomes wider, more varied, more flexible, and with it, the objects that are part of it are also increasingly changing.

We have, thus, a digital image, no longer a tributary of the real. We have an audience, gathered together to consume in only a virtual way. In addition we have an exchange with other media that widens the field of action but dilutes its identity as well. This is what the cinema has become—or rather, what the Cinema 2.0 has become. Its presence is still relevant, though sandwiched between the interstices of the great media territories. Film becomes more and more a reference for writers and essayists; cinema is taught in universities; prémieres gain large coverage in many newspapers. We continue to speak—and speak a lot—of the cinema. Even its role is still relevant. Its images often possess a sort of "high definition," compared with the quality of the depictions offered by other media. This allows these images to assure the communicative field's aesthetic dimension, a hundred years after they made the communicative emerge in the vast field of aesthetics. Similarly, these images are still able to fine-tune strongly meaningful emblems, particularly when it is a question of giving an account of the instability the old realities encounter. I am thinking especially of the representations of the human body and its now uncertain limits, in sagas from Alien on—a representation that deals more with a de-figuration than the refiguration it had previously concerned.[4] Finally, filmic images are still the bearers of narrative, where other media are inclined to entertainment with a narration that is implicit (such as in television *reality shows*), or only *a posteriori* (as in videogames), or folded into information (the Net). Lying hidden at the cinema, there is a pressing residual need for stories. For this, the *Cinema 2.0* continues to be an influential presence, despite the profound transformations it has encountered. Moreover, it is able to carry on a history that began over one hundred years ago, giving it new and sometimes problematic depths.[5] There are at least a couple of aspects of *Cinema 1.0* that, thanks to *Cinema 2.0*, now become clearer. It is on these points that I would like to conclude.

The first concerns foresight. The many-sidedness of the current cinema—caught between new forms of production and consumption—permits us also to see how the old cinema was less unified than described here. Though it has worked primarily in a dimension of negotiating—well attested to by its oxymoronic gaze—there has been no lack of opposing paths characterized by radicalness, search without mediations, seemingly impossible proposals. The *Cinema 1.0* was also a restless field of utopia and discontent. But it is precisely these aspects, which in the past might have seemed slightly eccentric, that today reveal their productivity within the new media landscape. These scandalous presences anticipated a panorama such as the one in which we are immersed, made of differences without remains. This need to leave the logic of compromise behind anticipated a more fluid and shapeless time such as the one in which we now live. If I have insisted on a cinema that negotiates—arguing that its identity can be located in this function—this does not mean that there was not another cinema (and another modernity) for which we need to account, today more than ever, as it is today that we are seeing its aftereffects.[6]

The second feature relates instead to cinema's legacy. If there is something that the cinema did do along the path of the twentieth century, it was to revisit the universe in which we are immersed, as much in its realities as its possibilities, and to transform these into spectacle. This spectacle of the world in one way gave us back reality, thanks to a photographic image that established itself as its *trace*. In another way, it has systematically imposed a *representation*—concrete, yes, but only a representation nonetheless—over reality. It is not difficult to gather in this gesture, carried out with a hitherto untested radicalness, the echo of a dual need that has undoubtedly marked the twentieth century: on the one hand, the need to preserve the sense of the real, threatened by the advance of new ways of life, the horrors of history, the loss of social memory, the difficulties of reconstructing the levels of existence; on the other, though preserving the sense of the real, the predilection for subtly participating in its decline. The cinema seemed to respond to this dual need. And while it assured us that the world continued to be in some way present on the screen, through signs born as its trace, it also clarified that, in some respects, the world was no longer there. Thanks to these signs, the cinema seemed to leave the last word to the world, almost as if things could narrate themselves; at the same time, it narrated the world, leaving room for it only through signs. We were thus able to have an idea of keeping the real within our hands, even becoming its master, while it nonetheless mutated in its deepest features. Rudolf Arnheim offers a beautiful synthesis of this maneuver when he writes: "Up to a certain degree [film] gives the impression of real life. . . . On the other hand, it partakes strongly of the nature of a painting. . . . It is always at one and the same time a flat postcard and the scene of a living action."[7] Arnheim adds: "film gives simultaneously the effect of an actual happening and of a picture."[8] Hugo Münsterberg sees other implications: "The massive outer world has lost its weight; it has been freed from space, time, and causality, and it has been clothed in the forms of our own consciousness. The mind has triumphed over matter, and the pictures roll on with the ease of musical tones. It is a superb enjoyment which no other art can furnish us."[9] Thanks to film, we continue to deal with the real. In dealing with it, however, we let it become something else. In this way, of course, it became more our own; yet, in changing, it slipped through our fingers.

In this respect, the cinema went beyond its role of being a device through which vision regulated its own internal contradictions, new categories of thought emerged, and a true "direction of the eye" took place. The cinema, more radically still, was the instrument through which we preserved a relationship with the world and, at the same time, we reflected on its loss. In other words, the cinema is what sought to retain the real at the moment in which it left the horizon of our experience, and that contemporaneously inserted itself in the most general feeling of loss, which the century labeled as "loss of experience" or an "experience of loss." The cinema was a machine that, exploring the world, preserved it and made it available (I have insisted on its function as explorer and witness), but also a machine that has revealed how the world is becoming ever more indistinct (incomplete, as we see from the fragment; evasive, as we see from the point of view; unrecognizable, as we see from the shock). In other words, a device that offered us images so that they might perpetuate the presence of the real; yet one that, reducing the world to its images, also revealed how it was by then a tender or cruel illusion.

The Italian essayist Giovanni Papini concludes a 1907 article dedicated to the cinema in this way:

> Contemplating those ephemeral and brilliant images of ourselves, we feel almost as gods contemplating their own creations, made in their image and likeness. Involuntarily, it occurs to us that there is someone who watches us as we watch the small figures of the cinema and before whom we—who feel concrete, real, eternal—would not be but colored images, running swiftly toward death to create pleasure for his eyes. Couldn't the universe be, with few changes of program, a grandiose cinematographic performance made for the enjoyment of a crowd of powerful unknowns? And how we discover, thanks to photography, the imperfection of certain movements, the ridiculousness of some mechanical gestures, the grotesque vanity of human grimaces, so that those divine spectators will smile at us while we become restless on this small earth, running around furiously in every sense restless, stupefied, avid, comical, until our part ends and we are lowered one by one into the silent obscurity of death.[10]

How better to recount the cinema's capacity to return the world to us, as well as to take it away in reducing it to a spectacle? How better to express the sense of possession and loss that pursue one another and overlap, in an oxymoron that lies at the foundation of all the others that we have examined one by one? How better to evoke the pleasure of filling one's eyes, together with the sorrow before this race to the death of things? Yet what comes to light in those ephemeral and luminous images on the screen is precisely the splendor and the farewell, the exaltation and the mourning. In other words, the seizing hold and the vanishing, the conquest and the loss, in a game that is realized before our eyes and in which we ourselves are bound—a sumptuous game reserved, all in all, for the last gods.

Yes, the cinema was precisely and primarily this game of conquest and loss. And in this game, it offered itself as a lesson for its century, the *twentieth century*: as its *eye*.

NOTES

A HUNDRED YEARS, A CENTURY

1. Craquebille (Enrico Thovez), "L'arte di celluloide," *La Stampa* 42.209, Turin (July 29, 1908).
2. Let's recall some of the most influential contributions: Leo Charney and Vanessa R. Schwartz, eds., *Cinema and the Invention of Modern Life* (Berkeley: U of California P, 1995); Dudley Andrew, ed., *The Image in Dispute: Art and Cinema in the Age of Photography* (Austin: U of Texas P, 1997); Miriam Hansen, *Babel and Babylon: Spectatorship in American Silent Film* (Cambridge: Harvard UP, 1991); Tom Gunning, "The Cinema of Attractions: Early Film, Its Spectator, and the Avant-Garde," *Wide Angle* 8.3–4 (1986); Tom Gunning, "Le style non continu du cinéma des premiers temps," *Les Cahiers de la Cinémathèque* 29 (1979); Anne Friedberg, *Window Shopping: Cinema and the Postmodern* (Berkeley: U of California P, 1993); Charles Musser, *The Emergence of Cinema: The American Screen to 1907* (New York: Maxwell Macmillan International, 1990); Mary Ann Doane, *The Emergence of Cinematic Time: Modernity, Contingency, the Archive* (Cambridge: Harvard UP, 2002); Pierre Sorlin, *Les fils de Nadar: Le "siècle" de l'image analogique* (Paris: Nathan, 1997); Lauren Rabinovitz, *For the Love of Pleasure: Women, Movies, and Culture in Turn-of-the-Century Chicago* (New Brunswick: Rutgers UP, 1998); Antonio Costa, *I leoni di Schneider: Percorsi intertestuali nel cinema ritrovato* (Rome: Bulzoni, 2002); Antonio Costa, *Il cinema e le arti visive* (Turin: Einaudi, 2002); Alberto Abruzzese, *Forme estetiche e società di massa: Arte e pubblico nell'età del capitalismo* (Venice: Marsilio, 1973); Alberto Abruzzese, *Archeologie dell'immaginario: Segmenti dell'industria culturale tra '800 e '900* (Naples: Liguori, 1988); Thomas Elsaesser, "Cinema—The Irresponsible Signifier or The Gamble with History: Film Theory and Cinema Theory," *New German Critique* 40 (Winter 1987); Richard Allen, "The Aesthetic Experience of Modernity: Benjamin, Adorno, and Contemporary Film Theory," *New German Critique* 40 (Winter 1987): 225–40.

   Besides film studies, debate on modernity has in the last few years been very intense: at least see Marshall Berman, *All That Is Solid Melts into Air: The Experience of Modernity* (New York: Simon & Schuster, 1982); Stephen Kern, *The Culture of Time and Space, 1880–1918* (Cambridge: Harvard UP, 1983); Antoine

Compagnon, *The Five Paradoxes of Modernity* (New York: Columbia UP, 1994) / *Les cinq paradoxes de la modernité* (Paris: Seuil, 1990); David Frisby, *Fragments of Modernity: Theories of Modernity in the Work of Simmel, Kracauer, and Benjamin* (Cambridge: Polity Press, 1985); David Harvey, *The Condition of Postmodernity* (London: Blackwell, 1990).

3. I refer to the expression "the period eye" (translated as "occhio del Quattrocento" or "oeil du Quattrocento" in Italian and French translations) used by Michael Baxandall in *Painting and Experience in Fifteenth Century Italy: A Primer in the Social History of Pictorial Style* (Oxford: Clarendon Press, 1972). Baxandall speaks also of "the public eye" of the epoch (109).

4. On this issue, see Jonathan Crary, *Techniques of the Observer: On Vision and Modernity in the Nineteenth Century* (Cambridge and London: MIT Press, 1990), and Crary, *Suspension of Perception: Attention, Spectacle, and Modern Culture* (Cambridge: MIT Press, 1999).

5. Eugenio Giovannetti, *Il cinema e le arti meccaniche* (Palermo: Sandron, 1930), 39.

6. See two contributions in the special section devoted to historiography of cinema in *Cinema Journal*: Charles Musser, "Historiographic Method and the Study of Early Cinema," *Cinema Journal* 44.1 (Fall 2004): 101–107, with an open reference to the history of theatrical exhibitions and to the history of moving images, and Janet Staiger, "The Future of the Past," *Cinema Journal* 44.1 (Fall 2004): 126–29, with a reference to the history of media.

7. According to Thovez, this is precisely the reason why film is a mirror of its age: celluloid, "in its seeming and not being, in its deceiving with such glossy ease, in its sweet surrender to every need, it is really the symbol of the modern mentality and life." Thovez, "L'arte di celluloide."

8. Bela Balász, *Der Geist des Films* (Halle: Verlag Wilhelm Knapp, 1930), reprinted in in *Schriften zum Film*, vol. 2: 1926–1931 (Budapest: Akadémiai Kiadó, 1983), 63.

9. On this topic, see Rick Altman, "Dickens, Griffith, and Film: Film Theory Today," in Jane Gaines, ed., *Classical Hollywood Narrative: The Paradigm Wars*, 9–47 (Durham, N.C., and London: Duke UP, 1992). In particular, speaking of the classical novel and its influence on cinema, Altman claims that, "Though the protagonist trajectory may be what holds the novel together, assuring its 'classical' nature, the novel's internal dialectic is completed by the presence of an unpsychologized, dual focus tradition that the protagonist continually confronts." Altman, "Dickens," 21.

10. The idea that Hollywood, facing a set of tensions both in terms of social and gender identity as well as stylistic and narrative trends, provided different solutions every decade—some based on convergent and coherent solutions, some others displaying more conflictual patterns—is explored by Veronica Pravadelli in her *La grande Hollywood: Stili di vita e di regia nel cinema classico americano* (Venice: Marsilio, 2007). See also Gaines, ed., *Classical Hollywood Narrative*.

11. On the paradoxical nature of modernity, see Compagnon, *The Five Paradoxes*.

1. THE GAZE OF ITS AGE

1. Bela Balázs, *Der sichtbare Mensch oder die Kultur des Films* (Vienna and Leipzig: Deutsch-Österreichischer Verlag, 1924), reprinted in *Schriften zum Film*, vol. 1: 1922–1926 (Budapest: Akadémiai Kiadó, 1982), 51–53 (italics in original).
2. Sebastiano A. Luciani, *L'antiteatro: Il cinematografo come arte* (Rome: La Voce Anonima Editrice, 1928), 76.
3. Jean Epstein, "Le regard du verre," *Les Cahiers du mois* 16–17 (1925). The argument will then be continued and developed the following year in *Le cinématographe vue de l'Etna* (Paris: Les Ecrivains Réunis, 1926).
4. Abel Gance, "Le temps de l'image est venu," *L'art cinématographique* 2:94 (Paris: Alcan, 1927).
5. The idea would, however, continue on even after the 1920s, and would in some way inspire one of the seminal books of reflection on cinema, *Theory of Film* by S. Kracauer, a key passage which I would evoke: "Film renders visible what we did not, or perhaps even could not, see before its advent. It effectively assists us in discovering the material world with its psychophysical correspondences. We literally redeem this world from its dormant state, its state of virtual nonexistence, by endeavoring to experience it through the camera." Siegfried Kracauer, *Theory of Film: The Redemption of Physical Reality* (Oxford: Oxford University Press, 1960), 300.
6. I use the expression "spirit of the time," particularly with regard to the age of modernity, but with the greatest caution, mindful of, if nothing else, what Franco Moretti suggests: "A long way from Hegel's spirit of the times, in the singular, recurring in every picture, every novel, and every symphony! Literary history is a battlefield—and especially, as we shall see, in the years of modernism." Franco Moretti, *Modern Epic: The World-System from Goethe to Garc'ia Marquez* (London and New York: Verso, 1996), 150.
7. Luciani, *L'antiteatro*, 76.
8. Erwin Panofsky, "Style and Medium in the Motion Picture," *Bulletin of the Department of Art and Archaeology*, Princeton University (1934), then reprinted in *Critique* 3 (1947), and in Daniel Talbot, ed., *Film: An Anthology* (Berkeley: U of California P, 1966), and in Gerald Mast, Marshall Cohen, and Leo Braudy, eds., *Film Theory and Criticism* (New York and Oxford: Oxford UP, 1992), 247.
9. The quotation comes from the famous article "The Little Shopgirls Go to the Movies" ("Die kleinen Ladenmädchen gehen ins Kino"), in which Kracauer recalls recurrent themes of the film of the age. The essay, which synthesizes a series of articles appearing in the *Frankfurter Zeitung* in March 1927, is part of the collection, *The Mass Ornament: Weimar Essays* (Cambridge and London: Harvard UP, 1995), 294 (*Das Ornament der Masse* [Frankfurt: Suhrkamp Verlag, 1963]). Also memorable is his vast work of film criticism featured in the same journal; the reviews are available in part in the volume Siegfried Kracauer, *Kino: Essays, Studien, Glossen zum Film* (Frankfurt: Suhrkamp, 1974).
10. Léon Moussinac, *Naissance du cinéma* (Paris: Povolozky, 1925), 7.

11. The essay, which appeared in various forms (the genesis and rewritings of which were brought to light by Miriam Hansen) has its best-known version in Walter Benjamin, "L'oeuvre d'art à l'époque de sa reproduction mécanisée," *Zeischrift für Sozialforschung* 1 (1936). The *Selected Writings* volumes present the two main versions of this essay: "The Work of Art in the Age of Its Technological Reproducibility: Third Version," in *Selected Writings, 1938–1940*, vol. 4, 251–82 (Cambridge and London: Belknap Press of Harvard UP, 2003); and the earlier "The Work of Art in the Age of Its Technological Reproducibility: Second Version," in *Selected Writings, 1935–1938*, vol. 3, 101–133 (Cambridge and London: Belknap Press, 2002). Here, we may refer to both versions.

12. Benjamin, "Work of Art: Third Version," 255; "Work of Art: Second Version," 104. Andrea Pinotti, in *Piccola storia della lontananza: Benjamin storico della percezione* (Milan: Cortina, 2001), brought to light this Benjaminian idea's debt to Aloïs Riegl and Heinrich Wölfflin.

13. Benjamin, "Work of Art: Third Version," 255. In the "Second Version" we read: "both linked to the increasing emergence of the masses and the growing intensity of their movements," 105.

14. Benjamin, "Work of Art: Third Version," 255; "Third Version" omits a part of the sentence.

15. Benjamin, "Work of Art: Third Version," 265; "Second Version," 117.

16. Benjamin, "Work of Art: Third Version," 265; "Second Version," 117.

17. Benjamin, "Work of Art: Third Version," 267; "Second Version," 119.

18. Benjamin, "Work of Art: Third Version," 262. In ""Second version" we read: "In the case of film, the newsreel demonstrates unequivocally that any individual can be in a position to be filmed," 114.

19. Benjamin, "Work of Art: Third Version," 26; "Second Version," 113.

20. "Clearly, there is another nature which speaks to the camera as compared with the eye. 'Other' above all in the sense that a space informed by human consciousness gives way to a space informed by the unconscious." Benjamin, "Work of Art: Third Version," 266; "Second Version," 117.

21. For the difference between cultural value and exhibition value, and of the shift of art in age of mechanical reproduction from the first to the second, see Benjamin, "Work of Art: Third Version," 257 ff.; "Second Version," 106 ff.

22. If I rely on the theoretical texts of the period, it is because I find that here (as well as in the broader picture of the vast web of social discourse) the cinema begins to be perceived as a complex but precise reality. It becomes a common reference; it is "that" thing with which we would reckon for the next seventy years. On the production side, there was a similar "institutionalization" of cinema, analogous in its function, though not always in its contents.

23. The expression "fifth art" is Delluc's, while "eighth art" belongs to Canudo, who then opted for the most noted "seventh art." For more information on the latter, see in particular Ricciotto Canudo, *L'usine aux images* (Paris: Chiron, 1927).

24. See Canudo's "Lettere d'arte: Il trionfo del cinematografo," *Nuovo giornale* (November 25, 1908), reprinted in *Filmcritica* 28.278 (1977): 296–302; a subsequent version of this essay would become his most famous text, "La naissance d'une sixième art: Essai sur le cinématographe," *Les Entretiens Idéalistes* (October 25, 1911). The tendency of twentieth-century intellectuals to apply to film categories developed close to the traditional arts, together with their often ambiguous perception that film constitutes a totally new terrain, in which the emergence and development of a cultural industry and a medial system are at stake, has been well emphasized on several occasions by Alberto Abruzzese, beginning with *Forme estetiche e società di massa* and *L'immagine filmica: Materiali di studio* (Rome: Bulzoni, 1974). More recently the topic was taken up again in Sergio Brancato, *Introduzione alla sociologia del cinema* (Rome: Luca Sossella Editore, 2001).

25. The essay was published for the first time in 1919 in *Le film*, and reissued the following year in *Cinéma et Cie* as "L'art du cinema." See Louis Delluc, "L'art du cinéma," reprinted in *Écrits cinématographiques* vol. 2 (Paris: Cinémathèque Française, Ed. de l'Etoile Cahiers du Cinéma, 1990), 114–18.

26. For an analysis of the media as instrument of transmission, representation, and relation, see Francesco Casetti, "Lettera ad Enzensberger," in Alberto Abruzzese and Gabriele Montagano, eds., *Caro Enzensberger: Il destino della televisione* (Milan: Lupetti, 1992).

27. Benjamin points out a medium's ability to organize human sensory perception in a certain way: if it is the representational dimension that is privileged, the context of his discourse provides nevertheless for making clear the other functions of medium as well.

28. On this subject, we must remember Benjamin's cutting irony toward film theorists. "Though commentators had earlier expended much fruitless ingenuity on the question of whether photography was an art—without asking the more fundamental question of whether the invention of photography had not transformed the entire character of art—film theorists quickly adopted the same ill-considered standpoint" (Benjamin, "Work of Art: Third Version," 258). Benjamin adds: "It is instructive to see how the desire to annex film to 'art' impels these theoreticians to attribute elements of cult to film—with a striking lack of discretion" (259). What Benjamin did not anticipate is that film, sixty years later, would become once again cult object, even before display object.

29. Let us think for example how elsewhere Benjamin contrasts fashion to art, attributing to the former a greater capacity to understand the processes of the moment, if for nothing else than by virtue of the group of consumers for whom it is intended (and for the fact that it is intended for a group of consumers): "It is well known that art will often—for example, in pictures—precede the perceptible reality by years. . . . Moreover, the sensitivity of the individual artist to what is coming certainly far exceeds that of the *grande*

dame. Yet fashion is in much steadier, much more precise contact with the coming thing, thanks to the incomparable nose which the feminine collective has for what lies waiting in the future. Each season brings, in its newest creations, various secret signals of things to come. Whoever understands how to read these semaphores would know in advance not only about new currents in the arts but also about new legal codes, wars, and revolutions." Walter Benjamin, *The Arcades Project* (Cambridge: Belknap Press of Harvard UP), 63–64; "Das Passagen Werk," in *Gesammelte Schriften*, vols. 1–2 (Frankfurt am Main: Suhrkamp Verlag, 1982).

30. On the "mediazation" of art, see also this biting observation of Benjamin's: "for the first time in world history, technological reproducibility emancipates the work of art from its parasitic subservience to ritual. To an ever-increasing degree, the work reproduced becomes the reproduction of a work designed for reproducibility." Benjamin, "The Work of Art: Third Version," 256.

31. Benjamin, at least it seems to me, does not clearly explore this path, which seems especially interesting today. On this new task of both action and aesthetic reflection, see the works of Pietro Montani, in particular *L'immaginazione narrativa: Il racconto del cinema oltre i confini dello spazio letterario* (Milan: Guerini, 1999).

32. Louis Delluc, "Le cinéma, art populaire," reprinted in *Écrits cinématographiques* 2:279–88.

33. "Rio Jim . . . ordinary as Orestes, moves within an eternal tragedy without psychological 'hitches.' I spoke to you about *Pour sauver sa race*. Did the terrible woman who played Louise Glaum not have the fatal splendor of Clytemnestra? Did Bessie Love not evoke the modesty and savage energy of Electra?" Delluc, "Le cinéma, art populaire," 286.

34. On the "in-forming" process, carried out by each medium, see Francesco Casetti and Ruggero Eugeni, "I media in forma: Il lavoro della pubblicità dalla réclame alla pubblicità," in Fausto Colombo, ed., *I persuasori non occulti* (Milan: Lupetti, 1989).

35. Rollin Summers, "The Moving Picture Drama and the Acted Drama: Some Points of Comparison as to Technique," *Moving Picture World* (September 19, 1908); reprinted in Stanley Kauffmann and Bruce Henstell, eds., *American Film Criticism: From the Beginnings to " Citizen Kane"* (New York: Liveright, 1972), 10.

36. David Bordwell, *On History of Film Style* (Cambridge and London: Harvard UP, 1997).

37. Giovannetti, *Il cinema e le arti meccaniche*, 23.

38. Panofsky, "Style and Medium in the Motion Picture," in Talbot, ed., *Film: An Anthology*, 240. Let's recall that, like Summers, Panofsky also speaks of "legitimate, that is, exclusive, possibilities and limitations" of the medium (240).

39. Rudolf Arnheim, *Film* (London: Faber & Faber, 1933), then republished with changes as *Film as Art* (Berkeley: U of California P, 1957); originally, *Film als Kunst* (Berlin: Ernst Rowohlt Verlag, 1932). Clearly, it would be Marshall McLu-

han, in the wake of Innis, who extended the idea of a "specificity" or at least a "characteristic" of each medium.

40. I have tried to show film's ties to the more general circuits of social discourse (and social practices) in Casetti, "Adaptations and Mis-adaptations: Film, Literature, and Social discourses," in Robert Stam and Alessandra Raengo, eds., *A Companion to Literature and Film* (Oxford: Blackwell, 2005), 81–91.

41. Louis Delluc, "La photoplastique au cinéma," *Paris-Midi*, July 6, 1918, reprinted in *Écrits cinématographiques* 2:210–12.

42. Berman's *All That Is Solid Melts into Air* is a good introduction to the great processes that mark modernity; see also Kern, *The Culture of Time and Space*; Compagnon, *The Five Paradoxes of Modernity*; Frisby, *Fragments of Modernity*; and Harvey, *The Condition of Postmodernity*.

43. Benjamin, "The Work of Art: Third Version," 267; "Second Version," 119.

44. Benjamin, "The Work of Art: Third Version," 269; "Second Version," 120.

45. Benjamin, "The Work of Art: Third Version," 266; "Second Version," 117.

46. Benjamin, "The Work of Art: Third Version," 263; "Second Version," 115.

47. Siegfried Kracauer, "Cult of Distraction: On Berlin's Picture Palaces," *The Mass Ornament: Weimar Essays* ("Kult der Zerstreuung" originally published in *Frankfurter Allgemeine*, March 4, 1926, then included in *Das Ornament der Masse*, 1963). For a better understanding of Kracauer's positions and evolution in the years of *Frankfurter Zeitung* (years that spanned practically the entire second decade of the century), see in particular Miriam Hansen, "America, Paris, the Alps: Kracauer (and Benjamin) on Cinema and Modernity," in Charney and Schwartz, eds., *Cinema and the Invention of Modern Life*, 363–402.

48. Raymond Spottiswoode, *A Grammar of the Film: An Analysis of Film Technique*, (London: Faber & Faber, 1935), 257.

49. On the avant-garde's deep functionality to mass culture, see Abruzzese, *Forme estetiche* and *L'immagine filmica*. On the necessity of a reconsideration of classical cinema in a tone that renders less "classical" its action, see Miriam Hansen, "The Mass Production of the Senses: Classical Cinema as Vernacular Modernism," in Christine Gledhill and Linda Williams, eds., *Reinventing Film Studies* (New York: Arnold; London: Oxford University Press, 2000), 332–50. For a rearticulation of the "classical paradigm," see Gaines, ed., *Classical Hollywood Narrative*.

50. On negotiation in communicative processes, see Francesco Casetti, *Communicative Negotiation in Cinema and Television* (Milan: Vita e Pensiero, 2002); see also Christine Gledhill, "Pleasurable Negotiations," in Sue Thornham, ed., *Feminist Film Theory: A Reader* (New York: New York UP, 1999), 166–79.

51. See Hansen, *Babel and Babylon*, and "The Mass Production of the Senses."

2. FRAMING THE WORLD

1. Balász, *Der sichtbare Mensch* (1924), reprinted in *Schriften zum Film*, vol. 1: 1922–1926 (1982); and Balász, *Der Geist des Films* (1930), reprinted in *Schriften zum*

Film, vol. 2: 1926–1931 (1983). All quotations are from the reprint volumes. On Balász and his position as film theorist, see Malcom Turvey, "Balász: Realist or Modernist?" *October* 115 (Winter 2006): 77–87.

2. Balász, *Der sichtbare Mensch*, 83.

3. Balász, *Der sichtbare Mensch*, 76.

4. Balász, *Der sichtbare Mensch*, 83.

5. Balászv *Der sichtbare Mensch*, 88. The idea of lining up a series of shots devoted to a fuller perception of the real leads Balász to theorize the *Querschnittfilm* ("horizontal film"), which gives a cross section of life through a progressive extension of examples. Adding gazes upon gazes, it "can literally become an art of Weltanschauung, as it is able to go over—so quickly, as to give the impression of simultaneity—the contiguities that constitute the most far-ranging faces of life. Balász, "Vorstoß in eine neue Dimension," *Die literarische Welt* 5 (November 1926), reprinted in *Schriften zum Film* 2:213.

6. Balász, *Der Geist des Films*, 70.

7. Balász, *Der Geist des Films*, 71.

8. Balász, *Der Geist des Films*, 71. See also: "The images captured reveal the director's intentions with respect to the object that they capture: his sympathy or aversion, his emotion or irony. In this, it is the propagandistic strength of the film that must not demonstrate a thesis conceptually, but must make it be absorbed visually" (73).

9. Balász, *Der Geist des Films*, 70–71.

10. Balász, *Der Geist des Films*, 146.

11. Erwin Panofsky, *Perspective as Symbolic Form* (New York: Zone Books, 1991); originally, "Die Perspektive als 'symbolishe Form,'" in *Vortäge der Bibliothek Warburg: Voraäge, 1924–25* (Leipzig and Berlin: Teubner, 1927). For a new consideration of perspective and point of view, see the excellent introduction by Christopher Wood for the English translation of Panofsky's work. See also Antonio Somaini, *Rappresentazione prospettica e punto di vista: Da Leon Battista Alberti a Abraham Bosse* (Milan: CUEM, 2004); and Antonio Somaini, "L'immagine prospettica e la distanza dello spettatore," in Antonio Somaini, ed., *Il luogo dello spettatore* (Milan: Vita e Pensiero, 2005), 53–92.

12. Panofsky, *Perspective*, 67. Panofsky adds: "Perspective mathematizes this visual space, and yet it is very much *visual* space that it mathematizes; it is an ordering, but an ordering of the visual phenomenon" (71).

13. "Plato condemned [the perspectival view of space] already in its modest beginnings because it distorted the true proportions of things, and replaced reality and the nomos (law) with subjective appearance and arbitrariness; whereas the most modern aesthetic thinking accuses it, on the contrary, of being the tool of a limited and limiting rationalism." Panofsky, *Perspective*, 71.

14. Henry James, "Prefaces to the New York Edition (1907–1909)," in *Literary Criticism*, vol. 2 (New York: Literary Classics of the United States, 1984), 1035–1341.

15. The coincidence between the birth of cinema and the Jamesian theory of the novel has been stressed by many, among them Keith Cohen, *Film and Fiction: The Dynamics of Exchange* (New Haven: Yale UP, 1979). A revival of the Jamesian theory takes place in years in which Balázs writes his major works: see Joseph Warren Beach, *The Method of Henry James* (New Haven: Yale UP, 1918); and Percy Lubbock, *The Craft of Fiction* (New York: J. Cape & H. Smith, 1929).

16. In the preface to *The Ambassadors*, James clarifies this condition: "But Strether's sense of these things, and Strether's only, should avail me for showing them; I should know them but through his more or less groping knowledge of them, since his very gropings would figure among his most interesting motions, and a full observance of the rich rigour I speak of would give me more of the effect I should be most 'after' than all other possible observance together. It would give me a large unity, and that in turn crown me with the grace to which the enlightened story-teller will at any time, for his interest, sacrifice if need be all other graces whatever." James, "Prefaces," 1313.

17. James, "Prefaces," 1075 (Preface to *Portrait of a Lady*). It goes without saying that Leon Battista Alberti as well, when speaking of perspective, proposes the image of the painting as an open window on the world.

18. One might call that "a subjective vision"; except, in James's view, what ensures a story's objectivity is precisely the fact that it is anchored to information that is in some way certain.

19. Crary, *Techniques of the Observer*. I would add that, for Crary, this idea of the eye as a simple passageway finds its principal confirmation in the fifteenth-century *camera obscura*. In the first half of the nineteenth century, there was a repudiation of this device and the philosophies of knowledge that were reshaped with it (as in Locke or in Descartes). Scientists advanced a new conceptual paradigm that would find its defining moment in new mechanisms such as the stereoscopic device and then the cinema.

20. An example: Impressionism is inconceivable outside of this epistemological turn. For an analysis of Impressionism in this light, and for a reading of it as film's forerunner, see Jacques Aumont, *L'oeil interminable: Cinéma et peinture* (Paris: Séguier, 1989).

21. See, in particular, the brief but dense essay "Experience and Poverty," in Walter Benjamin, *Selected Writings*, vol. 2: *1927–1934* (Cambridge and London: Belknap Press of Harvard UP, 1999), 731–36.

22. E[nrico] Toddi, "Rettangolo-Film (25 x 19)," In *Penombra* 1.3 (August 25, 1918): 121–23.

23. Sergei M. Eisenstein, "The Dynamic Square," *Close-Up* (March-June 1931).

24. Even the reduction carried out by the photogram follows a logic analogous to that of the point of view. As Toddi suggests, "we 'aim at' an object" even when we have under our vision ample portions of space, and thus in the focusing we construct a point of view within the visual field. Toddi, *Rettangolo-Film*, 122.

25. Jean Epstein, "Le sens 1bis," *Cinéa* (July 22, 1921), then in *Bonjour cinéma* (Paris: Éditions de La Sirène, 1921), reprinted now in *Écrits sur le cinéma*, vol. 1 (Paris: Cinéma club/Seghers, 1974) 93.

26. Epstein, "Le sens 1bis," 92–93.

27. In the vast bibliography on *Napoléon*, see at least the book written by Gance on his own film (Abel Gance, *Napoléon vu par Abel Gance: Épopée cinégraphique en cinq époques,* Paris: Plon, 1927), and the book by Kevin Brownlow devoted to the film restored by him, *Napoléon: Abel Gance's Classic Film* (London: Cape, 1983). See also Richard Abel, *French Cinema: The First Wave, 1915–1919* (Princeton: Princeton UP, 1984); Abel takes into account the film's project, as well as its production structure, linguistic construction, reactions to its release, and finally, its successive restorations. Interesting critical remarks are found in Steven Garrett, "Leaving History: Dickens, Gance, Blanchot," *Yale Journal of Criticism* 2.2 (Spring 1989): 145–90.

28. Earlier, the film offered an image of the friars intent on following the snowball fight. They are seen through a glass door, each of them behind a different frame: it is the perfect prefiguration of the split screen

29. Abel Gance, *Napoléon: Épopée cinématographique en cinq époques* (Paris: Jacques Bertoin, 1991; new edition of Gance's *Napoléon vu*), 4. On superimposition, see also the superb analysis in Marc Vernet, *Figures de l'absence* (Paris: Ed. de l'Etoile, 1988).

30. Blaise Cendrars, *L'ABC du cinéma* (Paris: Les Écrivains réunis, 1926); now in *Aujourd'hui, 1917–1929,* in *Oeuvres complètes*, vol. 4 (Paris: Denoël, 1960), 162–66. The text is dated 1917–1921.

31. Benjamin, "Work of Art: Third Version" (*Selected Writings*, vol. 4), 282; see also the "Second Version" (*Selected Writings*, vol. 3), 132. See also the acute analysis of aerial vision in twentieth-century culture in Franco La Polla, "Il cinema e le arti popolari," in *Stili americani* (Bologna: Bonomia UP, 2002).

32. Blaise Cendrars, "The Modern: A New Art, the Cinema," in Richard Abel, ed., *French Film Theory and Criticism*, vol. 1 (Princeton: Princeton UP, 1984), 182–83 (originally, "Modernités—Un nouveau art: le cinéma," *La rose rouge* 7.12, [June 1919]: 108). See also in Cendrars: "A hundred worlds, a thousand movements, a million events entering simultaneously into the field of that eye given to man by the cinema. And that eye is more marvelous, though arbitrary, than the faceted eye of a fly" (Cendrars, *L'ABC*, 164). And also Jean Epstein: "I descended as if through the facets of an immense insect's eye" (Epstein, *Le cinématographe vue de l'Etna* [1926], reprinted in *Écrits sur le cinéma* 1:136).

33. Gance, "Appel adressée le 4 juin 1924 a tous ces collaborateurs," in *Napoléon: Épopée*, 8.

34. As Gance's companion Nelly Kaplan would remember almost thirty years later in an affectionate posthumous homage: "Only one art exists—the most wonderful as it combines and condenses all of them—that possesses the richness and poetry necessary to translate, reflect and sublimate the movement and becoming of the atomic age, in which speed, ubiquity, and hereto-

fore unknown sensations become or will become an everyday thing. This art is the cinema." Nelly Kaplan, *Manifeste d'un art nouveau: la Polyvision* (Paris : Caractéres, 1955).

35. Abel, *French Cinema*, 441, effectively highlights this passage.

36. *Translator's note:* In Italian, to play blindman's bluff is *giocare a mosca cieca* (literally, "to play the blind fly").

37. Blaise Cendrars, *La fin du monde filmée par l'ange N.-D.* (Paris: Éditions de la Sirène, 1919); reprinted in *Édition complete*, vol. 2 (Paris: Denoël, 1960), 7–50.

38. Abel, *French Cinema*, 435.

39. François Truffaut, *Hitchcock* (New York: Simon & Schuster, 1967); originally, *Le Cinéma selon Hitchcock* (Paris: R. Laffont, 1966).

40. Hugo Münsterberg, *The Photoplay: A Psychological Study* (New York: Appleton, 1916), 73–74.

41. Münsterberg, *The Photoplay*, 85.

42. Münsterberg, *The Photoplay*, 89.

43. Münsterberg, *The Photoplay*, 87.

44. Münsterberg, *The Photoplay*, 91.

45. "The particular, the detail, will be always a synonym of intensification": Vsevelod I. Pudovkin, *Film Technique* (London: G. Newnes, 1933), 63; the volume synthesizes two booklets by Pudovkin: *Kinorežissër i kinomaterial* (Moscow: Kinopeciat, 1926) and *Kinoscenari* (Moscow: Kinopeciat, 1926). The quoted sentence comes from the former.

46. Crary, *Suspension of Perception*.

47. Crary, *Suspension*, 4.

48. Crary, *Suspension*, 12.

49. Crary, *Suspension*, 12.

50. Crary, *Suspension*, 17.

51. Jean Epstein, "Grossissement," in *Bonjour cinéma* (1921), reprinted in *Écrits sur le cinéma* 1:98.

52. Beyond the close-up, there is also the *iris*; in it, most of the image is obfuscated. Only a small portion is left, on which the gaze inevitably concentrates.

53. Pudovkin, *Film Technique*, 41; the passage belongs to *Kinoscenari* (1926).

54. André Bazin, "William Wyler ou le janséniste de la mise en scène," *Revue du Cinema* (1948), reprinted in *Qu'est ce que le cinéma*, vol. 1: *Ontologie et langage* (Paris: Éd. du Cerf, 1958). Bazin recognizes that, with découpage, the camera behaves like our eye; it "settles in spatially on the important point of the event . . . and proceeds on to successive investigations"; this means that a director who uses découpage "takes control of the discrimination that lies with us in real life" (157). Bazin, however, adds that we "unconsciously accept this analysis because it conforms to the laws of attention. Yet it strips us of a privilege equally grounded in psychology, which we have without realizing it: the freedom, at least virtual, to modify in each moment our system of découpage" (158)

55. Bazin does not know it, but his battle for the active role of the spectator can be read as a response to Benjamin and his idea that a film with excessive pressure provokes a "reception in distraction." For the latter, see Benjamin, "Work of Art: Third Version," 269; "Second Version," 120.

56. I would make two observations on modern film's banalization of the center of the attention. On the one hand, it seems to find compensation in the discovery of an image—any image even—capable of making an entire field of forces converge on it. The image-crystal theorized by Gilles Deleuze in *Time-Image* (Minneapolis: U of Minnesota P, 1989) is a perfect example. On the other hand, the compensation operates at a theoretical level: in the 1980s the theme of attention would be revived, thanks to studies like those of François Jost, *L'oeil-camera: Entre film et roman* (Lyon: Presses Universitaries de Lyon, 1987).

57. In the vast bibliography on M, see at least Tom Gunning, "M: The City Haunted by Demoniac Desire," *The Films of Fritz Lang: Allegories of Vision and Modernity* (London: BFI, 2000); Anton Kaes, M (London: BFI, 2000); and Bernard Eisen-schitz, *M le maudit, un film de Fritz Lang* (Paris: Le Cinématheque Française/ Éditions Plume, 1990). See also Stephen Jenkins, ed., *Fritz Lang: The Image and the Look* (London: BFI, 1981); and Paolo Bertetto and Bernard Eisenschitz, eds., *Fritz Lang: La messa in scena* (Turin: Lindau, 1993).

58. Bazin summarizes this double function of the filmic image's edges, saying that they are both *frame* (*cadre*) and mask (*cache*). André Bazin, "Painting and Cinema," in *What Is Cinema?* 1:164–69; originally, "Peinture et cinéma," in *Qu'est ce que le cinéma* 2:127–32.

59. On the offscreen and its structural role, see the essential Noel Burch, *Theory of Film Practice* (Princeton: Princeton UP, 1981); originally, *Praxis du cinema* (Paris: Gallimard, 1969). On the offscreen as implicit, see also Francesco Casetti, "I bordi dell'immagine," *Versus* 29 (May-August 1981): 93–115.

60. On the composition of classical cinema, see the stimulating pages of David Bordwell, Janet Staiger, and Kristin Thompson, *Classical Hollywood Cinema: Film Style and Mode of Production to 1960* (London: Routledge & Kegan Paul, 1985). On the role of the center, see Rudolf Arnheim, *The Power of the Center: A Study of Composition in the Visual Arts* (Berkeley: U of California P, 1982).

61. On the disappearance of single photograms and interspace, see the classic article by Thierry Kuntzel, "Le defilement du film," *Revue d'estetique* 2–4 (1973): 97–110.

62. Beyond the spatial offscreen, there is also the temporal offscreen: it is the ellipsis, that moment between two actions or two phases of an action that editing often loses to render the story more solid. On the ellipsis, see Casetti, "I bordi dell'immagine".

63. On the invisible as the sense horizon to which the filmic image tends, see two works with different accents: Virgilio Melchiorre, *L'immaginazione simbolica* (Bologna: Il Mulino, 1972), and Elio Franzini, *Fenomenologia dell'invisibile* (Milan: Cortina, 2001). I cite Franzini in particular to point out the difference,

but also a correlation, between the stylistic approach to the offscreen (such as Burch) and a more "philosophical" approach: in the first case, what the image does not offer the spectator's eye (though evoking it) is considered fundamentally implicit; in Franzini's study, beyond what we see there is the pre-categorical dimension of the image. Finally, next to an implicit invisible and a pre-categorical invisible, there is also a censured invisible: on the mechanisms that are produced by a "social exclusion" of entire segments of reality to the "emphasis" of others, see Pierre Sorlin, *Sociologie du cinema* (Paris: Aubier, 1977).

64. Victor O. Freeburg, *The Art of Photoplay Making* (New York: Macmillan, 1918); see in particular ch. 6, "The Appeal to the Imagination," 90–111.
65. Freeburg, *Art of Photoplay*, 94.
66. Freeburg, *Art of Photoplay*, 90. The following quotation is from the same page.
67. Mario Ponzo, "Di alcune osservazioni psicologiche fatte durante rappresentazioni cinematografiche," *Atti della R. Accademia delle scienze di Torino* 46 (1910–11) (Turin: Vincenzo Bona, 1911), 943–48.
68. Robert Bresson, *Notes sur le cinématographe* (Paris: Gallimard, 1975), 89.
69. Bresson, *Notes*, 95.
70. Bresson, *Notes*, 55.
71. Bresson, *Notes*, 90.
72. Bresson, *Notes*, 51.
73. Bresson, *Notes*, 56.
74. I will return to this subject. However, on imagination at the cinema, see the important contribution by Pietro Montani, *L'immaginazione narrativa*, to which here I am in debt.
75. It might be useful to reread in this light a contribution such as the one by Rudolf Arnheim, *Film*. Arnheim emphasizes the filmic image's incapacity to return the captured object to us as it *actually* is. Yet it is precisely this incapacity that constitutes the aesthetic basis of film.
76. The stereoscopic viewer, as common as the player piano, was found in many homes at the second half of the nineteenth century.
77. The relative bibliography is immense. I will indicate only those in the field of film studies. Antonio Costa, ed., *La meccanica del visibile: Il cinema delle origini in Europa* (Florence: La Casa Usher, 1983); Laurence Mannoni, *Le grand art de la lumière et de l'ombre: Archéologie du cinéma* (Paris: Nathan, 1995); and Gian Piero Brunetta, *Il viaggio dell'icononauta* (Venice: Marsilio, 1997). On optical devices in nineteenth-century culture, see also Lucilla Albano, *La caverna dei giganti* (Parma: Pratiche, 1982). For a history of lighting in the nineteenth century, see Wolfgang Schivelbusch, *Disenchanted Night: The Industrialization of Light in the Nineteenth Century* (Berkeley: U of California P, 1988); originally, *Lichtblicke: Zur Geschichte der Künstlichen Helligkeit im 19. Jahrhundert* (Munich: Carl Hanser Verlag, 1983). For a history of the railroad, with particular emphasis on the kind of visual experience that it brought, see Wolfgang Schivelbusch, *Railway*

Journey: Trains and Travel in the 19th *Century* (New York: Urizen, 1979); origi-nally, *Geschichte der Eisenbahnreise* (Munich: Carl Hanser Verlag, 1977).

78. Verlaine describes this sensation in some splendid verses: "The scene behind the carriage window-panes/Goes flitting past in furious flight; whole plains/ With streams and harvest-fields and trees and blue/Are swallowed by the whirlpool, whereinto/The telegraph's slim pillars topple o'er,/Whose wires look strangely like a music-score." "La bonne chanson" (1870), in *Poems of Paul Verlaine,* translated by Gertrude Hall (New York: Duffield, 1906). Schivel-busch, *Railway Journey,* dedicated some extraordinary pages to the "loss of landscape" tied to train voyages.

79. The field of literature offers significant examples: in Hoffman's stories, so rich in visual references, Max Milner, *La fantasmagorie* (Paris: PUF, 1982), shows that the optical instruments crush the idea of visual perception. They are presented as a constant font of deception, perdition, and death; knowl-edge passes through vision, but vision does not always offer correct and pro-ductive knowledge. Milner reminds us that the source of this contradiction lies in an epistemological revolution: "Everything changes—and the revolu-tion began with Kant—when man is no longer conceived as a being who receives knowledge of a world governed by the laws of optics, but as a being who receives, through the different senses, messages to gather and inter-pret information in order to construct an image of the world that requires the participation of all his being. The eye is not an optical apparatus that transmits to the brain images that exist as they are externally. It is instead an instrument of codification and decodification that transmits information, which must be continually interpreted and whose interpretation varies ac-cording to the nature of the signals received and the internal dispositions of the being who receives them." What Milner relates back to Kant, Crary in *Techniques of the Observer* relates back to physiologists in the first decades of the nineteenth century.

80. On *décadrage,* see Pascal Bonitzer, *Décadrages: Peinture et cinéma* (Paris: Édi-tions de l'Etoile/Seuil, 1985).

81. Serge Daney, *Persévérance* (Paris: P.O.L. Éditeur, 1994), 26.

82. The flashbacks are, respectively, those of Thatcher (through written memo-ries), Bernstein, Leland, Susan Alexander, Raymond, in addition to a lost wit-ness, Thompson's first meeting with Susan, and the newsreel that functions as testimony not reducible to a single subject-narrator.

83. It is curious to recall that critics of the age had difficulty seeing the name on the sled: "I did not catch it, nor did any other reviewer I have read. On the way home, Mrs Spectator told me about the name on the burning sleigh." Walford Beaton, in *Hollywood Spectator* 15.7 (May 1, 1941): 7; reprinted in Anto-ny Slide, *Selected Film Criticism,* 1941–1950 (Metuchen, N.J., and London: Scare-crow Press, 1983), 42.

84. Fausto Maria Martini, "La morte della parola," *La Tribuna* (February 16, 1912).

3. DOUBLE VISION

1. Balász, *Der Geist des Films* (1930), reprinted in *Schriften zum Film*, vol. 2 (1983). All quotations are from the reprint version.

2. Balász, *Der Geist*, 71.

3. Balász, *Der Geist*, 74.

4. See this passage: "Is it therefore impossible for us to see things as pure and simply as they really are?" The answer is: "The single frames can be a simple documentation of the naked object, but the general principle of form comes from the subject." Balázs, *Der Geist*, 124.

5. Balázs, *Der Geist*, 125.

6. Elena Dagrada maintained that the idea of subjectivity at the cinema emerges in relation to the popularization of the story-form. Cf. Elena Dagrada, "Le figure dell''io' e la nascita della soggettiva," in Lucilla Albano, ed., *Modelli non letterari nel cinema* (Rome: Bulzoni, 1999), 63–80.

7. René Allendy, "La valeur psychologique de l'image," in *L'art cinématographique*, vol. 2 (Paris: Alcan, 1926), 75–103.

8. Allendy, "La valeur," 75.

9. Allendy, "La valeur," 75.

10. Allendy, "La valeur," 77.

11. Georg Lukács, "Thoughts on an Aesthetic for the Cinema." *Frameworks* 14 (Spring 1981); originally, "Gedanken zu einer Ästhetik des 'Kino,'" *Frankfurter Allgemeine Zeitung* 251 (September 10, 1913): 1–2, reprinted in *Schriften zur Literatursoziologie* (Neuwied: Luchterhand, 1961), 75–80. There is a previous version in *Pester Lloyd* 90, Budapest (April 16, 1911): 45–46, reprinted in Jörg Schweinitz, ed., *Prolog vor dem Film: Nachdenken über ein neues Medium, 1909–1914* (Lipsi: Reclam Verlag, 1992), 300–305.

12. Lukács, *Schriften*, 77.

13. Lukács, *Schriften*, 79.

14. Epstein, "Le sens 1bis," *Cinéa* (July 22, 1921), reprinted in *Écrits sur le cinéma*, vol. 1 (1974), 85–93. Quotations are from *Écrits*.

15. Paul Souday, "Bergsonisme et cinéma," *Paris-Midi* (October 12, 1917): 3; reprinted in Pascal-Manuel Heu, *Le temps du cinéma: Émile Vuillermoz, père de la critique cinématographique, 1910–1930* (Paris: L'Harmattan, 2003), 232–33.

16. Pierre Deschanel, president of the Chamber of Deputies, "Discours prononcé au banquet de la Chambre syndicale française de cinématographie et des industries s'y rattachant, mars 26, 1914," in Marcel L'Herbier, *Intelligence du cinématographe* (Paris: Corrêa, 1946), 95.

17. Epstein, "Le sens 1bis," 86.

18. Epstein, "Le sens 1bis," 91

19. Epstein, "Le sens 1bis," 91.

20. Epstein, "Le sens 1bis," 91.

21. Epstein, "Le sens 1bis," 92.

22. Epstein, "Le sens 1bis," 92. Forty-two years later, Stan Brakhage will echo the idea of the camera as a subject lacking hesitation, scruples, venality, and possible errors, with these words: "Imagine an eye unruled by man-made laws of perspective, an eye unprejudiced by compositional logic, an eye which does not respond to the name of everything but which must know each object encountered in life through an adventure of perception." Stan Brakhage, *Metaphors on Vision* (New York: Film Culture, 1963).

23. Abel, *French Cinema*, 456. Abel dedicates an insightful analysis to Epstein's film. On *La glace à trois faces*, see also Regis Labourdette, "Le Temps de quelques analogies dans *La glace à trois faces* de Jean Epstein," in Jacques Aumont, ed., *Jean Epstein: Cinéaste, poète, philosophe* (Paris: Cinématèque Française, 1998).

24. Erving Goffman, *The Presentation of Self in Everyday Life* (Edinburgh: U of Edinburgh P, 1956).

25. Of the many explorations on the subject, I would refer to the study by Lauren Rabinovitz, *For the Love of Pleasure*, which connects fin de siècle urban life to the forms of cinematic representation.

26. Fantasio, "Cinémas," *Le Film* (June 12, 1914), reprinted in L'Herbier, *Intelligence du cinématographe*, 74–77.

27. Richard Abel notices Epstein's preoccupation with alternating different styles and opposes it to the idea of an immediate recovery of the real in French cinema. Abel, *French Cinema*, 458.

28. On *Dark Passage*, see Dana Polan, "Blind Insights and Dark Passages: The Problem of Placement in Forties Films," *Velvet Light Trap* 20 (Summer 1983): 27–33; and Jay P. Telotte, "Seeing in a Dark Passage," *Film Criticism* 9.2 (Winter 1984–85): 15–27. See also Edward Dimendberg, *Film Noir and the Spaces of Modernity* (Cambridge: Harvard UP, 2004).

29. Spottiswoode, *A Grammar of the Film*.

30. Pudovkin, *Film Technique*, 63; and Arnheim, *Film*.

31. Spottiswoode, *A Grammar*, 170.

32. Münsterberg, *The Photoplay*, 97.

33. Jean Epstein, "Grossissement," *Promenoir* 1–2 (February-March 1921), reprinted in *Bonjour cinéma* (1921), then in *Écrits sur le cinéma* 1:95 (1974).

34. Robert Bataille, *Le savoir filmer* (Lille-Paris: Taffin Lefort, 1944); Robert Bataille, *Grammaire cinégraphique* (Lille: Taffin-Lefort, 1947). André Berthomieu, *Essai de grammaire cinématographique* (Paris: La Nouvelle Édition, 1946).

35. Renato May, *Il linguaggio del film* (Milan: Il Poligono, 1947); by the same author, see also "Per una grammatica del montaggio," *Bianco e Nero* 2.1 (1938): 24–65.

36. May also adds that "objective shots ... are distinguished into the 'real' and the 'unreal,' according to whether they are seen by points accessible to man's eye or not." May, *Il linguaggio del film*, 99–100.

37. May, *Il linguaggio del film*, 100.

38. On *The Man Who Shot Liberty Valance*, see Jean Luis Leutrat, *L'homme qui tua Liberty Valance, John Ford: étude critique* (Paris: Nathan, 1995); and Edward Bus-

combe and Roberta Pearson, *Back in the Saddle Again: New Essays on the West-ern* (London: BFI, 1998).

39. For a history of the flashback, see Maureen Turim, *Flashbacks in Film: Memory and History* (New York and London: Routledge, 1989); for an analysis of the point-of-view shot, see Edward Branigan, *Point of View in the Cinema: A Theory of Narration and Subjectivity in Classical Film* (Berlin and New York: Mouton de Gruyter, 1984).

40. Johann Wolfgang von Goethe, *Faust: Parts One and Two*, trans. George Madison Priest (New York: Knopf, 1941). For a modernist rereading of Faust, see the pages on Goethe of Marshall Berman, *All That Is Solid Melts into Air*, and the first part of Franco Moretti, *Modern Epic*.

41. Boleslaw Matuszewski, *Una Nouvelle Source de l'Histoire historique* (Paris: Noisette, 1898). See the following passage: "The 'family film' belongs to the future, if not to the present. The fathers and mothers who can, will want to preserve the memory of their children playing with the abandon particular to their age. They will be the true family archives, which will allow us to review years later the ways of living, the particular habits and the dearly departed." Matuszewski, *La Photographie animée: Ce qu'elle est, ce qu'elle doit être* (Paris: Noisette, 1898).

42. Lucio D'Ambra, "Il museo dell'attimo fuggente," *La Tribuna illustrata* 22.20, Turin (May 17–24, 1914).

43. Deschanel, "Discours prononcé," 95.

44. Elie Faure, *The Art of Cineplastics* (Boston: The Four Seas Company, 1923); originally, "De la cinéplastique," in *L'Arbre d' Eden* (Paris: Ed. Crès, 1922), reprinted in L'Herbier, *Intelligence du cinématographe*, 266–78.

45. André Bazin, "Ontologie de l'image photographique," in *Qu'est ce que le cinéma*, vol. 1 (1958).

46. "Impenetrable if not for poets, and nevertheless those privileged and rare creatures who have a far-reaching gaze and an excellent nose": Alberto Savinio, *Galleria* (January 1924), reprinted in Vanni Scheiwiller, ed., *Il sogno Meccanico* (Milan: Libri Scheiwiller, Quaderni della Fondazione Primo Conti, 1981).

47. Jacques de Baroncelli, "Le cinéma au service d'une humanité meilleure," *Les Cahiers du mois* 16–17 (1925; special issue on cinema), reprinted in L'Herbier, *Intelligence du cinématographe*, 126–27.

48. Vachel Lindsay, *The Art of the Moving Picture* (New York: Macmillan, 1915). The author takes up the work again in 1922, with some changes. The citation comes from the reissue of 2000 (New York: Modern Library), 183–84.

49. On the relationship between memory and truth, I would refer to Deleuze and his reading of Proust's *In Search of Lost Time*. For Deleuze, memory is not only an exploration of the past or the unraveling of reason; it reflects the desire to interpret and decipher the signs that time has left. It therefore reflects the dimension of a real search for the truth. Memory is knowledge and understanding of the truth of the past, which gives meaning to the present. For

this reason, though its function is important, memory intervenes only as an instrument of an apprenticeship that surpasses it in both its aims and principles. Gilles Deleuze, *Proust and Signs* (Minneapolis: U of Minnesota P, 2000); originally, *Marcel Proust et les signes* (Paris: Presses Universitaires de France, 1964).

50. Jean Painlevé, "Le cinéma au service de la science," *La Revue des Vivants* (October 1931), reprinted in L'Herbier, *Intelligence du cinématographe*, 406. On film's capacity to restore to us the truth of things, see also the debate on the cinema in the circles of research on witness psychology cited, among others, by Allendy, "La valeur."

51. Painlevé, "Le cinema au service de la science," 407.

52. On the relationship between the ideology of restoration and film theory, see the excellent chapter in the book by Philip Rosen, *Change Mummified: Cinema, Historicity, Theory* (Minneapolis: U of Minnesota P, 2001).

53. For more on the cine-photographic image as a "digital imprint" of reality, see Bazin, "Ontology of the Photographic Image." For more on the trace-image, see Roland Barthes, *Camera Lucida: Reflections on Photography* (New York: Hill & Wang, 1981); originally, *La chambre claire: Note sur la photographie.* (Paris: Gallimard–Seuil, 1980). Barthes tends to differentiate between the photographic and filmic image: "In the Photograph, something has posed in front of the tiny hole and has remained there forever . . . ; but in cinema, something has passed in front of the same tiny hole: the pose has been swept away and denied by the continuous series of images: it is a different phenomenology, and therefore a different art which begins here, though derived from the first one" (78). I would add that Barthes shows some perplexity over the fact that photography can make the past "live again" and, in this sense, can even "remember" it; its functions would be that of simple testimonial: "Photography does not call up the past (nothing Proustian in a photograph). The effect it produces upon me is not to restore what has been abolished (by time, by distance) but to attest that what I see has indeed existed." And yet this "reality in past state" is "at once the past and the real" (82). That notwithstanding, his book is indispensable for the subject at hand.

54. Anonymous, "La cinematografia dal vero," *Cine-gazzetta* 1.52, Rome (September 1, 1917): 4; reprinted with some variations under the signature Gio:livo (Giovanni Livoni) and with the title "Pellicole dal vero," *La cine-fono* 376 (September 15–25, 1918) and, from this, now in *Tra una film e l'altra* (Venice: Marsilio, 1980), 345–47.

55. See the following passage in particular: "Cinema of the real must be not only beautiful, but interesting as well. One easily perceives that it is much more difficult for it (as opposed to a dramatic, comic, or sentimental piece or, at any rate, one that allows for plot development and performances by a certain number of actors) to present a wide and justifiable concern. The shots that make up 'the real' must be brief, and—tied together by the film title, and

thus consistent with it—they must each present a particular interest, different from the others." Anonymous, "La cinematografia."

56. Ricciotto Canudo, "L'esthétique du septième art," *Film* 180 (April 1921), reprinted in *L'usine aux images*, 20 (emphasis in the original).

57. Canudo, "L'esthétique," 23–24.

58. Ricciotto Canudo, "Réflexions sur le septième art," in *L'usine aux images*, 43.

59. Canudo, "L'esthétique," 21.

60. It is not a coincidence that Jean Epstein pays tribute to Canudo when speaking specifically of animism: see Jean Epstein, *Le Cinématographe vue de l'Etna* (1926), reprinted in *Écrits sur le cinéma* 1:131–52 (1974).

61. Hugo von Hofmannsthal, "Das Ersatz für die Traüme," *Das Tagenuch* 2 (1921).

62. Antonin Artaud, *Sorcellerie et cinéma* (1927), now in *Oeuvres complètes III* (Paris: Gallimard, 1970).

63. Let us remember one of the most celebrated definitions of the photogenic quality: "I define as photogenic any aspect of things, beings, and feelings that enhance the moral quality through the cinematographic reproduction": Jean Epstein, "De quelques conditions de la photogénie," *Cinéa-Ciné pour tous* (August 15, 1924), reprinted in *Écrits sur le cinéma* 1:137 (1974).

64. Epstein, *Le Cinématographe*, 137.

65. Luigi Pirandello's *Si gira* was published in serial form in *Nuova Antologia* (June-August 1915). It was published with the same title by Fratelli Treves (Milan, 1916), and finally became *Quaderni di Serafino Gubbio operatore* (Florence: Edizioni Bemporad, 1925). My citation comes from the volume *Shoot! The Notebooks of Serafino Gubbio: Cinematograph Operator*, trans. C. K. Scott Moncrieff (Chicago: U of Chicago P, 2005).

66. Epstein, *Le Cinématographe*.

67. Pirandello, *Shoot!*, 319.

68. On *Vertigo*, see Charles Barr, *Vertigo* (London: BFI, 2002), and Jean-Pierre Esquenazi, *Hitchcock et l'aventure de Vertigo: L'invention à Hollywood* (Paris: CNRS, 2001). See also Raymond Bellour, *L'analyse du film* (Paris: Albatros, 1979).

69. Jean-Pierre Oudart, "L'effet de réel," *Cahiers du cinéma* 228 (1971); see also "La suture," *Cahiers du cinéma* 211 (1969), and "La suture II," *Cahiers du cinéma* 212 (1969).

70. Edgar Morin, *Cinema; Or, the Imaginary Man* (Minneapolis: U of Minnesota P, 2005), 102; originally, *Le cinéma ou l'homme imaginaire: Essai d'anthropologie sociologique* (Paris: Minuit, 1956).

71. Morin, *Cinema*, 156.

72. Münsterberg, *The Photoplay*.

73. Christian Metz, *The Imaginary Signifier: Psychoanalysis and the Cinema*, trans. Celia Brittan, Annwyl Williams, Ben Brewster, and Alfred Guzzetti (Bloomington: Indiana UP, 1982); originally, *Le signifiant imaginaire: Psychanalyse et cinéma* (Paris: Union générale d'éditions, 1977).

4. THE GLASS EYE

1. L. Pirandello's *Si gira* (*Shoot!*) was first published in serial form between June and August of 1915 in *La Nuova Antologia*; it was published under the same name by Treves (Milano, 1916); it was subsequently released under the title *Quaderni di Serafino Gubbio operatore* (*The Notebooks of Serafino Gubbio, Operator*) by Edizioni Bemporad in 1925. All English translations come from *Shoot! The Notebooks of Serafino Gubbio, Cinematograph Operator* (Chicago: U of Chicago P, 2005).

2. Pirandello, *Shoot!*, 9.

3. Pirandello, *Shoot!*, 105–106.

4. Pirandello, *Shoot!*, 9.

5. Pirandello, *Shoot!*, 105–106.

6. The quotations are from pages 7, 215, and 112, respectively.

7. The examples are on pages 112, 27, and 28, respectively.

8. The expression "mechanism of life" recurs frequently in the novel; the first time on page 4 (cited here). For more on the excitation that machines create, see the Kosmograph actresses' description of the automobile: "the machinery intoxicates them and excites this uncontrollable vivacity in them" (Pirandello, *Shoot!*, 78). The description of the "the external, that is to say the mechanical framework of the life which keeps us clamorously and dizzily occupied and gives us no rest," appears on page 4.

9. Pirandello, *Shoot!*, 194.

10. Pirandello, *Shoot!*, 84.

11. The six portraits of Varia Nestorova painted by Giorgio Mirelli realize, in fact, "The assumption of that body of hers into a prodigious life, in a light by which she could never, even in her dreams, have imagined herself as being bathed and warmed, in a transparent, triumphant harmony with a nature round about her" (Pirandello, *Shoot!*, 263). The cinema instead offers a portrait of Varia that has no revelatory power: "She herself remains speechless and almost terror-stricken at her own image on the screen, so altered and disordered. She sees there someone who is herself but whom she does not know. She would like not to recognize herself in this person, but at least to know her" (Pirandello, *Shoot!*, 61).

12. Pirandello, *Shoot!*, 151. The observations are accompanied by a proposal: that of filming "the actions of life as they are performed without a thought, when people are alive and do not know that a machine is lurking in concealment to surprise them"—a sort of candid camera that allows us to see forms of contemporary life, with an intent that is almost pedagogical: "A man who is alive, when he is alive, does not see himself: he lives. . . . To see how one lived would indeed be a ridiculous spectacle!" (Pirandello, *Shoot!*, 151).

13. Pirandello, *Shoot!*, 77.

14. It is perhaps interesting to remember this passage written by an intellectual destined to become a successful cineaste: "In less than a century, the cre-

ative genius of a few men has given us the railroad and the electric tram, the light and the telephone, the transatlantic liner and the wireless telegraph, the automobile and the airplane, the gramophone and the cinema. All this grace of God has fallen upon us with such simplicity in so few years, and has so quickly and radically transformed our lives, that we have not even had the time to marvel." Lucio D'Ambra, "Il museo dell'attimo fuggente," *La Tribuna illustrata* 22.20, Turin (May 17–24, 1914): 309.

15. For the difference between tool, machinery, and technical macrosystem, see Alain Gras and Sophie L. Poirot-Delpech, *Grandeur et dépendance: Sociologie des macro-systemes techniques* (Paris: PUF, 1993). See also the interesting observations in the introduction by Michela Nacci and Peppino Ortoleva to the Italian edition of the book; in addition, Ingo Brown and Bernward Joerges, "Techniques du quotidien et macrosysèmes techniques," in Alain Gras, Bernward Joerges, Victor Scardigli, eds., *Sociologie des techniques de la vie quotidienne* (Paris: L'Harmattan, 1992).

16. Romano Guardini published the single letters in the journal *Schildgenossen* between early 1923 and the fall of 1925; they were republished under the title *Briefe vom Comer See* (Mainz: Gruenewald, 1927).

17. Lewis Mumford, *Technics and Civilization* (New York: Harcourt, Brace, 1934), 323.

18. Toddi, "Rettangolo-Film (25 x 19)," *In Penombra* 1.3 (August 25, 1918): 121–23.

19. Giovannetti, *Il cinema e le arti meccaniche*, 25.

20. Giovannetti, *Il cinema,* 62.

21. It is evidently an internal game, seeing that *The Cameraman* is a film produced by MGM. Keaton considered his move to this production house disastrous; thus, it is not difficult to see a ferocious criticism of his producers in the reference. See Buster Keaton and Charles Samuels, *My Wonderful World of Slapstick* (Garden City, N.Y.: Doubleday, 1960); and Robert Knopf, *The Theatre and Cinema of Buster Keaton* (Princeton: Princeton UP, 1999).

22. On photography and personal identification at the birth of cinema, see Tom Gunning, "Tracing the Individual Body: Photography, Detectives, and Early Cinema," in Charney and Schwartz, eds., *Cinema and the Invention of Modern Life* , 15–45.

23. Walter Benjamin, "A Short History of Photography," *Selected Writings* 2:520. "A Short History of Photography" is also published, in a different translation, in *One-Way Street and Other Writings* (London: Harcourt Brace Jovanovich, 1978); originally, "Eine Kleine Geschichte der Photographie," *Die literarische Welt* (1931).

24. "Sander's work is more than a picture book. It is a training manual." Benjamin, "Photography," 520.

25. The expression "machine à imprimer la vie" appears in Marcel L'Herbier, "Hermès et le silente," first published in *Le Temps* (February 23, 1918), then in *Mercure de France* and republished in its entirety in *Intelligence du cinématographe,* 199–212 (Paris: Correa, 1946). Émile Vuillermoz responds to L'Herbier in

"Hermès et le silence," *Le Temps* (March 9, 1918), now in Pascal-Manuel Heu, *Le Temps du cinéma*, 221–24: "The documentary cinema, faithful witness to our everyday existence, can render the considerable service of mechanically 'printing' life; the cinema, however, is not worthy of our interest if it does not become, on the contrary, the 'machine for printing dreams.'"

26. Luigi Pirandello, *The Late Mattia Pascal* (New York: New York Review Books, 2005). "Il fu Mattia Pascal" by Pirandello was serialized from April to June 1904 in *Nuova Antologia*, and then published (Milano: Treves, 1910). Marcel L'Herbier's *Feu Mattia Pascal* is from 1925.

27. "Couldn't they do without this hand? Couldn't you be eliminated, replaced by some piece of machinery?" (Pirandello, *Shoot!*, 7).

28. Bazin, "Ontology of the Photographic Image," in *What Is Cinema?*, vol. 1.

29. Alberto Luchini, "Lettera sul cinematografo," *Solaria* 3 3.2 (1927; emphasis in the original). The passage continues: "It is certainly a merit of the cinema—negative, though not irrelevant—to have freed the arts from such a nightmare. The production of sensations that correspond to such a congenital and perpetual need belongs exclusively to the Cinema."

30. Dziga Vertov, "Vystuplenie na prosmotre dokumental'nogo fil'ma 'Chelovek s kinoapparatom,'" in RGALI (Russian State Archive of Literature and Art), f. 2091, op. 2, d. 204, ll. 1–3. The unpublished manuscript of this introduction to the film, prepared by Dziga Vertov in 1929, was discovered by John MacKay; I thank him for his generosity in allowing me to use this citation.

31. Vertov, "Vystuplenie."

32. Vertov, "Vystuplenie."

33. Vertov, "Vystuplenie."

34. Dziga Vertov, "Kinoks: A Revolution," in *Kino-Eye: The Writings of Dziga Vertov* (Berkeley: U of California P, 1984), 15; originally, "Kinoki: Perevoròt," *Lef* 3 (1923): 139, reprinted in *Stat'i, dnevniki, zamysly* (Moscow: Iskusstvo, 1966).

35. Vertov, "Kinoks," 17.

36. Vertov, "Kinoks," 16.

37. Vertov, "Kinoks," 17–18.

38. Vertov, "Kinoks," 15.

39. Vertov, "Kinoks," 17.

40. Vertov, "Kinoks," 19.

41. Jacques Aumont underscores this and other points in his "Le film comme site théorique: L'homme à la camera," in *A quoi pensent les films* (Paris: Séguier, 1996), 47–67. On the film, see also Annette Michelson, "'The Man with the Movie Camera': From Magician to Epistemologist," *Artforum* 10.7 (1972); Jury Tsivian, "L'Homme à la camera en tant que texte constructiviste," *Révue du cinéma* (June 1980); and Vlada Petric, *Constructivism in Film: "The Man with the Movie Camera"— A Cinematic Analysis* (Cambridge and New York: Cambridge UP, 1987).

42. Vertov, "Vystuplenie."

43. Jacques Aumont summarizes this point very well: "Vertov did not want to show the world so much as its functioning, both real and, at another level, imagined or hoped for." Aumont, "Le film comme site théorique," 66.

44. Mikhail Kaufman was Dziga Vertov's brother and his chief cameraman; Elizaveta Svilova was Vertov's wife and lifelong collaborator, especially for editing.

45. Luchini, "Lettera sul cinematografo."

46. Dziga Vertov, "The Essence of Kino-Eye," in Kino-Eye: The Writings of Dziga Vertov, 50; originally, "Osnovnoe Kinoglaza," Kino (February 3, 1925).

47. Vertov, "Vystuplenie."

48. Vertov, "Vystuplenie."

49. "Hence, the performance of the actor is subjected to a series of optical tests. . . . Consequently, the audience takes the position of the camera: its approach is that of testing." Benjamin, "The Work of Art: Third Version" (Selected Writings, vol. 4), 259 and 260.

50. Dziga Vertov, "The Birth of Kino-Eye," in Kino-Eye: The Writings of Dziga Vertov, 41–42; originally, Roždenie Kinoglaza (1924). And from the same text: "Kino-Eye as the possibility of making the invisible visible, the unclear clear, the hidden manifest, the disguised overt, the acted nonacted; making falsehood into truth" (41).

51. "Starting today we are liberating the camera and making it work in the opposite direction—away from copying." Vertov, "Kinoks," 16.

52. Among the works in the large bibliography on King Kong, I want to focus upon two excellent close readings of the film. The first is provided by Fatimah Tobing Rony in her "King Kong and the Monster in Ethnographic Cinema," in Third Eye: Race, Cinema, and Ethnographic Spectacle (Durham, N.C., and London: Duke UP, 1996), 157–91. Tobing Rony moves from the idea that "the mode of representation of the 'ethnographic' in spectacular commercial cinema takes the form of teratology—the study of monstrosity" (160); she focuses on many issues that I discuss here, among them the self-referentiality of the film.

    The second close analysis is provided by James Snead in his "Spectatorship and Capture in King Kong: The Guilty Look," in White Screen, Black Images, 1–27 (New York and London: Routledge, 1994). Snead unfolds the racial implications in King Kong, highlighting many of the sequences on which I insist. Even though I will limit myself to a specific issue—King Kong as an illustration of the capitalist mode of production in cinema—I deeply agree with Snead's reading.

53. It is useful to remember that the name of the ship is Venture.

54. James Snead points out: "The ship, as we learn in the first few minutes, is leaving with dangerous 'cargo' (dynamite, guns, and bombs), and will likely return with tamed 'cargo' (in the event, black cargo). This transaction is the very definition of 'trade,' and no less of the slave trade. Denham's expedition, eccentric on the surface, is intimately linked (as in the establishing shots of New York harbor) with the centers of world trade, and the very authority of

American commerce and enterprise." Snead, "Spectatorship and Capture," 17.

55. G. Fossa, "Orizzonti cinematografici avvenire," *La Scena Illustrata* 43.5, Florence (March 1, 1907).

56. On the function of the spectacle in modern culture, which offers participation in the action without compromising spectators' safety, see also the celebrated essay by Erving Goffman, "Where the Action Is," in *Interaction Ritual: Essays on Face-to-Face Behavior* (Garden City, N.Y.: Anchor, 1967).

57. W. Troy, *The Nation*, March 22, 1933, reprinted in Stanley Kauffmann and Bruce Henstell, eds,, *American Film Criticism: From the Beginnings to "Citizen Kane"* (New York: Liveright, 1972).

58. Including human sacrifice. In Skull Island's premodern system, this constitutes an offering of reparatory value with respect to what they receive, even in terms of self-defense, from the presence of the Great Ape. On the meaning of sacrifice as a form of balancing Nature, countering the savage exploitation carried out by modern technology, see Gras and Poirot-Delpech, *Grandeur et dépendance*.

59. Alberto Abruzzese, *La grande Scimmia: Mostri, vampiri, automi, mutanti: l'immaginario collettivo dalla letteratura al cinema all'informazione* (Rome: R. Napoleone, 1979).

60. Enrico Thovez, "L'arte di celluloide," *Stampa* 42.209 (July 29, 1908).

61. Many scholars, James Snead among them, insist on the idea that it is precisely this attitude that makes Carl Denham a self-portrait of *King Kong*'s director and producer, Meriam Cooper.

62. Paul Souday, "Bergsonisme et cinéma," *Paris-Midi* (October 12, 1917): 3; reprinted in Heu, *Le temps du cinema*, 232–33.

63. Ricciotto Canudo, "Trionfo del cinematografo," *Nuovo Giornale*, Florence (November 25, 1908), reprinted in *Filmcritica* 278 (1977): 299.

64. Within the considerable bibliography on the film, see Alberto Farassino, *Jean-Luc Godard* (Milan: Il Castoro, 2002); see also Joachim Paech, *Passion, oder, Die Einbildungen des Jean-Luc Godard* (Frankfurt am Main: Deutsches Filmmuseum, 1989); Harun Farocki and Kaja Silverman, "To Love to Work and To Work to Love—A Conversation about 'Passion,'" *Discourse* 3.15 (Spring 1993): 57–75. For the importance of the film for its themes of modernity, see the vast and detailed reading by Giorgio De Vincenti, *Il concetto di modernità nel cinema* (Parma: Pratiche, 1993), in particular ch. 6, "Gli anni Ottanta di Jean Luc Godard: *Passione* del cinema, architettura dell'anima," 114–28.

65. On the dialectic between the copy and the original in modern cinema, see Giorgio Tinazzi, *La copia originale: cinema, critica, tecnica* (Venice: Marsilio, 1983).

66. Godard, quoted in Wim Wenders, "On Painters, Montage, and Dustbins: A Conversation between Wim Wenders and Jean-Luc Godard," in *The Act of Seeing: Essay and Conversations* (London: Faber & Faber, 2001); originally, *Texte und Gespräche* (Frankfurt am Main: Verlag der Autoren, 1992).

67. Naturally, the complicated relationship between Godard and his alter ego Jerzi should be analyzed in a more dialectical way. For example, Jerzi, represents the postmodern director who moves in a world that has become a museum. In addition, he likely illustrates the tragic face of the modern poet who does not know how to speak of the unspeakable. For Godard, this is the horror of the concentration camps, which are never made visible for him, as they are radically "obscene." As Pietro Montani has pointed out, this closing-off in a self-reflexive exercise (that is, his construction of images of images) is the most effective way of constructing a "structure that welcomes the other and the outside": in waiting for the other, one speaks of the self. I thank Montani for this observation, which coincides with a subject that he investigates splendidly in *Il debito del linguaggio* (Venice: Marsilio, 1985).
68. Giovannetti, *Il cinema*, 132.
69. Heinrich von Kleist, *Über das Marionettentheater* (1810), reprinted in *Kleists Aufsatz uber das Marionettentheater: Studien und Interpretationen* (Berlin: E. Schmidt, 1967).

5. *STRONG SENSATIONS*

1. Siegfried Kracauer, "Cult of Distraction: On Berlin's Picture Palaces" (1926), in *The Mass Ornament: Weimar Essays*, 323–28. For Kracauer's positions and evolution in the *Frankfurter Zeitung* years (which includes practically all of the second decade of the twentieth century), see in particular Miriam Hansen, "America, Paris, the Alps," in Charney and Schwartz, eds., *Cinema and the Invention of Modern Life*, 363–402.
2. Kracauer, "Cult of Distraction," 323 (emphasis in the original).
3. Kracauer, "Cult of Distraction," 323.
4. Kracauer, "Cult of Distraction," 324.
5. Kracauer, "Cult of Distraction," 326.
6. Kracauer, "Cult of Distraction," 326 (emphasis in the original).
7. "Indeed the very fact that the shows which aim at distraction are composed of the same mixture of externalities as the world of the urban masses; the fact that these shows lack any authentic and materially motivated coherence, except possibly the glue of sentimentality, which covers up this lack but only in order to make it all the more visible; the fact that these shows convey precisely and openly to thousands of eyes and ears the disorder of the society—this is precisely what would enable them to evoke and maintain the tension that must precede the inevitable and radical change." Kracauer, "Cult of Distraction," 326–27.
8. Kracauer, "Cult of Distraction," 326.
9. Kracauer, "Cult of Distraction," 327.
10. Kracauer, "Cult of Distraction," 328.
11. Kracauer, "Cult of Distraction," 327.
12. Kracauer, "Cult of Distraction," 328.

13. Georg Simmel, "The Metropolis and Mental Life," in *Simmel on Culture: Selected Writings* (Thousand Oaks, Calif., and London: Sage, 1997), 175; originally, "Die Großstädte und das Geistlesleben," *Jahrbuch der Gehe-Stiftung* 9 (1903).

14. Simmel, "The Metropolis," 175.

15. Simmel, "The Metropolis," 176.

16. Simmel, "The Metropolis," 178.

17. Simmel, "The Metropolis," 183.

18. Simmel, "The Metropolis," 183.

19. It might be useful to remember the portrait of the new urban universe offered by Robert Musil at the beginning of *The Man Without Qualities*. In speaking of Vienna (but we are also asked not to limit ourselves too much to such an identification), he writes: "Like all big cities, it consisted of irregularity, change, sliding forward, not keeping in step, collisions of things and affairs, and fathomless points of silence in between, of paved ways and wilderness, of one great rhythmic throb and the perpetual discord and dislocation of all opposing rhythms, and as a whole sembled a seething, bubbling fluid in a vessel consisting of the solid material of buildings, laws, regulations, and historical traditions." Robert Musil, *The Man Without Qualities*, vol. 1 (London: Pan Books, 1983), 4.

20. Edgar Allan Poe, "The Fall of the House of Usher," in *Tales of the Grotesque and Arabesque* (Philadelphia: Lea and Blanchard, 1840), and "The Tale-Tell Heart," in *The Works of the Late Edgar Allan Poe*, vol. 1 (New York: Redfield and Hall, 1850). Both texts appear in their definitive editions in Edgar Allan Poe, *The Complete Works of E.A. Poe*, 9 vols. (New York: Sproul, 1902).

21. Walter Benjamin, "On Some Motifs in Baudelaire," in *Illuminations*, ed. Hannah Arendt (New York: Harcourt Brace & World, 1968), 155–200; originally, "Über einige Motive bei Baudelaire," in *Zeitschrift für Sozialforschung* 1–2 (1939).

22. Sigmund Freud, *Beyond the Pleasure Principle* (London: Hogarth Press and the Institute of Psycho-Analysis, 1961), 20–21; originally, *Jenseits des Lustprinzips* (Leipzig and Vienna and Zurich: Internationaler Psycoanalytischer Verlag, 1920).

23. Freud, *Beyond the Pleasure Principle*, 21. See also: "The main purpose of the *reception* of stimuli is to discover the direction and nature of the external stimuli; and for that it is enough to take small specimens of the external world, to sample it in small quantities" (21). And: "It is characteristic of [the sense organs] that they deal only with very small quantities of external stimulation and only take in *samples* of the external world. They may perhaps be compared with feelers which are all the time making tentative advances towards the external world and then drawing back from it" (22). For further elaboration, see pages 18–27.

24. Freud, *Beyond the Pleasure Principle*, 11.

25. Tom Gunning, "Cinema of Attractions: Early Film, Its Spectator, and the Avant-Garde," in Adam Barker and Thomas Elsaesser, eds., *Early Cinema: Space, Frame, Narrative* (London: BFI, 1990), 56–62. The relationship between

early cinema and "excitement" has been studied exhaustively in the past few years: see also Ben Singer, "Modernity, Hyperstimulus, and the Rise of Popular Sensationalism," in Charney and Schwartz, eds., *Cinema and the Invention of Modern Life*, 72–99.

26. Jean Epstein, "Rapidité et fatigue de l'homme spectateur," in *Mercure de France* (November 1, 1948); reprinted in *Écrits sur le cinéma* 2:45–53.

27. I am also thinking of the presence in this part of the film of actual narrative suspensions: we have a capital execution that seems to take forever; a courting between Belshazzar and the Princess that goes forward as if nothing were happening; a Crucifixion that suddenly becomes a hieratic icon, even if these suspensions reinforce, by contrast, the sense of movement that pervades the whole. On the film, see Richard Koszarski, *An Evening's Entertainment: The Age of the Silent Feature Picture, 1915–1928* (New York: Maxwell Macmillan, 1990); and William M. Drew, *D.W. Griffith's "Intolerance": Its Genesis and Its Vision* (Jefferson: McFarland, 1986).

28. Among the numerous contributions on the role of velocity in the modern world, see the exhaustive chapter dedicated to the subject by Stephen Kern, *The Culture of Time and Space*.

29. This ambiguity is found, for example, in many of the metaphors of modern life that refer to speed: I am thinking of the idea of the whirlwind, which Marshall Berman discusses in the introduction to his *All That Is Solid Melts into Air*.

30. Filippo Tommaso Marinetti, "Fondazione e Manifesto del Futurismo," *Figaro* (Februrary 20, 1909), reprinted in Umbro Apollonio, ed., *Futurist Manifestos* (Boston: MFA Publications, 2001), 21. The same manifesto reads, "Up to now literature has exalted a pensile immobility, ecstasy, and sleep. We intend to exalt aggressive action, a feverish insomnia, the racer's stride, the mortal leap, the punch and the slap" (21). And more: "We want to hymn the man at the wheel, who hurls the lance of his spirit across the Earth, along the circle of its orbit" (21). See also by Marinetti, "The New Moral-Religion of Speed" ("La nuova religione-morale della velocità"), the 1916 manifesto in which there is a list of "places inhabited by the divinity" of speed, "cinematographic film" among them. See also his film script, "Velocità," examined by Giovanni Lista in "Un inedito marinettiano: *Velocità*, film futurista." Both appear in *Fotogenia* 2 (1995).

31. Schivelbusch, *Railway Journey*.

32. It was Kern, *The Culture of Time and Space*, who read the tragedy of the Titanic as a tragedy of speed.

33. Münsterberg, *The Photoplay*, 219.

34. Lindsay, *The Art of the Moving Picture*, 41.

35. On crosscutting, see Bordwell, Staiger, and Thompson, *The Classical Hollywood Cinema* (New York: Columbia UP, 1987), 210–12. For an appraisal of Bordwell on this point, see Slavoj Žižek, *The Fright of Real Tears: Krzysztof Kieslowski Between Theory and Post-Theory* (London: BFI, 2001). See also Raymond Bellour,

"To Alternate/To Narrate," in Barker and Elsaesser, eds., *Early Cinema*, 360–74; André Gaudreault, "Temporality and Narrativity in Early Cinema," in Roger Holdman, ed., *Cinema, 1900–1906: An Analytical Study* (Brussels: FIAF, 1982), 201–218; André Gaudreault, "Detours in Film Narrative: Cross-Cutting," *Cinema Journal* 19.1 (1979): 39–59; and Christian Metz, *Film Language: A Semiotics of the Cinema* (New York: Oxford UP, 1974), originally, *Essais sur la signification au cinema* (Paris: Klincksieck, 1968). On ubiquity, see Jean Epstein, "Logique du fluide," in "Alcool et Cinéma" (unpublished manuscript), now in *Écrits sur le cinéma* 2:210–15; and Blaise Cendrars, "The Modern: A New Art, the Cinema," in Abel, ed., *French Film Theory and Criticism* 1:182–83.

36. J. Johnson, "*Intolerance*," in *Photoplay* 11.1 (December 1916): 78, reprinted in Slide, ed., *Selected Film Criticism, 1912–1920*, 133.

37. F.J. Smith, in *New York Dramatic Mirror* 76.1969 (September 16, 1916): 22, reprinted in Slide, ed., *Selected Film Criticism*, 140.

38. On suspense, see Pascal Bonitzer, *Le champ aveugle: Essais sur le cinéma* (Paris: Gallimard, 1982), 45–71; Xavier Pérez, *El suspens cinematogràfic* (Barcelona: Portic, 1999); Gordon Gow, *Suspense in the Cinema* (New York: A.S. Barnes, 1968).

39. Ricciotto Canudo, "Lettere d'arte: Trionfo del cinematografo" (1908), reprinted in *Filmcritica* 28.278 (November 1977): 297.

40. Canudo, "Trionfo," 297.

41. Canudo, "Trionfo," 298 (all quotations).

42. Canudo, "Trionfo," 298.

43. On the adoption of universal time, see Kern, *The Culture of Time and Space*. On the advent of a collective temporality that eradicates the subjective one, as well as on punctuality and the calculability of the life of the modern metropolitan man, see Simmel, "The Metropolis," 177: "If all clocks and watches in Berlin would suddenly go wrong in different ways, even if only by one hour, all the economic life and communication of the city would be disrupted for a long time."

44. On the interlacing of "too late" and "just in time" in the "last second rescue" (in particular for *Way Down East*, David W. Griffith, USA, 1920), see Linda Williams, "Melodrama Revised," in Nick Browne, ed., *Refiguring American Film Genres* (Berkeley: U of California P, 1998), 42–88.

45. Pudovkin, *Film Technique*, 49.

46. Freeburg, *The Art of Photoplay Making*, 218.

47. On anguish as tied to waiting, see in particular some texts by Sigmund Freud: *Beyond the Pleasure Principle* and *Inhibitions, Symptoms and Anxiety* (London: Hogarth Press and the Institute of Psycho-Analysis, 1948); originally, *Hemmung, Symptom und Angst* (Vienna: Internationaler Psychoanalytischer Verlag, 1926); and Sigmund Freud, *Civilization and Its Discontents* (London: L. and Virginia Woolf at the Hogarth Press, 1930); originally, *Das Unbehagen in der Kultur* (Vienna: Internationaler Psychoanalytischer Verlag, 1930).

48. Perhaps the most beautiful inversion of a chase film remains *Seven Chances* by (Buster Keaton, USA, 1925), in which the protagonist, forced to find a wife

to collect an inheritance, runs like the wind from hundreds of admirers hot on his heels, from a slave who throws herself on him, and so on.

49. Benjamin, *The Arcades Project*, 62.

50. Benjamin, *The Arcades Project*, 105.

51. Benjamin, *The Arcades Project*, 105.

52. For Lyotard, cinema's apex rests in fireworks or in tableux vivants: Jean-François Lyotard, "L'acinéma," *Revue d'Esthétique* 2–4, reprinted in *Des Dispositifs pulsionnels* (Paris: Union générale d'éditions, 1973).

53. See in particular, Sergei Eisenstein, *Nonindifferent Nature: Film and the Structure of Things* (Cambridge and New York: Cambridge UP, 1987); originally, *Neravnodušnaja priroda*, in *Izbrannye proizvedenija v šesti tomach*, vol. 3 (Moscow: Iskusstvo, 1963–1970).

54. Compagnon, *The Five Paradoxes of Modernity*.

55. Compagnon explains quite well how modernity experiments with first an approval of what is current, then with the religion of the future (see Compagnon, *The Five Paradoxes of Modernity*)—the relationship between art and the current in Stendhal and then in Baudelaire, and the passage from an identification with the present to a projection in the future realized by the avant-garde.

56. *Excelsior*, with music by Romualdo Marenco and choreography by Luigi Manzotti, was a highly successful ballet. Composed in 1881, it is a lavish tribute to the scientific and industrial progress of the nineteenth century.

57. "For fashion was never anything other than the parody of the motley cadaver, provocation of death through the woman, and bitter colloquy with decay whispered between shrill bursts of mechanical laughter. That is fashion. And that is why she changes so quickly; she titillates death and is already something different, something new, as he casts about to crush her" (Benjamin, *The Arcades Project*, 63). Benjamin returns to the dialectic newness/negation at various moments: for example, in regard to the need for information ("Why does everyone share the newest thing with someone else? Presumably, in order to triumph over the dead. This only where there is nothing really new" (112).

58. On modern temporality, see the excellent study by Mary Ann Doane, *The Emergence of Cinematic Time*. On the connection between speed and change, I would like to observe that the two terms bring to light two complementary characteristics of temporality—that is, the rhythmic dimension (the steps that time takes in its racing forward) and the dimension of waiting in the strict sense (the articulation of a "before" and an "after"); we can add that, on the one hand, acceleration is the most evident sign that the world has assumed new trends, and that thus it has changed; on the other hand, that acceleration facilitates change, and renders it in some way indispensable.

59. Benjamin emphasizes the connections between the idea of change and that of the eternal return: "The belief in progress—in an infinite perfectibility understood as an infinite ethical task—and the representation of eternal re-

turn are complementary. They are the indissoluble antimonies in the face of which the dialectical conception of historical time must be developed." Benjamin, *The Arcades Project*, 119.

60. This element has been sufficiently examined by Pietro Montani, *L'immaginazione narrativa*, 24–26, particularly through the analysis of the ball sequence in *Staroe i novoe*.

61. It must be said that, for Eisenstein, an organic structure's capacity to go outside itself (ecstasy) and touch the apex of pathos is not a trait exclusive to art; it is found in nature as well, where all organisms develop passing from one mature state to the next, with a growth based on one of the "qualitative leaps," just as it is found in thought, which proceeds through successive processes, in which each eliminates and reabsorbs the preceding one. In this sense, the organic-pathetic work recalls nature and thought, as well as the processes of transformation of these domains.

62. For a survey of the musical, and in particular its narrative structure, see Rick Altman, *The American Film Musical* (Bloomington: Indiana UP, 1987), which contains an analysis of the "narrative syntax" of *Gold Diggers of 1933* (229–30). On the backstage musical, see the still-influential observations by John Belton, "The Backstage Musical," *Movie* 24 (Spring 1977). On *Gold Diggers of 1933*, see James Seymour, *Gold Diggers of 1933* (Madison: U of Wisconsin P, 1980). An important reading of the film is offered by Franco La Polla, "Negare il piacere: l'erotismo negli anni '30 e '40," in *L'età dell'occhio: Il cinema e la cultura Americana* (Turin: Lindau, 1999), 177–85, which emphasizes how Busby Berkeley pursues an "eroticization of the musical." On this subject, see also Patricia Mellecamp, "The Sexual Economics of 'Gold Diggers of 1933,'" in Peter Lehman, ed., *Close Viewings: An Anthology of New Film Criticism* (Tallahassee: Florida State UP, 1990), 177–99.

63. Giuseppe Pellizza da Volpedo was an Italian painter whose *The Fourth State* (1901) became a "manifesto" for the socialist movement.

64. Simmel, "The Metropolis," 175.

65. We have only to think of two things: the misunderstandings between the two lovers, tied mostly to the fact that he is rich but does not want it known, as well as the confusion that leads to the suspension of the initial show, due to the fact that the dancers thought there was money for the production (which then disappeared).

66. *Translator's Note:* The Italian word *storia* means both history and story.

67. This opposition between image and narrative shows the traces of many influences, from Roland Barthes ("The Third Meaning: Notes on Several Eisenstein Stills," in *The Responsibility of Forms: Critical Essays on Music, Art, and Representation* [Oxford: Blackwell, 1986], 41–62), to Gilles Deleuze (*Time-Image*), to Lyotard ("L'acinéma"). For a good summary of this contrast, see Sandro Bernardi, *Introduzione alla retorica del cinema* (Florence: Le Lettere, 1994), and Mario Pezzella, *Estetica del cinema* (Bologna: Il Mulino, 1996). See also the op-

position between "figuratif" and "figurale" in Philippe Dubois, "L'écriture figurale dans le cinéma muet des années vingt," *Art&Fact* 18 (1999).

68. For this cinema, see the essential work by Gunning, "Cinema of Attractions," 56–62; the formula is, however, borrowed explicitly from Eisenstein. For the passage from the early cinema to the institutional-narrative cinema, see Burch, *Life to Those Shadows* (Berkeley: U of California P, 1990); for a definition of the classical cinema within its relationship to narrativity, see Bordwell, Staiger, and Thompson, *The Classical Hollywood Cinema*.

69. Luigi Pirandello, "Se il film parlante abolirà il teatro" ("If talking film will eliminate the theater"), *Corriere della Sera* (June 16, 1929), reprinted in Francesco Callari, *Pirandello e il cinema* (Venice: Marsilio, 1991), 120–25. On the theoretical hypotheses that the cinema did not follow, see Leonardo Quaresima, ed., "Dead Ends/Impasses," *Cinema & Cie* 2 (Spring 2003).

70. On the subject (which I would summarize in another way as the problem of "sense" of filmic discourse beginning from the dimension of "as-yet-sensible" and "no-longer-sensible"), Montani has written some essentials, in particular his *L'immaginazione narrativa*. For a reflection on the subject that extends beyond the cinema, see Franzini, *Fenomenologia dell'invisibile*.

71. For this reading of the musical, see in particular a classical work such as Richard Dyer, "Entertainment and Utopia," *Movie* 24 (1977), part of Steven Cohan, ed., *Hollywood Musicals: The Film Reader* (London and New York: Routledge, 2002). Dyer suggests that the genre's uniqueness lies precisely in "working on the level of sensitivity," using signs both representational and nonrepresentational, and to bury its utopian design on this level.

72. The bibliography on the passage from silent to sound is immense: I would like to cite the series of essays by Rick Altman, precisely because they validate my argument: "Toward a Theory of the History of Representational Technology," *Iris* 2.2 (1984); "The Technology of Voice," *Iris* 3.1 (1985); "The Technology of Voice," *Iris* 4.1 (1986). See also Rick Altman, ed., *Sound Theory/ Sound Practice* (New York: Routledge and the American Film Institute, 1992); and Rick Altman, "The State of Sound Studies/Le son au cinéma, état de la recherche," *Iris* 27 (1999).

73. On the subject, see Francesco Casetti, "Tra l'opera d'arte totale e il mondo quotidiano: I paradossi del cinema sonoro," *La valle dell'Eden* 1 (1999): 7–21.

74. Sergei M. Eisenstein, "Vertical Montage," in *Selected Works* 2:327–99 (London: BFI, 1991; and Bloomington: Indiana UP, 1991); the section devoted to the "yellow rhapsody" appears on 350ff.; originally, "Vertikal'nyi montaž, stat'ja vtoraja," *Iskusstovo kino* 12 (1940): 27–35. On color, see also Eisenstein, *Cvet* in *Izbrannye proizvedenija v šesti tomach* 3.

75. Léon Pierre-Quint, "Signification du cinéma," in *L'art cinématographique* 2:1–28 (Paris: Alcan, 1926).

76. Pierre-Quint, "Signification du cinéma," 20. The following quotations come from pages 20, 21 and 26. I would emphasize that, for Pierre-Quint, this situ-

ation pushes the cinema towards an expression of extreme and instinctive emotions, and makes the fantastic its chosen land.

77. Sergei M. Eisenstein, "The Montage of Film Attractions," in *Selected Works*, vol. 1, 1922–34 (London: BFI, 1988; Bloomington: Indiana UP, 1988); originally, "Montaž kino-attrakcionov" (October 1924).

78. Eisenstein, "The Montage of Film," 40–41.

79. It might be useful to compare Eisenstein's suggestion with Barthes' reflection in "The Third Meaning" (*Le troisième sens*). It seems to me that Barthes' lesson consists in telling us that emotions, in fact, involve the senses, but it is not for this that they eliminate meaning: if anything, they question it on another level, that of its capacity "to make felt," beyond its capacity "to make known" and "to make understood." From this perspective, they bring out its "obtuse" form, which is added to the denotative and the symbolic. In Barthes, this action can seem "punctual" (I am referring to his notion of *punctum*); otherwise, it is random and disorganized.

80. "We must fully recall the characteristics of cinema's effect . . . that establish the montage approach as the essential, meaningful, and sole possible language of cinema, completely analogous to the role of the word in spoken material" (Eisenstein, "The Montage of Film," 46). For the notion of editing in Eisenstein (on which there is an exhaustive bibliography), see the entire corpus of writings: "Towards a Theory of Montage," in *Selected Works*, vol. 2. An insightful reading of Eisenstein's concept can be found in Jacques Aumont, *Montage Eisenstein* (Paris: Albatros, 1979).

81. The filmic flow's capacity (and a changing flow, thanks also to editing) to accentuate the shock value of the onscreen images is well understood by Benjamin: "the train of associations in the person contemplating these images is immediately interrupted by new images. This constitutes the shock effect of film, which, like all shock effects, seeks to induce heightened attention." Walter Benjamin, "The Work of Art: Third Version," 267.

82. See the dense reflection on this topic in Serge Daney, *Persévérance*, especially in the chapter "The Travelling of *Kapò*," 15–39.

83. "The visual is essentially pornographic, which is to say that it has its end in rapt, mindless fascination; thinking about its attributes becomes an adjunct to that, if it is unwilling to betray its object; while the most austere films necessarily draw their energy from the attempt to repress their own excess (rather than from the more thankless effort to discipline the viewer). Pornographic films are thus only the potentation of films in general, which ask us to stare at the world as though it were a naked body." Fredric Jameson, *Signatures of the Visible* (New York and London: Routledge, 1990), 1.

6. THE PLACE OF THE OBSERVER

1. Epstein, *Le cinématographe vue de l'Etna* (1926), reprinted in *Écrits sur le cinéma* 1:131–52 (quotations from *Écrits*). For a recent study of the work of Jean Ep-

stein, see Jacques Aumont, ed., *Jean Epstein*. On this specific text, see Stuart Liebman, "Visiting of Awful Promise: The Cinema Seen from Etna," in Richard Allen and Malcolm Turvey, eds., *Camera Obscura, Camera Lucida: Essays in Honor of Annette Michelson* (Amsterdam: Amsterdam UP, 2003).

2. Epstein, *Le cinématographe*, 131; the following quotation is from the same page.
3. Epstein, *Le cinématographe*, 133.
4. Epstein, *Le cinématographe*, 134.
5. Epstein, *Le cinématographe*, 133.
6. Epstein, *Le cinématographe*, 134; the following quotation is from the same page
7. Epstein, *Le cinématographe*, 135.
8. Epstein, *Le cinématographe*, 136; the two following quotations are from the same page.
9. Epstein, *Le cinématographe*, 135.
10. Epstein, *Le cinématographe*, 136.
11. Epstein, *Le cinématographe*, 136.
12. Epstein, *Le cinématographe*, 137; the following quotation is from the same page
13. Hans Blumenberg, *Shipwreck with Spectator: Paradigm of a Metaphor for Existence* (Cambridge: MIT Press, 1997); originally, *Schiffbruch mit Zuschauer: Paradigma einer Daseinsmetapher* (Frankfurt am Main: Suhrkamp, 1979).
14. In this line of interpretation, see also the introduction by Remo Bodei to Blumenberg's Italian translation, *Naufragio con spettatore: Paradigma di una metafora dell'esistenza* (Bologna: Il Mulino, 2001).
15. Paul's film is also recorded as *The Country Man and the Cinematograph* (R. W. Paul, Great Britain, 1901).
16. Though, as Epstein shows, it obviously gives it an interpretation of its own or, if you will, its own symbolic coding. Every description is also an interpretation and a definition: to describe is always to transcribe things as they are seen, just as it is of course to prescribe a certain way of seeing things.
17. On *Uncle Josh at the Moving Picture Show* (E. Porter, USA, 1902), see Charles Musser, *The Emergence of Cinema*, 321–22, in which the self-publicizing value of film is also emphasized.
18. Freeburg, *The Art of Photoplay Making*. The description is in chapter 2, "The Psychology of the Cinema Audience" (7–25).
19. Freeburg, *Art of Photoplay*, 11.
20. Freeburg, *Art of Photoplay*, 12. Freeburg insists on the idea that "the eye is especially pleased by certain types of physical movement which the motion picture can transmit, and which cannot be transmitted through any other medium" (11).
21. Freeburg, *Art of Photoplay*, 14.
22. Freeburg, *Art of Photoplay*, 15.
23. Freeburg, *Art of Photoplay*, 15.

24. Freeburg, *Art of Photoplay*, 18.

25. Freeburg, *Art of Photoplay*, 19.

26. Freeburg concludes the chapter affirming: "Let us learn how best to please the eye, how to stir the self-emotion of the individual in the crowd, how to arouse and maintain his social sympathies, how to give him intellectual entertainment without mental fatigue; and let us constantly remember that if our photoplay is to become a classic it must possess beneath the attractive surface which appeals to the crowd the permanent values of illuminating truth, universal meaning, and unfading beauty." Freeburg, *Art of Photoplay*, 25.

27. For those years, the conventional distance between camera and filmed object was nine to eleven feet. It was obviously possible to capture the object from a smaller distance; in this case, however, we would have "magnified visions" meant to evoke wonder, more than close-ups able to direct the narrative, as will happen in classical cinema. This confirms the fact that the same type of shot can assume meanings that are, in part, different, during the course of film history. On the close-up in early cinema, see Giulia Carluccio, *Verso il primo piano: Attrazioni e racconto nel cinema americano, 1908–1909: il caso Griffith-Biograph* (Bologna: Clueb, 1999). Among the most recent studies on the close-up, see at least Jacques Aumont, *Du visage au cinema* (Paris: Éd. de l'Étoile, 1992), which offers a useful summary, and Pascal Bonitzer, *Le champ aveugle*.

28. Epstein, "Grossissement" (1921), in *Bonjour cinéma*, reprinted in *Écrits sur le cinéma* 1:93–99 (quotations from *Écrits*).

29. Epstein, "Grossissement," 98.

30. Epstein, "Grossissement," 97.

31. Epstein, "Grossissement," 98.

32. Epstein, "Grossissement," 93. On the same topic, and in the same year, Jean Epstein writes an intense paragraph devoted to the "Aestetics of Proximity" in *La poésie d'aujourd'hui, un nouvel état d'intelligence*, 171–72 (Paris: Éditions de la Sirène, 1921).

33. An idea so ably demonstrated at the time by Hugo Münsterberg in *The Photoplay*.

34. On the permanence of lines of division in a world that seems to eliminate them, see Benjamin's splendid observations on the nineteenth-century metropolis: "The city is only apparently homogeneous. Even its name takes on different sounds from one district to the next. Nowhere, unless perhaps in dreams, can the phenomenon of the boundary be experienced in a more originary way than in cities. To know them means to understand those lines that, running alongside railroad crossings and across privately owned lots, within the park and along the riverbank, function as limits; it means to know these confines, together with the enclaves of the various districts. As threshold, the boundary stretches across streets; a new precinct begins like a

step into the void—as though one had unexpectedly cleared a low step on a flight of stairs." Benjamin, *The Arcades Project*, 87.

35. On awareness of the spectator, Hugo Münsterberg is explicit. See at least this passage regarding depth of field in an image that is in itself flat: "Nevertheless we are never deceived: we are fully conscious of the depth, and yet we do not take it for real depth." Münsterberg, *The Photoplay*, 54.

36. The camera movement is not altogether continuous, even if it maintains the effect of continuity: before the camera moves, there is a gap between the close-up of the couple and a slightly larger field, which is still on them, but also includes the son and some spectators to the side; moreover, the camera movement is rendered with two shots, joined by a half fade-over. Yet, I repeat, the effect of continuity is preserved. On the film, see Raymond Durgnat, "The Crowd," *Film Comment* 9.4 (July-August 1973): 15–17; Heinrich Von Beck, "'History' zu 'Hysteria'—King Vidor's *The Crowd*," in *Amerikastudien/American Studies* 37.1 (1992): 85–93; and Giulia Carluccio, "City Films: New York nel cinema americano degli anni Venti: Il caso di *The Crowd*," in Giaime Alonge and Federica Mazzocchi, eds., *Ombre metropolitane: Città e spettacolo nel Novecento* (Turin: Lexis, 2002).

37. Freeburg, *Art of Photoplay*, 7.

38. The close-up seems to cancel all portions of the surrounding world; nonetheless, it succeeds in making us aware of it: "The setting is not seen in close-ups, but its atmosphere reverberates in the magnified image." Balász, *Der Geist des Films* (1930), reprinted in *Schriften zum Film* 2:171–72.

39. For the transformation of the idea of space in modernity, see at minimum Stephen Kern, *The Culture of Time and Space*. Kern offers many references, both in the fields of scientific and artistic research, which illustrate this passage: he cites Umberto Boccioni and his sculpture *Development of a Bottle in Space* to demonstrate how objects not only occupy a certain position but also literally absorb the surrounding context; he cites Munch and *The Scream* to show how space is taken up by the presences of which it is constituted; he names Mallarmé and his *Calligrammes* to illustrate the equal dignity attained by words and the spaces between words.

40. On the idea of the world as an inclusive entity and the relevance of this idea to modern literature, see the intense analyses of Franco Moretti in *Modern Epic*.

41. On the individual adrift, and in particular the woman adrift, see the informative observations of Lauren Rabinovitz, *For the Love of Pleasure*, 20–46.

42. As Paolo Jedlowski reminds us, "[in the modern age] there is a rise of an ethic orientation that tends to emphasize more than ever first the essential freedom of each individual, his or her uniqueness, and his or her personal responsibility in the definition of one's own destiny and its realization." Paolo Jedlowski, *Il mondo in questione: Introduzione alla storia del pensiero sociologico* (Rome: Carrocci, 1998), 112.

But the singularity of the individual seems threatened by the presence of a second protagonist, precisely the mass, which presents itself as a decisive reality on the levels of production (the mass of workers), economy (mass consumption), politics (mass movements), military (mass troops), and knowledge (mass culture). The problem is then how the two terms relate to each other: is the mass—locus of pervasive anonymity—a negation of the individual, or does it constitute an extension of it? And in parallel, is the individual with his or her singularity integrated warmly into the mass, or can he or she only renounce him or herself to become part of it? For the dialectic between individual and mass, among the vast bibliography between the nineteenth and twentieth centuries, see at least Georg Simmel, "The Metropolis and Mental Life," in *Simmel on Culture*, 174–85.

43. Spottiswoode, *A Grammar of the Film*, 140. Here Spottiswoode speaks of the representation of the crowd in Soviet film.

44. There is a vaudeville number going on onstage; but nothing prevents us from imagining that, given the structure of the performances of the age, immediately after a screen will appear and a film will be projected.

45. Freeburg, *Art of Photoplay*, 7.

46. Freeburg, *Art of Photoplay*, 7.

47. Canudo goes on: "This oblivion will one day be aesthetic; it will be a religious day." Canudo, "Trionfo del cinematografo" (1908), reprinted in *Filmcritica* 28.278 (November 1977): 302.

48. And Romains adds: "The crowd is a being that remembers and imagines, a group that evokes other groups much like itself—audiences, procession, parades, mob in the streets, armies. They imagine that it is they who are experiencing all these adventures, all these catastrophes, all these celebrations. And while their bodies slumber and their muscles relax and slacken in the depths of their seats, they pursue burglars across the rooftops, cheer the passing of a king from the East, or march into a wide plain with bayonets or bugles." Jules Romains, "The Crowd at the Cinématograph," reprinted in Abel, *French Film Theory and Criticism* 1:53; originally, "La foule au cinématographe," in *Les Puissances de Paris* (Paris: Eugene Figuière, 1911).

49. Matilde Serao, "Parla una spettatrice," *L'arte muta* 1 (June 15, 1916): 31–32.

50. Freeburg, *Art of Photoplay*, 8.

51. Freeburg, *Art of Photoplay*, 8.

52. The last subject was recently taken up in cinematic debate: I am thinking in particular of contributions by Miriam Hansen, beginning with *Babel and Babylon: Spectatorship in American Silent Film*, in which she explores the idea that one of the great effects of the cinema was that of bringing some of the great private themes to the "public sphere" (which is not to be confused with the "public opinion" discussed by Freeburg, which has similar features). *The Crowd*, reread with Freeburg, seems a confirmation of the process brought to light by Hansen.

53. This dual axis of spectatorality, which demonstrates the dual nature of the receiver of film (spectator/audience), has recently and meticulously been explored by Reception Studies. Among the various contributions, I will limit myself to recalling the work of Janet Staiger, beginning with *Interpreting Films: Studies in the Historical Reception of American Cinema* (Princeton: Princeton UP, 1992), aimed at the study of historical forms of reception and interpretation of film; Douglas Gomery, directed at reviewing the ways in which the cinema was offered, in *Shared Pleasures: A History of Movie Presentation in the United States* (Madison: U of Wisconsin P, 1992)]; Annette Kuhn, focused on the exploration of the relationship between memory and consumption, in *Dreaming of Fred and Ginger: Cinema and Cultural Memory* (New York: NYU Press, 2002); the volume from Linda Williams, ed., *Viewing Positions: Ways of Seeing Film* (New Brunswick: Rutgers UP, 1994), on the act of seeing a film and its implications, etc.

    I cannot leave out the vast work in the Italian sector: Gian Piero Brunetta, *Buio in sala: Cent'anni di passioni dello spettatore cinematografico* (Venice: Marsilio, 1989), and the studies by Mariagrazia Fanchi and Elena Mosconi, *Spettatori: Forme di consumo e pubblici del cinema in Italia, 1930–1960* (Rome: Fondazione Scuola Nazionale di Cinema, 2002). This dual dimension of spectatoriality was recently taken up again by Ruggero Eugeni, in his beautiful exploration of the relationship between hypnosis and spectatorship: Eugeni notes how the "magnetic scene" revolves around the coexistence of two types of relations—those between hypnotizer and hypnotized and that between the two and an audience (Eugeni, *La relazione d'incanto: Studi su cinema e ipnosi* [Milan: Vita e Pensiero, 2002]).

54. The way in which we pass, in the filmic experience, from being mainly scopic subjects to social ones and vice versa was finally analyzed by Erich Feldmann in "Considérations sur la situation du Spectateur au Cinéma," *Revue Internationale de Filmologie* 26 (1956).

55. In this key, one can read phenomena such as the fan groups tied to cult films, ready to create ceremonies both around the representation of their love object (e.g., the weekly projection of *The Rocky Horror Picture Show*), as well as—in its absence—its reevocation (film buffs and cinephile chatter). Yet one can also read in this key the latently religious nature of the cinema (a completely secular religiosity) that, maintaining the desire to rejoin the object of the gaze, meanwhile makes scopic subjects members of a sort of "mystical body."

56. Robert Desnos, "Charlot," *Journal Littéraire* (June 13, 1925), reprinted in *Cinéma* (Paris: Gallimard, 1966), 145–46.

57. In point of view, the shot of the seeing subject can obviously also precede that of the object seen: it is important that the shot of the seen object perfectly reproduces the point of view of the seeing subject, and that the shot of the seeing subject clarify that the object is captured from his or her point

of view. On point of view, see Edward Branigan's essential *Point of View in the Cinema*. For a historical approach to point of view, see Elena Dagrada, *La rappresentazione dello sguardo nel cinema delle origini in Europa: nascita della soggettiva* (Bologna: CLUEB, 1998).

58. On the semi-subjective shot, see Jean Mitry, *Aesthetics and Psychology of the Cinema* (Bloomington: Indiana UP, 1997); originally, *Esthétique et psychologie du cinéma*, vol. 2 (Paris: Éditions Universitaires, 1966), 70ff. See also Francesco Casetti, *Inside the Gaze: The Fiction Film and Its Spectator* (Bloomington: Indiana UP, 1999), 102; originally, *Dentro lo sguardo: il film e il suo spettatore* (Milan: Bompiani, 1986).

59. Casetti, *Inside the Gaze*, 96–106. For a more extensive analysis of the strategies of the gaze in Antonioni, see Lorenzo Cuccu, *Antonioni: il discorso dello sguardo e altri saggi* (Pisa: ETS, 1997), and Seymour Chatman, *Antonioni, or the Surface of the World* (Berkeley: U of California P, 1985).

60. On the various scopic positions, see Jacques Fontanille, *Point de vue et subjectivité au cinéma* (Urbino: Centro Internazionale di semiotica and Università di Urbino, 1987), and *Un point de vue sur "croire" et "savoir": les deux systèmes de l'adéquation cognitive* (Besançon: Imprimé par l'Institut National de la Langue Française, 1982); Eric Landowski, *Jeux optiques: exploration d'une dimension figurative de la communication* (Paris: Centre national de la recherche scientifique, 1981); Vivian C. Sobchack, *The Address of the Eye: A Phenomenology of Film Experience* (Princeton: Princeton UP, 1992). See also Casetti, *Inside the Gaze*.

61. Jean-Paul Sartre, *Being and Nothingness: An Essay on Phenomenological Ontology* (New York: Citadel Press, 1956); originally, *L'être et le néant: Essai d'ontologie phénoménologique* (Paris: Gallimard, 1943).

62. Sartre, *Being and Nothingness*, 252.

63. Sartre, *Being and Nothingness*, 254.

64. Sartre, *Being and Nothingness*, 255.

65. Sartre, *Being and Nothingness*, 260.

66. Sartre, *Being and Nothingness*, 359. On the subject of self-reflexivity, also in regard to the cinema, see Montani's recovery of Merleau-Ponty in Pietro Montani, *L'immaginazione narrativa*, 63–67.

67. Sartre, *Being and Nothingness*, 263. Also, naturally, in the negative, so to speak: "And the one who I am—and who in principles escapes me—I am *in the midst of the world* in so far as he escapes me."

68. Sartre, *Being and Nothingness*, 257.

69. Maurice Merleau-Ponty, *Visible and the Invisible: Followed by Working Notes* (Evanston: Northwestern UP, 1968); originally, *Le visible et l'invisible* (Paris: Gallimard, 1964). Also: Jacques Lacan, *The Seminar of Jacques Lacan* (New York: Norton 1988–2007); originally, *Le séminaire, Livre XI: Les quatre concepts fondamentaux de la psychanalyse* (1964) (Paris: Seuil, 1973).

70. "Everything changes—and, with it, the revolution that began with Kant—when man is no longer conceived as a being who receives knowledge of a world held up by the laws of optics, but as a being who receives, through the

various senses, messages from which he gathers and interprets information in such as way as to construct an image of the world that demands the participation of all his being. The eye, then, is not an optical device that transmits images to the brain that exist as they are on the outside. It is an instrument of codification and decodification that transmits information, which needs to be continually interpreted and whose interpretation will vary according to the received signs and the internal dispositions of the being who receives them." Max Milner, *La Fantasmagorie*.

71. On the ability of the spectator to filter and integrate filmic data, see the classic observations by Münsterberg, *The Photoplay*, 71: "Depth and movement alike come to us in the moving picture world, not as hard facts but as a mixture of fact and symbol. They are present and yet they are not in the things. We invest the impressions with them."

72. On the intentional suspension of disbelief and the building of belief from the Freudian denegation, based on a structure such as "Yes, I know it is not true, but still . . . ," see at least Octave Mannoni, *Clefs pour l'immaginaire, ou L'autre Scène* (Paris: Éditions du Seuil, 1969).

73. The mechanism of projection-identification, as a constituent of the spectator's participation, is already analyzed by Hugo Münsterberg in *The Photoplay*. This will be the topic of many filmological studies in the fifties, and finds its most effective analysis in Edgar Morin, *Cinema; Or, the Imaginary Man*. For a survey of filmological studies, see Francesco Casetti, *Theories of Cinema*. *1945–1995* (Austin: U of Texas P, 1999); originally, *Teorie del cinema, 1945–1990* (Milan: Bompiani, 1993), 91–93 and 95–102. For the difference between secondary identification in the character of the film and primary identification, in the filmic gaze that catches the character, see Metz, *Imaginary Signifier*.

74. Roland Barthes, "Leaving the Movie Theater," in *The Rustle of Language* (Oxford: Blackwell, 1986), 345–49; originally, "En sortant du cinema," *Communications* 23 (1975): 104–107, then reprinted in *Le Bruissement de la langue: Essais critiques*, vol. 4 (Paris: Seuil, 1984), 407–412.

75. Barthes, "Leaving," 346.

76. Barthes, "Leaving," 346.

77. Barthes, "Leaving," 347.

78. Barthes, "Leaving," 348. Barthes continues the sentence: "The Real knows only distances, the Symbolic knows only masks; the image alone (the image-repertoire) is close, only the image is 'true' (can produce the resonance of truth)."

79. Barthes, "Leaving," 349.

80. Barthes, "Leaving," 345. And nevertheless, something still remains. The sentence continues: "he's sleepy, that's what he's thinking, his body has become something sopitive, soft, limp, and he feels a little disjointed, even . . . irresponsible."

81. On this aspect of the apparatus, see Jean-Louis Baudry, "The Apparatus: Metapsychological Approaches to the Impression of Reality in Cinema," *Camera*

Obscura 1 (Fall 1976): 104–128; originally, "Le dispositif: approches métapsychologiques de l'impression de réalité," Communications 23 (1975): 56–72. See also Baudry, "Ideological Effects of the Basic Cinematographic Apparatus," Film Quarterly 28.2 (Winter 1974–75): 39–47; originally, "Effets idéologiques produits par l'appareil de base," Cinéthique 7–8 (1970). For a continuation of Baudry, see Metz, Imaginary Signifier.

82. This idea has recently been put forward especially by Anne Friedberg in Window Shopping.

7. GLOSSES, OXYMORONS, AND DISCIPLINE

1. On the notion of "theoretical works" that put their device in play, see Omar Calabrese, La macchina della pittura: Pratiche teoriche della rappresentazione figurativa tra Rinascimento e Barocco (Rome: Laterza, 1985). See also the notion of "metapainting" in Victor I. Stoichita, Instauration du tableau: métapeinture à l'aube des temps modernes (Paris: Méridiens Klincksieck, 1993).

2. On films as nodes of "circuits of social discourse," see Francesco Casetti, "Cinema, letteratura e circuito dei discorsi sociali," in Ivelise Perniola, ed., Cinema e letteratura: percorsi di confine (Venice: Marsilio, 2002), 21–31. The concept of "circuits of social discourse" is an attempt to rethink the concepts of "discursive formation" and "episteme" discussed by Michel Foucault in Archaeology of Knowledge (London: Routledge, 1972); originally, Archèologie du Savoir (Paris: Gallimard, 1969), with stronger attention to interdiscursive and intermedial processes.

3. On theoretical reflection as "gloss" of the cinematographic phenomenon, see Francesco Casetti, "La teoria del cinema nella storia del cinema italiano," in Un secolo di cinema italiano (Milan: Il Castoro, 2000), 129–49.

4. I want to insist on the fact that the solutions proposed by the cinema, through its compromises, are neither pacific nor pacified. On the contrary, they inscribe within themselves the sense of tension and conflict from which they are born. Gian Piero Brunetta, in reconstructing the relationship between intellectuals and the cinema, emphasizes the work of confluence that the latter accommodates: "with respect to literature, the cinema redesigns and unifies the collective imagination, giving form to a type of visual story able to nourish in a deeper and more lasting way imagination and memory." I agree with him less on the fact that this locus of confluence is precisely a place outside of these conflicts: "More than a simple locus of memory, the cinema is a hyperlocus, a locus of loci, a space of spaces. It is a point of connection and congruency among real and imaginary spaces as perfect and self-sufficient world." The compromise is not always congruency and never self-sufficiency.

5. On the rearticulation, see this passage by Benjamin: "Modest methodological proposal for the cultural-historical dialectic. It is very easy to establish oppositions, according the determinate points of view, within the various

'fields' of any epoch, such that on one side lies the 'productive,' 'forward-looking,' lively, positive part of the epoch, and on the other side the abortive, retrograde, and obsolescent. The very contours of the positive element will appear distinctly only insofar as this element is set off against the negative. On the other hand, every negation has its value solely as background for the delineation of the lively, the positive. It is therefore of the decisive importance that a new partition be applied to this initially excluded, negative, component so that, by a displacement of the angle of vision (but not of the criteria!), a positive element emerges anew in it too—something different from that previously signified, And so on, ad infinitum, until the entire past is brought into the present in a historical apocatastasis." Benjamin, *The Arcades Project*, 459.

6. I am obviously referring to Gilles Deleuze, *The Movement-Image* and *The Time-Image* (Minneapolis: U of Minnesota P, 1986 and 1989). See also Jacques Aumont, *A quoi pensent les films*. On the idea that the cinema constitutes the locus of "philosophical reflection," see Stanley Cavell, "The Thought of Movies," in *Themes Out of School* (San Francisco: North Point Press, 1984), 3–26, reprinted in *Cavell on Film* (Albany: SUNY Press, 2005), 87–106.

7. Simmel, "The Metropolis and Mental Life," in *Simmel on Culture*, 183.

8. Simmel, "The Metropolis," 184.

9. Crary, *Techniques of the Observer*, and *Suspension of Perception*.

10. Michel Foucault, *Discipline and Punish: The Birth of the Prison* (New York: Pantheon, 1977); originally, *Surveiller et punir: Naissance de la prison* (Paris: Gallimard, 1975).

11. Pudovkin, *Kinorežissёr i kinomaterial* (1926) and *Kinoscenari* (1926). Pudovkin's work was immediately translated and had a rapid and influential impact on film theory: *Film Technique: Five Essays and Two Addresses* (London: George Newnes, 1933), followed by *Film Acting: A Course of Lectures Delivered at the State Institute of Cinematography* (London: G. Newnes, 1937), then both reprinted in *Film Technique and Film Acting: The Cinema Writings of V. I. Pudovkin* (New York: Lear, 1949) (citations below refer to this edition).

12. Pudovkin, *Film Technique*, 64 and 40.

13. Pudovkin, *Film Technique*, 40–41.

14. Pudovkin, *Film Technique*, 58 and 98.

15. Pudovkin, *Film Technique*, 64–65.

16. Pudovkin, *Film Technique*, 66.

17. Pudovkin, *Film Technique*, 41 and 47.

18. See, on this topic, the excellent study by David Bordwell, *On History of Film Style*.

19. This request underlies his entire volume: Hugo Münsterberg, *The Photoplay*.

20. Sergei Eisenstein, "The Montage of Film Attractions," in *Selected Works*, vol. 1: 1922–34, 39–58.

21. Georg Simmel, "Money in Modern Culture," in *Simmel on Culture*, 243–54; see also *Philosophie des Geldes* (Berlin: Duncker & Humblot Verlag, 1900).

22. Giovanni Papini, "La filosofia del cinematografo," La Stampa 41, Milan (May 18, 1907).
23. Anonymous, "Il pubblico del cinematografo," La rivista fono-cinematografica (February 11, 1908), reprinted in Tra una film e l'altra: Materiali sul cinema muto italiano, 1907–1920 (Venice: Marsilio, 1980), 43–45.
24. Anonymous, "Stile cinematografico," Il Corriere della Sera (March 27, 1912): 3.

REMAINS OF THE DAY

1. Zigmut Bauman, Liquid Life (Cambridge, Mass.: Polity, 2005).
2. Among the contributions on the digital image, see "Film Theory and the Digital Image," Iris 25 (1998); Thomas Elsaesser and Kay Hoffman, eds., Cinema Futures: Cain, Abel or Cable? The Screen Arts in the Digital Age (Amsterdam: Amsterdam UP, 1998); Laurent Jullier, Les images de synthèse (Paris: Nathan, 1998); Andrew Darley, Visual Digital Culture: Surface Play and Spectacle in New Media Genres (London and New York: Routledge, 2000). For an account about cinema as a field of "transition" toward the digital media, see Lev Manovich, The Language of New Media (Cambridge: MIT Press, 2001). Another critical (and highly interesting) account is John Belton's "Digital Cinema: A False Revolution," October 100 (Spring 2002): 98–114.
3. Even though digital images may still imply a strong component of indexicality. The surveillance camera is a good example of permanence of an indexical role—even transformed into a "temporal index." On this topic, see Thomas Levin, "Rethoric of the Temporal Index: Surveillant Narration and the Cinema of 'Real Time,'" in Thomas Y. Levin, Ursula Frohne, and Peter Weibel, eds., Ctrl (Space): Rhetorics of Surveillance from Bentham to Big Brother (Karlsruhe: ZKM Center for Art and Media, 2002; and Cambridge, Mass.: MIT Press, 2002), 578–93.
4. On this subject see Gianni Canova in L'alieno e il pipistrello: La crisi della forma nel cinema contemporaneo (Milano: Bompiani, 2000)
5. Even though there is also a shared sense that cinema has entered a new epoch. As Serge Daney writes, "The images are no longer on the side of the dialectical truth of 'seeing' and 'showing'; they have completely passed to that of promotion and advertising: in few words, to power. We have thus arrived at the point that we must begin to work on what remains; that is, the posthumous and golden legend of what was the cinema." Daney, Persévérance, 35.
6. On this subject, see in particular Paolo Bertetto, ed., Il cinema d'avanguardia (Venice: Marsilio, 1983).
7. Arnheim, Film, 32.
8. Arnheim, Film, 33.
9. Münsterberg, The Photoplay, 220.
10. Papini, "La filosofia del cinematografo," La Stampa 41 (May 18, 1907).

BIBLIOGRAPHY

Abel, Richard. *French Cinema: The First Wave, 1915–1919*. Princeton: Princeton UP, 1984.

——. *French Film Theory and Criticism*, vol. 1: *1907–1939*. Princeton: Princeton UP, 1984.

Abruzzese, Alberto. *Archeologie dell'immaginario: Segmenti dell'industria culturale tra '800 e '900*. Naples: Liguori, 1988.

——. *Forme estetiche e società di massa: Arte e pubblico nell'età del capitalismo.* Venice: Marsilio, 1973.

——. *La grande Scimmia: Mostri, vampiri, automi, mutanti: l'immaginario collettivo dalla letteratura al cinema all'informazione.* Rome: R. Napoleone, 1979.

——. *L'immagine filmica: Materiali di studio.* Rome: Bulzoni, 1974.

——. *Introduzione allo studio delle teoriche cinematografiche americane (1910–1929).* Venice: La Biennale di Venezia, 1975.

Abruzzese, Alberto and Gabriele Montagano, eds. *Caro Enzensberger: Il destino della televisione.* Milan: Lupetti, 1992.

Albano, Lucilla. *La caverna dei giganti: Scritti sull'evoluzione del dispositivo cinematografico.* Parma: Pratiche, 1992.

Albano, Lucilla, ed. *Modelli non letterari nel cinema.* Rome: Bulzoni, 1999.

Allen, Richard. "The Aesthetic Experience of Modernity: Benjamin, Adorno, and Contemporary Film Theory." *New German Critique* 40 (Winter 1987): 225–40.

Allen, Richard and Malcolm Turvey, eds. *Camera Obscura, Camera Lucida: Essays in Honor of Annette Michelson.* Amsterdam: Amsterdam UP, 2003.

Allendy, René. "La valeur psychologique de l'image." In *L'art cinématographique* 2:75–103 (1926).

Altman, Rick. *The American Film Musical.* Bloomington: Indiana UP, 1987.

——. "Dickens, Griffith, and Film: Film Theory Today." In Gaines, ed., *Classical Hollywood Narrative*, 9–47.

——. "The State of Sound Studies/Le son au cinéma, état de la recherche." *Iris* 27 (1999).

——. "The Technology of Voice." *Iris* 3.1 (1985) and *Iris* 4.1 (1986).

——. "Toward a Theory of the History of Representational Technology." *Iris* 2.2 (1984).

Altman, Rick, ed. *Sound Theory/Sound Practice*. New York: Routledge & the American Film Institute, 1992.

Andrew, Dudley. *Concepts in Film Theory*. Oxford and New York: Oxford UP, 1984.

Andrew, Dudley, ed. *The Image in Dispute: Art and Cinema in the Age of Photography*. Austin: U of Texas P, 1997.

Anonymous. "Il pubblico del cinematografo." *La rivista fono-cinematografica* (February 11, 1908), reprinted in *Tra una film e l'altra: Materiali sul cinema muto italiano, 1907–1920*, 43–45. Venice: Marsilio, 1980.

Anonymous. "Stile cinematografico." *Il Corriere della Sera* (March 27, 1912): 3.

Arnheim, Rudolf. *Film*. London: Faber & Faber, 1933, then republished with changes as *Film as Art* (Berkeley: U of California P, 1957). Originally, *Film als Kunst* (Berlin: Ernst Rowohlt Verlag, 1932).

Artaud, Antonin. *Sorcellerie et cinéma* (1927), reprinted in *Oeuvres complètes III*. Paris: Gallimard, 1970.

L'art cinématographique. 6 vols. Paris: Alcan, 1924–1926.

Aumont, Jacques. *A quoi pensent les films*. Paris: Séguier, 1996.

——. *Du visage au cinéma*. Paris: Éd. de l'Étoile, 1992.

——. *L'oeil interminable: Cinéma et peinture*. Paris: Séguier, 1989.

——. *Montage Eisenstein*. Paris: Albatros, 1979.

Aumont, Jacques, ed. *Jean Epstein: Cinéaste, Poète, Philosophe*. Paris: Cinémathèque Française, 1998.

Balázs, Bela. *Der Geist des Films*. Halle: Verlag Wilhelm Knapp, 1930. Reprinted in *Schriften zum Film*, vol. 2: *1926–1931*. Berlin and Budapest: Henschel Verlag and Akadémiai Kiadó, 1983.

——. *Der sichtbare Mensch oder die Kultur des Films*. Vienna and Leipzig: Deutsch-Österreichisches Verlag, 1924. Reprinted in *Schriften zum Film*, vol. 1: *1922–1926* (Berlin and Budapest: Henschel Verlag and Akadémiai Kiadó, 1982).

Barbera Alberto and Roberto Turigliatto, eds. *Leggere il cinema*. Milan: Mondadori, 1978.

Barker, Adam and Thomas Elsaesser, eds. *Early Cinema: Space, Frame, Narrative*. London: BFI, 1990.

Barthes, Roland. *Camera Lucida: Reflections on Photography*. New York: Hill & Wang, 1981; originally, *La chambre claire: Note sur la photographie* (Paris: Gallimard-Seuil, 1980).

——. "Leaving the Movie Theater." In *The Rustle of Language*, 345–49. Oxford: Blackwell, 1986. Originally, "En sortant du cinéma," *Communications* 23 (1975): 104–107, reprinted in *Le Bruissement de la langue: Essais critiques* 4:407–412 (Paris: Seuil, 1984).

——. "The Third Meaning: Research Notes on Several Eisenstein Stills." In *The Responsibility of Forms: Critical Essays on Music, Art, and Representation*, 41–62. Oxford: Blackwell, 1986. Originally, "Le troisième sens," *Cahiers du cinéma* 222 (1970), reprinted in *L'obvie et l'obtus: essais critique III* (Paris: Éditions du Seuil, 1982).

Bataille, Robert. *Grammaire cinégraphique*. Lille: Taffin-Lefort, 1947.

——. *Le savoir filmer.* Lille-Paris: Taffin Lefort, 1944.

Baudry, Jean-Louis. "The Apparatus: Metapsychological Approaches to the Impression of Reality in Cinema." *Camera Obscura* 1 (Fall 1976): 104–128. Originally, "Le dispositif: approches métapsychologiques de l'impression de réalité," *Communications* 23 (1975): 56–72.

——. "Ideological Effects of the Basic Cinematographic Apparatus." *Film Quarterly* 28.2 (Winter 1974–75): 39–47. Originally, "Effets idéologiques produits par l'appareil de base," *Cinéthique* 7–8 (1970).

Bazin, André. *Cinema of Cruelty: From Buñuel to Hitchcock.* Ed. and with an introduction by François Truffaut. Trans. Sabine d' Estrée with the assistance of Tiffany Fliss. New York: Seaver, 1982. Originally, *Cinéma de la cruauté: Eric von Stroheim, Carl Th. Dreyer, Preston Sturges, Luis Buñuel, Alfred Hitchcock, Akira Kurosawa* (Paris: Flammarion, 1975).

——. *What Is Cinema?* Berkeley: U of California P, 2005. Originally, *Qu'est ce que le cinéma?* (Paris: Ed. du Cerf): Vol. 1, *Ontologie et language* (1958); vol. 2, *Le cinéma et les autres arts* (1959); vol. 3, *Cinéma et Sociologie* (1961); and vol. 4, *Une esthétique de la réalité: le néo-réalisme* (1962).

Bellour, Raymond. *L'analyse du film.* Paris: Albatros, 1979.

——. "Segmenting/Analyzing." *Quarterly Review of Film Studies* 11 (August 1976): 331–53. Originally, "Alterner/raconter," in Bellour, ed., *Le cinéma americain* 1:69–88.

Bellour, Raymond, ed. *Le cinéma americain: Analyses de films.* 2 vols. Paris: Flammarion, 1980.

Belton, John. "The Backstage Musical." *Movie* 24 (Spring 1977).

Benjamin, Walter. *The Arcades Project.* Cambridge and London: Belknap Press of Harvard UP, 1999. Originally, "Das Passagenwerk," *Gesammelte Schriften* 1–2 (Frankfurt am Main: Suhrkamp Verlag, 1982).

——. "On Some Motifs in Baudelaire." In *Illuminations*, 155–200. Ed. Hannah Arendt. New York: Harcourt Brace & World, 1968. Originally, "Über einige Motive bei Baudelaire," in *Zeitschrift für Sozialforschung* 8.1–2 (1939).

——. "A Short History of Photography." In *One-way Street, and Other Writings.* Trans. Edmund Jephcott and Kingsley Shorter. London: NLB, 1979. Originally, "Eine Kleine Geschichte der Photographie," *Die literarische Welt* (1931)

——. "The Work of Art in the Age of Technological Reproducibility: Third Version." In *Selected Writings*, vol. 4: *1938–1940*, 251–82. Ed. Marcus Bullock and Michael W. Jennings. Cambridge and London: Belknap Press of Harvard UP, 2003. See also the previous version: "The Work of Art in the Age of Technological Reproducibility: Second Version," in *Selected Writings*, vol. 3: *1935–1938*, 101–133, ed. Bullock and Jennings (Cambridge and London: Belknap Press of Harvard UP, 2002). Originally, "L'oeuvre d'art à l'époque de sa reproduction mécanisée," *Zeischrift für Sozialforschung* 1 (1936).

Berman, Marshall. *All That Is Solid Melts into Air: The Experience of Modernity.* New York: Simon & Schuster, 1982.

Bernardi, Sandro. *Introduzione alla retorica del cinema.* Florence: Le Lettere, 1994.

Bertetto, Paolo, ed. *Il cinema d'avanguardia.* Venice: Marsilio, 1983.

Berthomieu, André. *Essai de grammaire cinématographique.* Paris: La Nouvelle Édition, 1946.

Blumenberg, Hans. *Shipwreck with Spectator: Paradigm of a Metaphor for Existence.* Trans. Steven Rendall. Cambridge: MIT Press, 1997. Originally, *Schiffbruch mit Zuschauer: Paradigma einer Daseinsmetapher* (Frankfurt am Main: Suhrkamp, 1979).

Bonitzer, Pascal. *Le champ aveugle: Essais sur le cinéma.* Paris: Gallimard, 1982.

———. *Décadrages: peinture et cinéma.* Paris: Éditions de l'Etoile/Seuil, 1985.

Bordwell, David. *On the History of Film Style.* Cambridge and London: Harvard UP, 1997.

Bordwell, David, Janet Staiger, and Kristin Thompson. *Classical Hollywood Cinema: Film Style and Mode of Production to 1960.* London: Routledge & Kegan Paul, 1985; New York: Columbia UP, 1985.

Branigan, Edward. *Point of View in the Cinema: A Theory of Narration and Subjectivity in Classical Film.* Berlin and New York: Mouton de Gruyter, 1984.

Bresson, Robert. *Notes on the Cinematographer.* København and Los Angeles: Distributed in the United States by Sun and Moon Press, 1997. Originally, *Notes sur le cinématographe* (Paris: Gallimard, 1975).

Browne, Nick, ed. *Refiguring American Film Genres.* Berkeley and London: U of California P, 1998.

Brownlow, Kevin. *Napoléon: Abel Gance's Classic Film.* London: Cape, 1983.

Brunetta, Gian Piero. *Buio in sala: Cent'anni di passioni dello spettatore cinematografico.* Venice: Marsilio, 1989.

———. *Il viaggio dell'icononauta.* Venice: Marsilio, 1997.

———. *Storia del cinema italiano.* 4 vols. Rome: Editori Riuniti, 1979.

Brunetta Gian Piero, ed. *Storia del cinema mondiale.* 5 vols. Turin: Einaudi, 1999–2001.

Bruno, Giuliana. *Atlas of Emotion: Journeys in Art, Architecture, and Film.* New York: Verso, 2002.

Burch, Noel. *Life to Those Shadows.* Berkeley: U of California P, 1990.

———. *Theory of Film Practice.* Princeton: Princeton UP, 1981. Originally, *Praxis du cinema* (Paris: Gallimard, 1969).

Callari, Francesco, ed. *Pirandello e il cinema.* Venice: Marsilio, 1991.

Campari, Roberto. *Film della memoria.* Venice: Marsilio, 2005.

Canosa, Michele, ed. *Cinéma: La creazione di un mondo.* Genoa: Le Mani, 2001.

Canova, Gianni. *L'alieno e il pipistrello: La crisi della forma nel cinema contemporaneo.* Milan: Bompiani, 2000.

Canudo, Ricciotto. "The Birth of the Sixth Art." *Frameworks* 13 (1980). Originally, "La naissance d'une sixième art: Essai sur le cinématographe," *Les Entretiens Idéalistes,* Paris (October 25, 1911).

———. "Lettere d'arte: Trionfo del cinematografo," *Nuovo giornale* (November 25, 1908); reprinted in *Filmcritica* 28.278 (November 1977): 296–302.

———. *L'usine aux images.* Paris: Chiron, 1927.

Carluccio, Giulia. *Verso il primo piano: Attrazioni e racconto nel cinema americano, 1908–1909: il caso Griffith-Biograph*. Bologna: Clueb, 1999.

Casetti, Francesco. "Adaptations and Mis-adaptations: Film, Literature, and Social Discourses." In Robert Stam and Alessandra Raengo, eds., *A Companion to Literature and Film*, 81–91. Oxford: Blackwell, 2005.

——. *Communicative Negotiation in Cinema and Television*. Milan: Vita & Pensiero, 2002.

——. *Inside the Gaze: The Fiction Film and Its Spectator*. Bloomington: Indiana UP, 1999. Originally, *Dentro lo sguardo: il film e il suo spettatore* (Milan: Bompiani, 1986).

——. *Theories of Cinema: 1945–1995*. Austin: U of Texas P, 1999. Originally, *Teorie del cinema, 1945–1990* (Milan: Bompiani, 1993).

Cavell, Stanley. *Cavell on Film*. Ed. and with an introduction by William Rothman. Albany: SUNY Press, 2005.

——. *The World Viewed: Reflections on the Ontology of Film*. New York: Viking, 1971.

Cendrars, Blaise. *L'ABC du cinéma* (1917–1921). Paris: Les Écrivains réunis, 1926. Now in *Aujourd'hui, 1917–1929*, in *Édition complète des œuvres de Blaise Cendrars* 4:162–66 (Paris: Denoël, 1960).

——. *La fin du monde filmée par l'ange N.-D.* Paris: Éditions de la Sirène, 1919. Now in *Édition complète des œuvres de Blaise Cendrars*, vol. 2 (Paris: Denoël, 1960), 7–50.

——. "The Modern: A New Art, the Cinema." In Abel, ed., *French Film Theory and Criticism* 1:182–183. Originally, "Modernités—Un nouveau art: le cinéma," *La rose rouge* 7.12 (June 12, 1919): 108.

Charney, Leo and Vanessa R. Schwartz, eds. *Cinema and the Invention of Modern Life*. Berkeley: U of California P, 1995.

Chatman, Seymour. *Antonioni, or the Surface of the World*. Berkeley: U of California P, 1985.

Christie, Ian and Richard Taylor, eds. *The Film Factory: Russian and Soviet Cinema in Documents*. Cambridge: Harvard UP, 1988.

Cohen, Keith. *Film and Fiction: The Dynamics of Exchange*. New Haven: Yale UP, 1979.

Colombo, Fausto. *Ombre sintetiche: Saggio di teoria dell'immagine elettronica*. Naples: Liguori, 1990.

Colombo, Fausto, ed. *I persuasori non occulti*. Milan: Lupetti, 1989.

Comolli, Jean-Louise. "Technique et idéologie." *Cahiers du Cinéma* 229 (1971), 230 (1971), 231 (1971), 233 (1971), 234–35 (1971–72), 241 (1972). "Technique and Ideology" (part 1), republished in *Film Reader* 2 (1977): 128–40; "Technique and Ideology: Camera, Perspective, Depth of Field" (parts 3 and 4), in Philip Rosen, ed., *Narrative, Apparatus, Ideology: A Film Theory Reader* (New York: Columbia UP, 1986).

Compagnon, Antoine. *The Five Paradoxes of Modernity*. Trans. Philip Franklin. New York: Columbia UP, 1994. Originally, *Les cinq paradoxes de la modernité* (Paris: Seuil, 1990).

Costa, Antonio. *Il cinema e le arti visive*. Turin: Einaudi, 2002.

——. *I leoni di Schneider: Percorsi intertestuali nel cinema ritrovato*. Rome: Bulzoni, 2002.

Costa, Antonio, ed. *La meccanica del visibile: Il cinema delle origini in Europa*. Florence: La Casa Usher, 1983.

Crary, Jonathan. *Suspension of Perception: Attention, Spectacle, and Modern Culture*. Cambridge: MIT Press, 1999.

——. *Techniques of the Observer: On Vision and Modernity in the Nineteenth Century*. Cambridge and London: MIT Press, 1990.

Cuccu, Lorenzo. *Antonioni: il discorso dello sguardo e altri saggi*. Pisa: ETS, 1997.

Dagrada, Elena. "Le figure dell' 'io' e la nascita della soggettiva." In Albano, ed., *Modelli non letterari nel cinema*, 63–80.

——. *La rappresentazione dello sguardo nel cinema delle origini in Europa: nascita della soggettiva*. Bologna: CLUEB, 1998.

D'Ambra, Lucio. "Il museo dell'attimo fuggente." *La Tribuna illustrata* 22.20, Torino (May 17–24, 1914).

Daney, Serge. *Persévérance*. Paris: P.O.L. Éditeur, 1994.

De Baroncelli, Jacques. "Le cinéma au service d'une humanité meilleure." *Les Cahiers du mois* 16–17 (1925; special issue on cinema); reprinted in L'Herbier, *Intelligence du cinématographe*, 126–27.

Deleuze, Gilles. *Movement-Image*. Trans. Hugh Tomlinson and Barbara Habberjam. Minneapolis: U of Minnesota P, 1986. Originally, *L'image-mouvement* (Paris: Éditions de Minuit, 1983).

——. *Proust and Signs*. Minneapolis: U of Minnesota P, 2000. Originally, *Marcel Proust et les signes* (Paris: Presses Universitaires de France, 1964).

——. *Time-Image*. Trans. Hugh Tomlinson and Robert Galeta. Minneapolis: U of Minnesota P, 1989. Originally, *L'image-temps* (Paris: Éditions de Minuit, 1985).

Delluc, Louis. *Cinéma & cie: confidences d'un spectateur*. Paris: Grasset, 1919.

——. *Écrits cinématographiques*. 4 vols. Paris: Cinémathèque Française, 1985–1990.

——. *Jungle du cinéma*. Paris: Éditions de la Sirène, 1921.

Deschanel, Pierre (president of the Chamber of Deputies). "Discours prononcé au banquet de la Chambre syndicale française de cinématographie et des industries s'y rattachant, 26 mars 1914." In L'Herbier, *Intelligence du cinématographe*, 94–97.

Desnos, Robert. *Cinéma*. Paris: Gallimard, 1966.

De Vincenti, Giorgio. *Il concetto di modernità nel cinema*. Parma: Pratiche, 1993.

Diodato Roberto. *Estetica del virtuale*. Milan: Bruno Mondadori, 2005.

Doane, Mary Ann. *The Emergence of Cinematic Time: Modernity, Contingency, the Archive*. Cambridge: Harvard UP, 2002.

Donald, James, Anne Friedberg, and Laura Marcus, eds. *Close-up, 1927–33: Cinema and Modernism*. London: Cassell, 1998.

Dotoli, Giovanni. *Nascita della modernità: Baudelaire, Apollinaire, Canudo, il viaggio dell'arte*. Fasano: Schena, 1995.

Dubois, Philippe. "L'écriture figurale dans le cinéma muet des années vingt." *Art&Fact* 18 (1999).

Dyer, Richard. "Entertainment and Utopia." *Movie* 24 (1977); reprinted in Steven Cohan, ed., *Hollywood Musicals: The Film Reader* (London and New York: Routledge, 2002).

Eisenstein, Sergei Mikhailovich. "The Dynamic Square." In *Selected Works*, vol. 1: *Writings, 1922–34*, 206–18. Ed. and trans. Richard Taylor. London: BFI, 1988; Bloomington: Indiana University Press, 1988. Originally published in *Close-Up* (March-June 1931): 39–58.

——. *The Film Form: Essays in Film Theory*. Ed. and trans. Jay Leyda. New York: Harcourt, Brace, 1949.

——. "The Montage of Attractions." In *Selected Works*, vol. 1: 1922–34, 33–38. Ed. and trans. by Richard Taylor. London: BFI, 1988; Bloomington: Indiana UP, 1988. Originally, "Montaž attrakcionov," *Lef* 3 (1923): 70–71, 74–75, reprinted in *Izbrannye proizvedenija v šesti tomach*, vol. 2 (Moscow: Iskusstvo, 1963–1970).

——. "The Montage of Film Attractions." In *Selected Works*, vol. 1: 1922–34, 39–58. Ed. and trans. Richard Taylor. London: BFI, 1988; Bloomington: Indiana UP, 1988. Originally, "Montaž kino-attrakcionov" (October 1924), partially published by Alexander Belenson under his own name in *Kino segodnja* (Moscow, 1925).

——. *Nonindifferent Nature*. Trans. Herbert Marshall. Cambridge and New York: Cambridge UP, 1987. Originally, "Neravnodušnaja priroda," in *Izbrannye proizvedenija v šesti tomach,* vol. 3 (Moscow: Iskusstvo, 1963–1970).

——. "Towards a Theory of Montage." In *Selected Works II*. Ed. Michael Glenny and Richard Taylor. Trans. Michael Glenny. London: BFI, 1991; Bloomington: Indiana UP, 1991 (the volume also includes "Montage 1937," "Montage 1938," and "Vertical Montage"; from manuscripts in Eisenstein Kabinett, Moscow; from "Montăz," in *Izbrannye proizvedenija v šesti tomach,* II, Moscow: Iskusstvo, 1963–1970; and then Naum Kleiman, ed., *Montăz*. Moscow: Muzei kino, 2000).

——. "Vertical Montage." In *Selected Writings* 2:327–99. Originally, "Vertikal'nyi montaž, stat'ja vtoraja." *Iskusstovo kino* 12 (1940): 27–35.

Elsaesser, Thomas. "Cinema—The Irresponsible Signifier, or The Gamble with History: Film Theory and Cinema Theory." *New German Critique* 40 (Winter 1987).

Epstein, Jean. *Bonjour cinéma*. Paris: Éditions de La Sirène, 1921. Reprinted in *Écrits sur le cinéma* 1:71–104.

——. *Le cinématographe vue de l'Etna*. Paris: Les Ecrivains Réunis, 1926. Reprinted in *Écrits sur le cinéma* 1:131–52 (1974).

——. "De quelques conditions de la photogénie." *Cinéa-Ciné pour tous* (August 15, 1924). Reprinted in *Le cinématographe vue de l'Etna* (1926), now in *Écrits sur le cinéma* 1:137–42.

——. *Écrits sur le cinéma*. 2 vols. Paris: Cinéma Club–Seghers, 1974–75.

——. *La poésie d'aujourd'hui, un nouvel état d'intelligence*. Paris: Éditions de la Sirène, 1921; now, partially, in *Écrits sur le cinéma* 1:65–69 (1974).

——. "Rapidité et fatigue de l'homme spectateur." In *Mercure de France* (November 1, 1948), reprinted in *Écrits sur le cinéma* 2.45–53.

——. "Le regard du verre." *Les Cahiers du mois* 16–17 (special issue on *cinéma*) (1925). Reprinted in *Écrits sur le cinéma* 1:125–26 (1974).

Eugeni, Ruggero. *La relazione d'incanto: Studi su cinema e ipnosi*. Milan: Vita & Pensiero, 2002.

Fanchi, Mariagrazia and Elena Mosconi. *Spettatori: Forme di consumo e pubblici del cinema in Italia, 1930–1960*. Rome: Fondazione Scuola Nazionale di Cinema, 2002.

Fantasio. "Cinémas." *Le Film* (June 12, 1914); reprinted in L'Herbier, *Intelligence du cinématographe*, 74–77.

Faure, Elie. *The Art of Cineplastics*. Boston: The Four Seas Company, 1923. Originally, "De la cinéplastique," in *L' Arbre d' Eden* (Paris: Éd. Crès, 1922), reprinted in L'Herbier, *Intelligence du cinématographe*, 266–78.

——. *De la cinéplastique suivi de: Le cinéma, langue universelle*. Paris: Séguier, 1995.

——. *Fonction du cinéma—De la cinéplastique à son destin social, 1921–1937*. Paris: Plon, Éditions d'Histoire et d'art, 1953.

——. *Histoire de l'Art*. Vol. 7. Paris: Le Livre de poche, 1976.

Feldmann, Erich. "Considérations sur la situation du Spectateur au Cinéma." *Revue Internationale de Filmologie* 26 (1956).

Fontanille, Jacques. *Point de vue et subjectivité au cinéma*. Urbino: Centro Internazionale di semiotica & Università di Urbino, 1987.

——. *Un point de vue sur "croire" et "savoir": les deux systèmes de l'adéquation cognitive*. Besançon: Imprimé par l'Institut National de la Langue Française, 1982.

Fossa, Giovanni. "Orizzonti cinematografici avvenire." *La Scena Illustrata* 43.5 (March 1, 1907).

Foucault, Michel. *Discipline and Punish: The Birth of the Prison*. Trans. Alan Sheridan. New York: Pantheon, 1977. Originally, *Surveiller et punir: Naissance de la prison* (Paris: Gallimard, 1975).

Franzini, Elio. *Fenomenologia dell'invisibile: Al di là dell'immagine*. Milan: Cortina, 2001.

Freeburg, Victor O. *The Art of Photoplay Making*. New York: Macmillan, 1918.

Freud, Sigmund. *Beyond the Pleasure Principle*. Ed. and trans. C. J. M. Hubback. New York: Boni and Liveright,1924. Originally, *Jenseits des Lustprinzips*. Leipzig, Vienna, and Zurich: Internationaler Psycoanalytischer Verlag, 1921).

——. *Civilization and Its Discontents*. Trans. Joan Riviere. London: L. and Virginia Woolf at the Hogarth Press, 1930. Originally, *Das Unbehagen in der Kultur* (Vienna: Internationaler Psychoanalytischer Verlag, 1930).

——. *Inhibitions, Symptoms and Anxiety*. Trans. Alix Strachey. London: Hogarth Press and the Institute of Psycho-Analysis, 1948. Originally, *Hemmung, Symptom und Angst* (Vienna: Internationaler Psychoanalytischer Verlag, 1926).

Friedberg, Anne. *Window Shopping: Cinema and the Postmodern*. Berkeley: U of California P, 1993.

Frisby, David. *Fragments of Modernity: Theories of Modernity in the Work of Simmel, Kracauer, and Benjamin.* Cambridge: Polity Press, 1985.

Gaines, Jane, ed. *Classical Hollywood Narrative: The Paradigm Wars.* Durham, N.C., and London: Duke UP, 1992.

Gance, Abel. *Napoléon vu par Abel Gance: Épopée cinégraphique en cinq époques.* Paris: Plon, 1927; new edition, Paris: Jacques Bertoin, 1991.

——. "Le temps de l'image est venu." In *L'art cinématographique* 2:83–102 (1926).

Gaudreault, André. "Detours in Film Narrative: Cross-Cutting." *Cinema Journal* 19.1 (1979): 39–59.

——. "Temporality and Narrativity in Early Cinema (1895–1908)." In Roger Holdman, ed., *Cinema, 1900–1906: An Analytical Study*, 201–218. Brussels: Fédération Internationale des Archives du Film (FIAF), 1982).

Giovannetti, Eugenio. *Il cinema e le arti meccaniche.* Palermo: Sandron, 1930.

Gledhill, Christine. "Pleasurable Negotiations." In Thornham, ed., *Feminist Film Theory*, 166–79.

Gledhill, Christine and Linda Williams, eds. *Reinventing Film Studies.* New York: Arnold, 2000; London: Oxford UP, 2000.

Goffman, Erving. *Interaction Ritual: Essays on Face-to-Face Behavior.* Garden City; N.Y.: Anchor, 1967.

——. *The Presentation of Self in Everyday Life.* Edinburgh: U of Edinburgh P, 1956.

Gomery, Douglas. *Shared Pleasures: A History of Movie Presentation in the United States.* Madison: U of Wisconsin P, 1992.

Gras, Alain and Sophie L. Poirot-Delpech. *Grandeur et dépendance: Sociologie des macro-systèmes techniques.* Paris: Presses Universitaires de France, 1993.

Guardini, Romano. *Briefe vom Comer See.* Mainz: Gruenewald, 1927.

Gunning, Tom. "Cinema of Attractions: Early Film, Its Spectator, and the Avant-Garde." *Wide Angle* 8.3–4 (1986). Reprinted in Barker and Elsaesser, eds., *Early Cinema: Space, Frame, Narrative*, 56–62.

——. *The Films of Fritz Lang: Allegories of Vision and Modernity.* London: BFI, 2000.

——. "Le style non continu du cinéma des premiers temps." *Les Cahiers de la Cinémathèque* 29 (1979): 108–125.

——. "Tracing the Individual Body: Photography, Detectives, and Early Cinema." In Charney and Schwartz, eds., *Cinema and the Invention of Modern Life*, 15–45.

Hansen, Miriam. "America, Paris, the Alps: Kracauer (and Benjamin) on Cinema and Modernity." In Charney and Schwartz, eds., *Cinema and the Invention of Modern Life*, 363–402.

——. *Babel and Babylon: Spectatorship in American Silent Film.* Cambridge: Harvard UP, 1991.

——. "The Mass Production of the Senses: Classical Cinema as Vernacular Modernism." In Gledhill and Williams, eds., *Reinventing Film Studies*, 332–50.

Harvey, David. *The Condition of Postmodernity.* London: Blackwell, 1990.

Heu, Pascal-Manuel. *Le temps du cinéma: Émile Vuillermoz pére de la critique cinématographique, 1910–1930.* Paris: L'Harmattan, 2003.

Hofmannsthal, Hugo von. "Das Ersatz für die Traüme." *Das Tagenuch* 2 (1921).

James, Henry. "Prefaces to the New York Edition (1907–1909)." In *Literary Criticism* 2:1035–1341. New York: Literary Classics of the United States, 1984.

Jameson, Fredric. *Signatures of the Visible*. New York and London: Routledge, 1990.

Jost, François. *L'oeil-camera: Entre film et roman*. Lyon: Presses Universitaries de Lyon, 1987.

Kaplan, Nelly. *Manifeste d'un art nouveau: La Polyvision*. Paris: Caractéres, 1955.

Kauffmann, Stanley and Bruce Henstell, eds. *American Film Criticism: From the Beginnings to "Citizen Kane."* New York: Liveright, 1972.

Kern, Stephen. *The Culture of Time and Space, 1880–1918*. Cambridge: Harvard UP, 1983.

Kracauer, Siegfried. *Kino Essays: Studien, Glossen zum Film*. Frankfurt am Main: Suhrkamp, 1974.

——. *Kleine Schriften zum Film*. 6 vols. Frankfurt am Main: Suhrkamp Verlag, 2004–2006.

——. *The Mass Ornament: Weimar Essays*. Edited and trans. Thomas Y. Levin. Cambridge: Harvard UP, 1995. Originally, *Das Ornament der Masse* (Frankfurt am Main: Suhrkamp Verlag, 1963).

——. *Theory of Film: The Redemption of Physical Reality*. New York: Oxford UP, 1960.

Kraiski, Giorgio, ed. *I formalisti russi nel cinema*. Milan: Garzanti, 1971.

Kuhn, Annette. *Dreaming of Fred and Ginger: Cinema and Cultural Memory*. New York: New York UP, 2002.

Kuntzel, Thierry. "Le defilement du film." *Revue d'estetique* 2–4 (1973): 97–110.

Lacan, Jacques. *The Seminar of Jacques Lacan*. Ed. Jacques-Alain Miller. New York: Norton, 1988–2007. Originally, *Le séminaire, Livre XI: Les quatre concepts fondamentaux de la psychanalyse* (1964; rpt., Paris: Seuil, 1973).

Landowski, Eric. *Jeux optiques: exploration d'une dimension figurative de la communication*. Paris: Centre national de la recherche scientifique, 1981.

La Polla, Franco. *Il nuovo cinema americano: 1967–1975*. Venice: Marsilio, 1985.

——. *L'età dell'occhio: Il cinema e la cultura americana*. Turin: Lindau, 1999.

——. *Stili americani*. Bologna: Bonomia UP, 2003.

L'Herbier, Marcel. "Hermès et le silence." *Le Temps* (February 23, 1918); reprinted in *Mercure de France* and in a complete version in *Intelligence du cinématographe*, 199–212.

——. *Intelligence du cinématographe*. Paris: Corrêa, 1946.

Liebman, Stuart. "Visiting of Awful Promise: The Cinema Seen from Etna." In Allen and Turvey, eds., *Camera Obscura, Camera Lucida*.

Lindsay, Vachel. *The Art of the Moving Picture*. New York: Macmillan, 1915 (2d rev. ed., 1922). Rpt., New York: Modern Library, 2000.

Luchini, Alberto. "Lettera sul cinematografo." *Solaria* 2.3 (1927).

Luciani, Sebastiano Arturo. *L'antiteatro: Il cinematografo come arte*. Rome: La Voce Anonima Editrice, 1928.

Lukács, Georg. "Thoughts on an Aesthetic for the Cinema." *Frameworks* 14 (Spring 1981) ("Gedanken zu einer Ästhetik des Kino," *Frankfurter Allgemeine Zeitung*, 251 [September 10, 1913]: 1–2. Originally, "Gedanken zu einer Ästhetik des 'Kino,'" *Pester Lloyd* (Budapest), 90 [April 16, 1911]: 45–46; then in *Schriften zur Literatursoziologie* [Neuwied: Luchterhand, 1961], 75–80).

Lyotard, Jean-François. "L'acinéma." *Revue d'Esthétique* 2–4 (1973), reprinted in *Des Dispositifs pulsionnels*. Paris: Union générale d'éditions, 1973.

Malraux, Andre. "Esquisse d'une psychologie du cinéma." *Verve* (1941).

Mannoni, Laurent. *Le grand art de la lumière et de l'ombre: Archéologie du cinéma*. Paris: Nathan, 1995.

Mannoni, Octave. *Clefs pour l'imaginaire, ou L'autre scène*. Paris: Éditions du Seuil, 1969.

Manovich, Lev. *The Language of New Media*. Cambridge: MIT Press, 2001.

Marie, Michel. "La séquence/le film." In Bellour, ed., *Le cinéma americain: Analyses de films* 2:27–44.

Marinetti, Filippo Tommaso. *Futurist Manifestos*. Ed. Umbro Apollonio. Boston: MFA Publications, 1973. Originally, "Fondazione e Manifesto del Futurismo," *Figaro*, Paris (February 20, 1909).

Martini, Andrea, ed. *Utopia e cinema: Cento anni di sogni, progetti e paradossi*. Venice: Marsilio, 1994.

Martini, Ferdinando Maria. "La morte della parola." *La Tribuna* (February 16, 1912).

Matuszewski, Boleslaw. "A New Source of History: The Creation of a Depository for Historical Cinematography." *Cultures* 2.1 (1974): 219–22. Originally, *Una Nouvelle Source de l'Histoire historique* (Paris: Noisette, 1898).

——. *La Photographie animée: Ce qu'elle est, ce qu'elle doit être*. Paris: Noisette, 1898.

May, Renato. *Il linguaggio del film*. Milan: Il Poligono, 1947.

——. "Per una grammatica del montaggio." *Bianco e Nero* 2.1 (1938): 24–65.

McLuhan, Marshall. *Understanding Media: The Extensions of Man*. New York: Mc-Graw-Hill, 1964.

Melchiorre, Virgilio. *L'immaginazione simbolica: Saggio di antropologia filosofica*. Bologna: Il Mulino, 1972.

Merleau-Ponty, Maurice. *Sense and Non-Sense*. Trans. Hubert L. Dreyfus and Patricial Allen Dreyfus. Evanston: Northwestern UP, 1964. Originally, *Sens et non-sens* (Paris: Nagel, 1948).

——. *Visible and the Invisible: Followed by Working Notes*. Ed. Claude Lefort. Trans. Alphonso Lingis. Evanston: Northwestern UP, 1968. Originally, *Le visible et l'invisible* (Paris: Gallimard, 1964).

Metz, Christian. *Film Language: A Semiotics of the Cinema*. Trans. Michael Taylor. New York: Oxford UP, 1974. Originally, *Essais sur la signification au cinema*, vol. 2 (Paris: Klincksieck, 1972).

——. *Imaginary Signifier: Psychoanalysis and the Cinema*. Trans. Celia Brittan, An-nwyl Williams, Ben Brewster, and Alfred Guzzetti. Bloomington: Indiana UP,

1982. Originally, *Le signifiant imaginaire: Psychanalyse et cinema* (Paris: Union générale d'éditions, 1977).

———. *Language and Cinema*. Trans. Donna Jean Umiker-Sebeok. The Hague: Mouton, 1974. Originally, *Essais sur la signification au cinema* (Paris: Klincksieck, 1968).

Michelson, Annette. "The Man with the Movie Camera: From Magician to Epistemologist." *Artforum* 10.7 (1972): 60–72.

Milner, Max. *La fantasmagorie: Essai sur l'optique fantastique*. Paris: Presses Universitaires de France, 1982.

Mitry, Jean. *Aesthetics and Psychology of the Cinema*. Trans. Christopher King, Bloomington: Indiana UP, 1997. Originally, *Esthétique et psychologie du cinéma*, 2 vols. (Paris: Éditions Universitaires, 1963–1966).

Montani, Pietro. *Il debito del linguaggio*. Venice: Marsilio, 1985.

———. *L'immaginazione narrativa: Il racconto del cinema oltre i confini dello spazio letterario*. Milan: Guerini, 1999.

Moretti, Franco. *Modern Epic: The World-System from Goethe to Garcia Marquez*. Trans. Hoare Quintin. London and New York: Verso, 1996. Originally, *Opere mondo: Saggio sulla forma epica dal Faust a Cent'anni di solitudine* (Turin: Einaudi, 1994).

Morin, Edgar. *Cinema; Or, the Imaginary Man*. Trans. Lorraine Mortimer. Minneapolis: U of Minnesota P, 2005. Originally, *Le cinéma ou l'homme imaginaire: Essai d'anthropologie sociologique* (Paris: Minuit, 1956).

Moussinac, Leon. *Naissance du cinéma*. Paris: Povolozky, 1925.

Mumford, Lewis. *Technics and Civilization*. New York: Harcourt, Brace, 1934.

Münsterberg, Hugo. *The Photoplay: A Psychological Study*. New York: Appleton, 1916.

Musser, Charles. *The Emergence of Cinema: The American Screen to 1907*. New York: Maxwell Macmillan International, 1990.

———. "Historiographic Method and the Study of Early Cinema." *Cinema Journal* 44.1 (Fall 2004): 101–107.

Ortoleva, Peppino. *Mediastoria*. Parma: Pratiche, 1995.

Oudart, Jean-Pierre. "La suture." *Cahiers du cinéma* 211 (1969). Also: "La suture II." *Cahiers du cinéma* 212 (1969).

———. "L'effet de réel." *Cahiers du cinéma* 228 (1971).

Painlevé, Jean. "Le cinéma au service de la science." *La Revue des Vivants* (October 1931). Reprinted in L'Herbier, *Intelligence du cinématographe*, 403–408.

Panofsky, Erwin. *Perspective as Symbolic Form*. New York: Zone Books, 1991. Originally, "Die Perspektive als 'symbolische Form,'" in *Vortäge der Bibliothek Warburg: Vortäge, 1924–25* (Leipzig and Berlin: Teubner, 1927).

———. "Style and Medium in the Motion Picture." *Bulletin of the Department of Art and Archaelogy*. Priceton University, 1934. Reprinted in *Critique* 3 (1947), then in Daniel Talbot, ed., *Film: An Anthology* (1966).

Papini, Giovanni. "La filosofia del cinematografo." *La Stampa* 41, Milan (May 18, 1907).

Pérez, Xavier. *El suspens cinematogràfic*. Barcelona: Portic, 1999.

Perniola, Ivelise, ed. *Cinema e letteratura: percorsi di confine*. Venice: Marsilio, 2002.

Petric, Vlada. *Constructivism in Film: "The Man with the Movie Camera"—A Cinematic Analysis*. Cambridge and New York: Cambridge UP, 1987.

Pezzella, Mario. *Estetica del cinema*. Bologna: Il Mulino, 1996.

Pierre-Quint, Leon. "Signification du cinéma." *L'art cinématographique* 2:1–28 (1926).

Pinotti, Andrea. *Piccola storia della lontananza: Benjamin storico della percezione*. Milan: Cortina, 2001.

Pirandello, Luigi. "Il fu Mattia Pascal." *Nuova Antologia* (April-June 1904; then Milan: Fratelli Treves, 1910. Rpt., Pirandello, *The Late Mattia Pascal* (New York: New York Review of Books, 2005).

——. "Se il film parlante abolirà il teatro." *Corriere della Sera* (June 16, 1929). Reprinted in Callari, ed., *Pirandello e il cinema*, 120–25.

——. *Shoot! The Notebooks of Serafino Gubbio, Cinematograph Operator*. Trans. C. K. Scott Moncrieff. Chicago: U of Chicago P, 2005. Originally, "Si gira," *Nuova Antologia* (June-August 1915; then Milan: Fratelli Treves, 1916); subsequently released under the title *Quaderni di Serafino Gubbio operatore* (Florence: Edizioni Bemporad, 1925).

Pisanti, Achille. *Periodici cinematografici in U.S.A. (1910–1930)*. Venice: La Biennale di Venezia, n.d.

Ponzo, Mario. "Di alcune osservazioni psicologiche fatte durante rappresentazioni cinematografiche." *Atti della R. Accademia delle scienze di Torino* 46 (1910–1911). Turino: Vincenzo Bona, 1911.

Pravadelli, Veronica. *La grande Hollywood: Stili di vita e di regia nel cinema classico americano*. Venice: Marsilio, 2007.

Pudovkin, Vsevolod Illarionovich. *Film Technique: Five Essays and Two Addresses*. Trans. Ivor Montague. London: G. Newnes, 1933. (Includes *Kinorežissër i kinomaterial* [Moscow: Kinopeciat, 1926] and *Kinoscenari* [Moscow: Kinopeciat, 1926]).

——. *Film Technique and Film Acting: The Cinema Writings of V. I. Pudovkin*. New York: Lear, 1949.

Quaresima, Leonardo, ed. "Dead Ends/Impasses." *Cinema & Cie* 2 (Spring 2003).

Rabinovitz, Lauren. *For the Love of Pleasure: Women, Movies, and Culture in Turn-of-the-Century Chicago*. New Brunswick: Rutgers UP, 1998.

Ray, Robert R. *A Certain Tendency of the Hollywood Cinema, 1930–1980*. Princeton: Princeton UP, 1985.

Romains, Jules. "The Crowd at the Cinématograph." Reprinted in Abel, *French Film Theory and Criticism*, vol. 1. Originally, "La foule au cinématographe," in *Les Puissances de Paris* (Paris: Eugene Figuière, 1911).

Rosen, Philip. *Change Mummified: Cinema, Historicity, Theory*. Minneapolis: U of Minnesota P, 2001.

Rosen, Philip, ed. *Narrative, Apparatus, Ideology*. New York: Columbia UP, 1986.

Sartre, Jean-Paul. *Being and Nothingness: An Essay on Phenomenological Ontology.* Trans. Hazel E. Barnes. New York: Citadel Press, 1956. Originally, *L'être et le néant: Essai d'ontologie phénoménologique* (Paris: Gallimard, 1943).

Savinio, Alberto. "Il sogno meccanico." *Galleria* (January 1924). Reprinted in Scheiwiller, ed., *Il sogno meccanico.*

Scheiwiller, Vanni, ed. *Il sogno meccanico: Scritti inediti cinematografici.* Milan: Libri Scheiwiller, Quaderni della Fondazione Primo Conti, 1981.

Schivelbusch, Wolfgang. *Disenchanted Night: The Industrialization of Light in the Nineteenth Century.* Trans. Angela Davies. Berkeley: U of California P, 1988. Originally, *Lichtblicke: Zur Geschichte der Künstlichen Helligkeit im 19. Jahrhundert* (Munich: Carl Hanser Verlag, 1983).

——. *Railway Journey: Trains and Travel in the 19th Century.* Trans. Anselm Hollo. New York: Urizen, 1979. Originally, *Geschichte der Eisenbahnreise: Zur Industrialisierung von Raum und Zeit im 19. Jahrhundert* (Munich and Vienna: Carl Hanser Verlag, 1977).

Serao, Matilde. "Parla una spettatrice." *L'arte muta* 1 (June 15, 1916): 31–32.

Simmel, Georg. "The Metropolis and Mental Life." In *Simmel on Culture: Selected Writings,* 174–85. Ed. David Frisby and Mike Featherstone. Thousand Oaks, Calif., and London: Sage, 1997. Originally, *Die Großstädte und das Geistesleben, Jahrbuch der Gehe-Stiftung* 9 (1903), then reprinted in *Brucke und tür* (Stuttgart: K. F. Koehler Verlag, 1957).

——. *The Philosophy of Money.* Trans. Tom Bottomore and David Frisby. London and Boston: Routledge & Kegan Paul, 1978. Originally, *Philosophie del Geldes* (Berlin: Duncker & Humblot Verlag, 1900).

Slide, Anthony. *Selected Film Criticism [1886–1960].* 6 vols. Metuchen, N.J., and London: Scarecrow Press,, 1982–1985.

Sobchack, Vivian C. *The Address of the Eye: A Phenomenology of Film Experience.* Princeton: Princeton UP, 1992.

Somaini, Antonio. *Rappresentazione prospettica e punto di vista: Da Leon Battista Alberti a Abraham Bosse.* Milan: CUEM, 2004.

Sorlin, Pierre. *Les fils de Nadar: Le "siècle" de l'image analogique.* Paris: Nathan, 1997.

——. *Sociologie du cinéma.* Paris: Aubier, 1977.

Souday, Paul. "Bergsonisme et cinéma." *Paris-Midi* (October 12, 1917): 3. Reprinted in Pascal-Manuel Heu, *Le temps du cinéma,* 232–33.

Spottiswoode, Raymond. *A Grammar of the Film: An Analysis of Film Technique.* London: Faber & Faber, 1935.

Staiger, Janet. "The Future of the Past." *Cinema Journal* 44.1 (Fall 2004): 126–29.

——. *Interpreting Films: Studies in the Historical Reception of American Cinema.* Princeton: Princeton UP, 1992.

Summers, Rollin. "The Moving Picture Drama and the Acted Drama: Some Points of Comparison as to Technique." *Moving Picture World* (September 19,1908). Reprinted in Kauffmann and Henstell, eds., *American Film Criticism.*

Talbot, Dan. *Film: An Anthology*. Berkeley: U of California P, 1966.

Teige, Karel. "K estetice filmu." *Studio* 6–10 (May-December 1929).

Thornham, Sue, ed. *Feminist Film Theory: A Reader*. New York: New York UP, 1999.

Thovez, Enrico (Craquebille). "L'arte di celluloide," *La Stampa* 42.209, Turin (July 29, 1908).

Tinazzi, Giorgio. *La copia originale: Cinema, critica, tecnica*. Venice: Marsilio, 1983.

Toddi, Emmanuele. "Rettangolo-Film (25 x 19)." In *Penombra* 1.3 (August 25, 1918): 121–23.

Tra una film e l'altra: Materiali sul cinema muto italiano, 1907–1920. Venice: Marsilio, 1980.

Troy, William. *The Nation* (March 22, 1933). Review reprinted in Kauffmann and Henstell, eds., *American Film Criticism*.

Truffaut, François. *Hitchcock*. New York: Simon & Schuster, 1967. Originally, *Le Cinéma selon Hitchcock* (Paris: R. Laffont, 1966).

Turim, Maureen. *Flashbacks in Film: Memory and History*. New York and London: Routledge, 1989.

Tsivian, Jury. "L'Homme à la camera en tant que texte constructiviste." *Révue du cinéma* (June 1980).

Un secolo di cinema italiano. Milan: Il Castoro, 2000.

Vernet, Marc. *Figures de l'absence*. Paris: Éd. de l'Étoile, 1988.

Vertov, Dziga. *Kino-Eye: The Writings of Dziga Vertov*. Ed. Annette Michelson. Berkeley: U of California P, 1984.

——. "Vystuplenie na prosmotre dokumental'nogo fil'ma 'Chelovek s kinoapparatom'" (unpublished). In RGALI (Russian State Archive of Literature and Art), f. 2091.

Von Kleist, Heinrich. *Über das Marionettentheater* (1810), reprinted in *Kleists Aufsatz uber das Marionettentheater: Studien und Interpretationen*. Berlin: E. Schmidt, 1967.

Vuillermoz, Émile. "Textes de Émile Vuillermoz." In Pascal-Manuel Heu, *Le Temps du cinéma*, 218–29.

Wenders, Wim. *The Act of Seeing: Essays and Conversations*. Trans. Michael Hofmann. London: Faber & Faber, 2001. Originally, *Texte und Gespräche* (Frankfurt am Main: Verlag der Autoren, 1992).

Williams, Linda. "Melodrama Revised." In Browne, ed., *Refiguring American Film Genres*, 42–88.

Williams, Linda, ed. *Viewing Positions: Ways of Seeing Film*. New Brunswick: Rutgers UP, 1994.

Williams, Raymon. *Television: Technology and Cultural Form*. London: Fontana–Collins, 1974.

Žiž]ek, Slavoj. *The Fright of Real Tears: Krzysztof Kieslowski Between Theory and Post-Theory*. London: BFI, 2001.

INDEX

FILM + CULTURE

A SERIES OF COLUMBIA UNIVERSITY PRESS

EDITED BY JOHN BELTON